THE POLITICAL SOCIOLOGY OF DALIT ASSERTION

THE POLITICAL SOCIOLOGY OF DALIT ASSERTION

PRAKASH LOUIS
Executive Director,
Indian Social Institute, New Delhi

GYAN PUBLISHING HOUSE
NEW DELHI - 110002

THE POLITICAL SOCIOLOGY OF DALIT ASSERTION
(Scheduled Caste)

Published by Gyan Publishing House
5, Ansari Road, Daryaganj,
New Delhi - 110 002
Phone : 23282060, 23261060
Fax : 011 - 23285914
E-mail : gyanbook@vsnl.com
Visit our website at : \\www.gyanbooks.com

First Published in India 2003

Rs. 495

ISBN : 81-212-0836-X

Laser Typesetting by : Varsha Graphics, Delhi

Printed by : Delux Offset Printers, Delhi-110035

Dedicated with gratitude to my parents
Mrs. Savariammal
and
Late Mr. D.S. Lazer
who continue to inspire me to be part of
the struggles of the
marginalised communities

Contents

The Agony and Anguish of the Dalits

We assist you in your birth pangs
we bring forth your children
we wash your linen
We clean / scrub your utensils
Yet we remain '*achuth*'.

We plough your field
We fill your large godowns
But, you in turn, starve us.

We cremate your ancestors
We do *mundan* for the clan
So that you can mourn the dead
Is this why you burn us alive?

As the lamentation were going on
I smelt the burning of flesh, which echoed:

Woe to you the touchables,
You burnt us alive,
Woe to you the *zamindars*,
The land that you grabbed from us
will be confiscated and distributed.

Woe to you the politicians
You sided with the dominant castes
Your power will be curtailed

Woe to you the police
You harassed us unnecessarily
You will be buried alive.

Woe to you the dalit leaders
You sold us for your survival
Your security will be shattered.

Slowly the woe turned into blessings
Blessed are the *bandhua-mazdur*

For you will break out from the
Perpetual bondage.

Blessed are the Dalit women
For you will mother the
Martyrs of Dalitsthan.

Blessed are you the activists
You shall be rewarded for
Your commitment.

Blessed are the Dalits
For you will create a Dalitsthan
From your burnt ashes.

Preface

Untouchability has been the historical curse of the outcastes of India. But the heart of the matter is that untouchability has also been the root cause of the degraded and degenerating Indian social order. The Indian mindset made itself to believe that by unleashing systemic violence and oppression on the Dalits and the outcastes, it can construct its world devoid of the Dalits and the downtrodden. For a long period of time it exerted all the pressure possible and invested all the energy at its disposal to construct a social order based on the principles of purity and pollution, inferior and superior, high and low, included and excluded, cooked and uncooked, mental and menial labour, upper and lower castes. Though the Indian social principles as well as the Indian philosophy is projected to be the most integrated and peace loving, violence was inbuilt in the entire system.

The institutional forms of discrimination and deprivation reduced the Dalits and the downtrodden to a state of lesser being, non-being and exist only for the well-being of the dominant castes and class. It is not simply illiteracy, poverty, malnutrition, ill health that became the lot of the Dalits, but in the ultimate analysis they are reduced to resourceless, powerless, and baseless people. Both the so-called mainline intellectuals, academicians and administrators project illiteracy, ignorance and poverty as the evils that affect the Dalit communities. By doing this they totally sideline the real issues of redistribution of resources, progressive political participation, and equity in cultural and economic wealth. Finally, the Dalits are deprived of social and human capital.

Over 160 million Dalits of India demanded a 'Dalit Discourse' in the Durban World Conference Against Racism. Even before the Durban conference, the Dalits were aware of the fact that the Durban Conference will not contribute in any substantial manner to their struggle for emancipation. But all the 'much ado about nothing' as the opponents of Dalit issue put it, was an attempt to highlight their plight at the international forum so that the Indian mindset gets exposed of its caste bias.

In the post-Durban phase, many questions are raised about the very utility and legitimacy of the 'hue and cry' raised before Durban. The 'dust storm' that was raised by Dalit discourse at Durban has not settled down. Possibly as claimed by some of the non-Dalits, the entire attempt by the Dalit activists and human rights activists was an exercise in futility. Times to come will decide on it. But one fact is for sure, Dalit discourse will continue for some more time, even if the non-Dalits resist it or even if the Dalits themselves do not raise the issue.

Taking into account, the various issues that have emerged over the years in general and the discourse that took place before Durban conference in particular, this book has been prepared to present the social facts from the perspectives of the Dalit masses. It is perceived that the next two decades are crucial to Dalit discourse in more than one sense. It is not assumed that this book will colour the emerging Dalit discourse. But it is hoped that it would provide the pointers for Dalit discourse from the perspectives of the Dalits.

Even before the Durban conference, I wrote a book with limited objectives trying to give shape to many of the issues that were emerging in the Indian scenario. That was a response to the false alarm raised by some of the social scientists who branded the attempts of the Dalits, Dalit activists and human rights activists who were raising the issue of caste at the international forum as an attempt to equate casteism with racism. Hence, I had titled the book "Casteism is more Horrendous than Racism".

In the post-Durban phase, I am bringing out this book in a revised and enlarged form with broader objectives. There were many interpretations about the outcome of the World Conference Against Racism. The dominant castes vehemently criticised the attempt to take the caste discrimination to the international forum. Some critiques went to the extent of saying that the entire exercise was futile. These opponents of the Dalit cause failed to correlate the outcome of the Durban Conference with the agenda of those who were engaged in this exercise. Among those who went to Durban to represent the Dalit cause, some were euphoric about the visibility the caste discrimination attained at the World Conference

Against Racism. They made themselves and others believe that the battle has been won. Once again they were busy pretending a phenomenal success, while in my reading the issue has only been 'discovered' and 'made visible'. This false propaganda needed to be countered with hard data.

While the Dalit activists and human rights activists provided visibility to caste discrimination at international arena, at the domestic front atrocities were unleashed on the Dalits. It is the common Dalit masses who were subjected to oppression, exploitation and repression on day to day basis. What needs to be done to alleviate their suffering continues to be the central question.

Caste discrimination and atrocities, identity formation and assertion among the Dalits are integral part of Dalit liberation and emancipation. But there are differences of opinion among Dalit activists about the path Dalit movement should take. This book attempts to identify some of these factors.

This book is based on secondary data and is designed more as a popular book. Moreover, this book like many other works of its time focuses on many of the historical, day-to-day, structural issues that affect the Dalits. It tries to examine these issues and the arena where these issues unfold themselves as part of the socio-political processes. It is hoped that this book would further the Dalit discourse for liberation and emancipation.

Prakash Louis

Acknowledgements

I take this opportunity to thank first and foremost the Dalit masses, who have been the mute witness of the entire Dalit discourse, for their ability to perceive the various discourses that are going on in the Indian society and polity. It is they who continue to challenge me to address the issues that are dear to them both at the theoretical level as well as at the practical area.

Many people have contributed in the preparation and presentation of this book. There are some among them who challenged my theoretical perception as well as the limitedness of the day to day experience.

I am grateful to Mr. Fidelis Tirkey, Ms. Seema Toppo, Mr. Malviya, Mr. Samu and Mr. Mohan who are the staff of the library, documentation and journal section of the Indian Social Institute, for providing me with the material needed for the preparation of this book. I thank Bijulal who went through the entire manuscript and provided valuable suggestions and corrections. I thank Ms. Ann King, Ms. Anjana Dua and Mr. Jacob for typing the text. I want to place in record my gratitude to Gyan Publishing House, who invited me to write this book and brought out this book in a record time. Finally, I am indebted to everyone who helped me in getting the manuscript ready and finally getting it published in book form. But I am solely responsible for the mistakes.

Prakash Louis

Introduction

Caste Discrimination

Six persons belonging to the Dalit community in Barabanki district, barely 22 kms from Lucknow the capital of Uttar Pradesh were subjected to brutal acid attack on the 24th October 2000. The dominant caste Thakurs who are also the landed gentry of the area carried out this barbarous assault because they were infuriated by the failure to procure a tender for fishing rights in a nearby pond. The Dalits who dared to challenge the hegemony and the monopoly of the Thakurs were 'taught the historical lesson'. A Dalit woman was stripped naked and beaten to death by two upper backward caste men in Negla village in Agra district. This woman made the mistake of crossing the path of Virendra Pal and Vijay Pal, carrying an empty pot.[1]

Similarly in Hasnapur of Varanasi district, five Dalits were beaten to death by the Thakurs because one of them 'defied the dictates of the Rajputs' and filed a FIR against the criminal assault made by a Rajput of the village.[2] This enraged the dominant caste Rajputs and they took law into their hands against the 'erring untouchables of the village'. Here it needs to be stated that by filing a FIR it is not assured that action will be taken against the offender. It is an age-old practice that more often than not even FIR lodged by the Dalits and the downtrodden are not registered by the police station. In this case, the dominant caste Rajputs were provoked because the Dalits dared to register their complain with the police.

These types of brutal and barbaric assaults heaped on the Dalits are not limited to Uttar Pradesh alone. Beating, bashing and branding of Dalit men, women and children go on unabated all over India everyday and in fact every minute. The barbers of many villages in Jodhpur district of Rajasthan even now do not allow the entry of the Dalits into the barbershops. Thus it is not just the 'holy of holies' that would become impure and contaminated by the very sight of the Dalits, but even the barbershops would be defiled and desecrated by their very presence. A group of upper caste Hindus beat up Dalit youth and women when they came to collect water from the only source of the village in Khambhala village in Amreli district of Saurashtra region of Gujarat. These incidents have once again reinforced the age-old caste barriers and caste discriminations.

It is of seminal significance to underscore this social fact that social segregation and caste exclusion are assuming their draconian face today than ever. In Bassapur a remote village in Bellari in Karnataka there are separate tumblers for caste Hindus and the Dalits. If you are an upper caste you will get 'Special Tea' in a steel tumbler. But if you are a Dalit you must settle for hindalium mugs kept in the corner outside the hotel.[3] In the past when hotels where not in existence in rural areas, there was no possibility of discrimination of this type. Now with changed circumstances the caste segregation has taken newer forms. Interestingly, the Bellari constituency attained maximum media attention during the 13th Lok Sabha elections. This was due to the high profile election contest, involving Ms. Sushma Swaraj and Ms. Sonia Gandhi. But the entire media did not care to expose the caste discrimination, which is continuing under new garb in one of the most progressive states in India.

"I will always remember the faces of my husband and his seven friends who were beheaded, after the bus they were in was stopped by the upper castes, who separated the Dalits from other villagers. This massacre was not committed because there was enmity between those who were beheaded and the upper castes. This heinous crime was committed because we are Dalits, the "untouchables" and my husband won the *panchayat* elections. While the rest of the village was rejoicing at the election of my husband, the upper caste men vowed that they would avenge this 'disgrace'. They carried out their death threat six months after the election. Now they continue to threat us with dire consequences if we seek legal justice to the atrocities committed against us". This was the gruesome tale recounted by Manimegalai, a delegate from the Dalit community who participated in the conference against racism at Durban in South Africa in September 2001. Through this testimony of Manimegalai, the discrimination suffered by 160 million Dalits in India was made visible for the first time in the international arena.[4] For the past few decades, Tamil Nadu had witnessed 'self-right' and 'self-determination' movements. But there is no scope for self-right movement for the Dalits of Tamil Nadu.

Progress: Myth and Reality

The above-narrated incidents provide only a glimpse of the daily occurrences of brutal atrocities in the lives of over 160 million Dalits[5] of India. On the one hand, India could boast of being one of the most progressive modern states, adept at introducing and engaging in modern technology. Based on the technological development, the United Nations Development Programme's (UNDP) Human Development Report 2001 has ranked India as one of the 72 countries, which is reported to have made 'real progress' over the last year.[6] Throughout the report India has been cited positively as one of the countries, which has made great strides especially in the area of information technology. Interestingly, Bangalore has been cited as a world class IT hub.

On the other hand, the atrocities committed against the Dalits and the downtrodden can shame even the greatest perpetrators of apartheid world has even known. While Bangalore could boast of being the centre of information technology, just at the outskirts of Bangalore (Kamabalahalli) seven Dalits were burnt to death by the upper caste Reddys. Here too the Dalits braved to organise themselves under caste forums, to do away with caste discrimination. It baffles a person with common sense that what was the wrong done by these seven victims that they should be subjected to such a monstrous 'punishment'.

Seeing a Dalit woman walking with an empty earthen vessel could trigger off a vicious and violent reaction from the so-called upper caste is a clear indication of the abhorrence the dominant castes have towards the Dalits and the downtrodden. It also exposes the age-old blind belief in omen that the empty pot is the indication of failure one would encounter in the mission towards which one is proceeding. It is significant to note that if an individual from the Dalit community or a group of Dalits were on their way and if they encountered a woman with empty pot, they would not think of penalising her for appearing before them with an empty vessel. But for the dominant castes the doors are always open to take laws into their own hands and 'do away with the culprit'. This also goes to state the fact that obscurantism is ruling the roost of the Indian mind set even in an age of modern education and technological development.

Going further, one also observes that India can claim to compete with the Silicon Valley, but has not got rid of its most detestable and despicable blind practices. But it is not just adhering to an unchallenged and cruel form of behaviour that haunts the mind of any human being but the Dalit woman becoming victim of this inhuman blind faith is the central question that needs to be faced squarely today. Vijay Pal and Virendra Pal did not commit this murderous crime only because the empty pot foretold a bad omen. They instantaneously engaged in this heinous crime because they were also absolutely sure of the fact that they could strip naked, bash up and murder the woman and get away with the crime. Going further, one can venture to state that these two men could even be ranked as 'upholders' of *varnashrama dharma*. This is irrespective of the fact that the woman had not committed any mistake except the fact that she hails from the untouchable community. On the other hand, one cannot imagine of similar treatment to be meted out to a woman from the dominant caste.

Caste: Discriminatory Behaviour

The word 'caste' is sometimes used as translation to varna, a term denoting the four groups or categories of Hindu society: Brahmins, whose duties are religious scholarship and priestcraft; Kshatriyas, the kings and soldiers who protect society and sponsor rituals; Vaishyas, the agriculturalists, cattle herders, and traders; and Shudras, who must serve the other three classes. The word jati, which exists in more Indian languages, literally means 'kind' or 'species' and can denote a range of social categories, although one of its primary references is 'caste'. Among the Hindus, the vast majority has taken it for granted that every one of them belongs to a caste. Caste divisions are also found among Muslims, Christians, Sikhs and other religious minorities, although generally not among the tribal peoples. Castes also exist in Pakistan, Bangladesh, Sri Lanka, and Nepal as well as among South Asians overseas.[7]

Social scientists in general and Louis Dumont[8] in particular continued to argue that caste system should be grasped in relation to ideas and values, as a system grounded in a distinctly religious ideology of hierarchy. This is a reality, because, caste system derives its sustenance from religious principles. But the social scientists of this tradition failed to examine the religious grounding of the system in its day-to-day operations. One of the most crucial and vital fact that was overlooked by even the later day analysts of the caste system in general and discrimination of the Dalits in particular was that the interpreters were from the dominant castes. Hence, it was a birds-eye view and not worms eye-view.

Some of the salient features of caste system are as follows: the most distinctive feature of caste system is that it is hierarchical in nature. That is castes are ascriptive status groups with no individual social mobility between them. Caste system is segmentary in so far as all larger castes are normally divided into sub-castes, and are sometimes further split into sub-sub-castes. From the point of view of economy, caste system also defines a division of labour, and many occupations are caste-specific, especially in the services and artisan sectors. Finally, caste system is predicated on social inequality and in principle all castes within a locality can be mutually ranked within a single hierarchy.[9]

Within the broader social interaction, there were and are different behavioural patterns practiced towards different social categories. This has been accepted as a social reality. These behaviour patterns did not emerge at random or where they the handy work of some individual with malice. These interactional behavioural patterns are historical and social. One can find some illustration of this fact from the code of Manu. "That a king shall never execute a Brahman though convicted of all possible crimes but may banish him with all his property secure and his body unhurt. No greater crime is known on the earth than slaying a Brahman;

and the king therefore must not even form in his mind an idea of killing a priest".[10]

Historically speaking, one sees a continuation in the attitude and behaviour of the dominant castes, which deny educational environment for the marginalised communities. This can be illustrated through some historical events. Due to the severity of caste discrimination special schools were opened for the children of lower castes so that they benefit through educational qualification. But the reaction of the caste Hindus was one of continuous opposition to the education of those who, in their eyes, were fated to a life of ignorance. Official reports in the late 19th and 20th centuries are replete with the accounts of the many trials and tribulations of untouchable children who persevered to receive an education even in 'special' schools set up exclusively for them. For instance, it is reported that the boys of *Cherumar*, that is, the ancient slave caste boys used to have their books snatched out of their hands as they went to schools established for them in Calicut in Kerala. In Kaira district of Gujarat, five or six large schools were closed down and the crops of the depressed people burnt whey they attempted to avail education. As late as 1931, the *Kallars* of Ramnad district in Tamil Nadu, laid down strictures like the children of the lower castes should not read and get themselves literate or educated'.[11]

It is also reported that the British government acknowledged that it was not religious sentiment, unclean habits and unpolished manners of the lower caste boys that drew objection to their education from the upper castes. They are also occasionally due to the desire of the upper castes to keep the low castes in a state of subjection and sovereignty. This view is validated by the later fact that once the social environment became conducive the lower castes entered into educational arena in a massive way. Night schools became the best centre in the early stages to impart education among the depressed castes.[12]

Caste discrimination was not and is not limited to Dalits or the untouchables, but it extends to all the lower communities. The backward castes, who were also the Shudras, were subjected to discriminatory treatment. Some of the British administrators have observed that the relationship between the upper caste and the upper backward castes[13] has been very strained. Lacey wrote, "In August 1926 feelings between the *Goalas* and *Babans* were reported to be very strained at Barh, and this tension was increased by the mysterious disappearance of a member of the *Goala* community". Collins observed that 'such incidents often enough culminated in serious riots'.[14] These reports also identify the issues that lie deeper than the one that sets the spark for violent confrontations between various caste groups. The backward castes demanded social equality and this was also expressed politically in terms of mobilizing votes for their caste candidates. They also refused to render *begari,* that is, forced labour and resisted the demand for illegal taxes. Thus, economic, social and political issues converged together in the assertion of the backwards to put an end to various forms of oppression by the upper caste landlords. This assertion of the G*oalas* had to face stiff reprisal from the landlords. They 1) deprived the *Goalas* from the *Khud kast* lands, 2) threw them out of their homes claiming that those houses belong to them, 3) refused the use of grazing grounds for G*oalas*' cattle, 4) refused drinking water from public tanks, 5) and finally, imposed social boycott.[15] If this was the case with the backward castes one can imagine the plight of the lower castes.

Education was not the only one sector that was denied to the Dalits. There was total ostracism and denial of rights to be human. In December 1930 the *Kallar*[16] in Ramnad propounded eight prohibitions the disregard of which led to the use of violence by the Kallars against the exterior castes whose huts were burnt, whose granaries and property were destroyed, whose livestock was looted. These eight prohibitions were as follows:

1. That the *Adi Dravidas*[17] should not wear ornaments of gold and silver;
2. That the males should not be allowed to wear their clothes below their knees or above their hips;
3. That their males should not wear coats or shirts or banyans;
4. No *Adi Dravida* shall be allowed to have his hair cropped;
5. That the *Adi Dravida* should not use other than earthen-ware vessels in their homes;

6. Their women shall not be allowed to cover the upper portion of their bodies;
7. Their women shall not be allowed to use flowers;
8. The men shall not use umbrellas for protection against sun and rain nor should they wear sandals.

Not satisfied with these injunctions the Kallars in June 1931 came up with more prohibitions.[18]

Kerala is one of the most literate states of India. It is also acclaimed for its socio-political awareness as well as the sense of equality among the people. But if one looks at historical records one realises this fact caste system and its abusive practices were in tact in here too. 'If a Pulayan (an untouchable) wishes to address a man of higher caste he must stand a far off and 'cry aloud'. If a Pulayan touched a Brahman, the Brahman must at once bathe and read much of the divine books and change his Brahminical thread'.[19] There are many social scientists and social activists who would shake their head vehemently and argue that this was in the past and now 'untouchability' is not practiced, which is contrary to the reality.

The upper caste Hindus refused to enumerate Dalits as Hindus. "Many of the more bigoted high caste Hindoos employed as census enumerators or supervisors objected to record such low persons as of the Hindoo religion. This was illustrated by numerous instances brought to my notice of such persons having been recorded as of the *Dher*, *Mang* or *Chandal* religion by mere repetition of their caste in the column for religion. Possibly some in their humility and ignorance may not even have claimed to be of the Hindoo religion. More probably they were not even asked".[20] This once again goes to establish the fact that even in census enumeration, the Dalits and the downtrodden were kept out. Further, this extreme practice of exclusion culminated in slavery and bondage.

The colonial administrators have also recorded the *malik-kamia*, that is, landlord-bonded labourer (which in extension could be stated to be the relationship between the dominant castes and dominated castes) interaction. The following description is self-explanatory: "The household of the *Raja* [in Palamu],[21] and every considerable *jageerdar*, that is, local chieftain cum landlord, was a perfect feudal establishment. It was a matter of pride to be surrounded by a train of "*burkundauzes*" (guards), "*fakirs*" (devotees), "*shikarees*" (huntsmen), and "*bhats*" and "*bad feroshes*" (family poets and bards), and a still larger retinue of *serfs* called *kumeas*, whose state of bondage is the counterpart of the condition of the *servi* of the eight and ninth centuries in Europe".[22] Thus, it is not only the slavery and bondage to which the Dalits and the downtrodden are reduced to which has rendered the discrimination irremovable, but the continuance of arrogant way of life, which has denied any scope for mitigation of the system.

It would be invidious to single out one factor as the determining aspect of social segregation of the Dalits and the downtrodden. But the one over arching mode of thought of this social exclusion and inclusion is that the exploited and subjugated masses were termed as savage, brute, anti-social, uncouth and crude. Those who termed the subjugated masses as savage etc. themselves were termed as *sabhya*, that is, polite, courteous, well bred and well mannered. Thus, the freedom enjoyed by the dominant castes and feudal landed gentry in the rural regions of India was not limited to political power, economic resources, social status and educational centers. But the power and the freedom to castigate the subjugated and marginalized masses in whichever from and manner they wanted.

It is this historical practice of reducing vast masses of the population to unfreedom, which is central to the social malaise of Indian society. The student of political sociology of India in her or his examination of the social reality of India becomes acutely aware of the fact that in the rural sector, feudal behaviour and practice have become the norm of operation between the landowning dominant castes and the landless dominated castes. In addition to this, feudalism in this scenario is not confined to landownership alone. But it is intimately linked to caste aggression and dominance and is also expression of a certain mindset. It is a way of being which enforces ruthless control over others' way of life, property and freedom.[23]

Dalits are subjected to atrocities of all forms is undisputable from the available data. But the agony undergone by the Dalits are only one side of the coin. The Dalit assertion also come of age and is also creating ripples in the Indian society. The fact of the matter is that Dalit assertion may be in limited sectors and geographical areas, but these revolts and protests, open up avenues for a long drawn-out struggle can not be denied. Javed Alam's argument amplifies this social process. 'The great merit of the concept of collective unfreedom is that it provides us with a historical basis as well as a heuristic tool to understand, what I would like to call, the great battle for bourgeois equality being fought out in the many terrains of Indian democracy, whether we look at the electoral battlefield, structure of power, institutions of parliamentary rule, bureaucratic set up, educational arena and so on. India, to note in passing, is the only country in the world (among those for which data is available) where the composition of the electorate has changed in favour of the vulnerable section of the population between 1971 and 1996.[24]

Elimination of Discrimination

The foregoing brief discussion illuminates this fact that while the suppression and marginalisation of the Dalits and the downtrodden are ongoing process, the resistance and struggle also go on unabated. Thus, the Dalits are assiduously attempting to change their state of unfreedom and subjugation. The Dalit discourse has inbuilt content and strategy for liberation and emancipation. These refer to the collective efforts by the Dalits and the downtrodden for enhancing their power for collective action. The various terms used to describe collective action carry many different inflections. They include attitudinal terms such as dissent, opposition, resistance, protest, defiance; terms emphasizing methods of action such as riot, violence, jacquerie, rebellion, mutiny, revolution, petition, demonstration, consciousness raising; general terms with normative or political overtones such as class struggle, liberation, emancipation, participation, empowerment; and social science terminology such as collective behaviour, collective action, social movement.[25]

Emancipation of the Dalits and the downtrodden from oppression and exploitation to become builders of an egalitarian, democratic and pluralistic social order is the central focus of empowerment today. Both at the national and international order, various attempts are being made.

At the international realm, the International Day for the Elimination of Racial Discrimination is commemorated on 21st March. The historical root of this commemoration is to honour the victims of Sharpeville massacre on 21st March 1960, in which 69 peaceful demonstrators against apartheid were killed by South African police forces. In his message on 21st March 2003, the UN Secretary-General Kofi Annan stated, 'The Sharpeville massacre marked an important watershed in the fight against racism, but the fight is not yet won. More than 40 years later, racial discrimination, xenophobia and related intolerance are still extremely serious problems. Indeed, discrimination is deeply imbedded in the economic, social and political structures of many societies, and has been among the root cause of a number of violent conflicts. Members of particular racial or ethnic groups continue to be more likely to be poor and to have less access to adequate health services and education than dominant groups. The persistence of old patterns of racism condemns many people to a life of marginalisation and humiliation. And in the last decade, new manifestations of hatred have emerged.'[26]

In brief and in essence, caste discrimination and caste oppression are not anything new to the Indian sub-continent. But what is extraordinary to the caste system and caste based deprivation is the newer forms these oppressions and exploitation can take in the everyday discourse and interaction. Interestingly social segregation based on casteism is not only operative in the social sphere. It is even more dominant in the political arena of modern state. While the ruling establishment engaged the marginalised communities in nation building, it thrived on the hard labour and toil of the masses. Even those who eloquently spoke against caste discrimination did not deem it imperative to eliminate the caste system.

The iron grip of caste system is so powerful that the Indians who have migrated to other countries practice caste discrimination in its totality. It is reported that 'In the United States, a rising number of caste-based groups –each with chapters throughout many major cities- also points to the importance of castes as an identifier for migrant Indian communities. Such caste-based associations in the United States are providing funds and political support for a resurgence of caste fundamentalism in South Asia as well'.[27] It is not at the economic or the political level the segregation and seclusion continues among the Diaspora, the by now infamous 'no temple entry' continues there too. For instance, in Britain emigrant Dalits must also worship in segregated temples and have thus formed an umbrella group for low-caste temples-Guru Ravidass UK. Twenty-two of these temples withheld (and ultimately redirected) funds raised for earthquake victims in Gujarat due to incidents of caste discrimination in the distribution of earthquake relief.[28]

Caste distinction and caste violence is not limited to India. In Britain caste tensions frequently erupt between high-caste Punjabis (Jats) and low-caste Punjabis (Ravidasis). Physical violence has also been known to erupt following intermarriage between the two communities. Caste consciousness becomes especially problematic given the sizeable population of both Jats and Ravidasis in the United Kingdom.[29] It is therefore clear that the death penalty imposed on those youngsters who cross the caste boundary in their attempt to search life partners is not limited to some parts of Uttar Pradesh and Rajasthan, but a global phenomenon as for as caste is concerned.

Mahatma Jotirao Phule, as early as 1870 presented scathing attack on the dominant castes because of their subjugation of the downtrodden. In the Preface to his book Slavery he wrote, "Since the advent of the rule of Brahmins for centuries, the Shudras and Atishudras are suffering hardships and are lading miserable lives. To draw people's attention to this and that they should think over their misfortune and that they should eventually set themselves free from this tyranny of the Bhats (Brahmins) perpetrated on them- is the main aim of this book".[30]

Jotirao Phule engaged in this sharp criticism not due to any personal enmity with the Brahmins. His criticism emanated from his comprehension of this Indian social reality that the dominant castes who appropriated material power have also taken control over mental power. Due to this, they determine the life, thought patterns, other activities economic, political etc. He argued, "The Brahman despoils the Shudra not only in his capacity of a priest, but does so in a variety of other ways. Having, by his superior education and cunningness monoplised all the higher places of emolument, the ingenuity of his ways is past finding out".[31]

Former President of India, Shri. K.R. Narayanan in his Address to the Nation on the eve of Republic Day – 2001 pointed out, "The awakening of the women and the youth of India is something that gives us hope. But the march of development is having different kinds of impact on different sections of our people. It tends to widen the existing inequalities and create new inequalities. The already marginalised sections, the Scheduled Castes and Scheduled Tribes, are the greatest sufferers in this process".[32] Thus, contrary to the myth propagated by the ruling establishment, the former President points to the social fact that instead of discrimination and deprivation being eliminated they are perpetuated in newer ways.

This process had and continues to have cumulative and longstanding impact on the Dalits. Those who make pronouncements in terms of the upliftment of the Dalits and the subjugated in India grossly mistake the fact that it is not just the denial of gainful employment or even access to economic resources, which have reduced the Dalits to the state of non-beings. It is the very denial of the right to self-determination, self-actualisation and self-respect, which is at the core of cultural and political poverty of the Dalits. Denial of basic opportunities for self-expression curtails self-confidence and social exclusion completes the picture by indoctrinating paralyzing fear. This is one of the most devastating aspects of caste discrimination on the Dalits.

Further, the political establishment of this country, instead of taking these aspects into examination and striving to bring necessary changes, is continuing to turn a blind eye to these issues. The dominant castes and ruling classes of India, had also taken unilateral decision that the issue 'caste discrimination is more horrendous than racial discrimination' should not be brought for examination and rectification in the international arena in the World Conference

Against Racism' that was held in Durban from 31st August to 7th September, 2001. The ruling class and dominant castes waged relentless war against the inclusion of caste discrimination in the agenda of WCAR.

Dalit individuals, activists and human rights activists were engaged in a discourse with the ruling dispensation that any issue that affects a vast segment of the population should be allowed to be taken up for debate both in the domestic and international forums. According to them, the issues of the common masses in general and that of the dalits and the downtrodden surpass, national boundaries. But the ruling castes and classes were bent on throttling this attempt from its very womb. The following pages try to spell out this discursive discourse of Dalit discrimination. This book also looks at the various attempts made by the Dalit communities as well as other human rights groups to ensure the rights of the Dalits to be human and live like human beings. An attempt is also made here to look at the post-Darban scenario of the dalit emancipation and liberation.

It is appropriate to conclude this section by quoting the prophetic words of Mahatma Jotirao Phule. "The potent remedy for this is as follows: All the Shudras and Ati-Shudras as also our other compatriots such as the tribals, the fishermen etc. who have been traditionally condemned as mean, ignoble and insignificant by the Aryan-Bhats/Brahmins for centuries, should send their sons and daughters to the schools where they will begin to learn the tenets of true knowledge. When, in due course of time, when all our sons and daughters will be properly educated in the tenets of the true knowledge a saintly character will arise from among the ranks of the Shudras and other allied classes, who will strew flowers over the graves of us all and will truly sanctify and glorify our names. I prophesy thus with my heart brimming over with joy and grateful thanks.'[33]

References

1. For analysis of similar incidents see, Prakash Louis, Dalit Human Rights are for Violation. State of Human Rights in India, 2000, Indian Social Institute, New Delhi, 2001, p. 33ff.

2. Anand Swarup Varma, *Hindutva ki Rajniti ka Sawarna prakar*. Jansatta, 1.7.2001, p. 6.
3. Bellary is a century behind, Untouchability is a way of life there. Indian Express, 1.9.1999, p. 1.
4. Prakash Louis. Globalising Caste or Nationalising Hypocrisy?, Subalterns, Indian Social Institute, New Delhi, July-September, 2001, p. 1.
5. The term 'Dalit' is and has been defined exclusively and inclusively. There are some Dalits and non-Dalits, who under exclusive definition refer only to the Scheduled Castes or erstwhile untouchables. There is another group of Dalits and non-Dalits who includes Scheduled Castes and Scheduled Tribes under the category Dalits. Thus, 160 million Scheduled Castes and 80 million Scheduled Tribes are at times clubbed together and called Dalits. This group of people at times in extension also includes all the exploited masses within the fold of Dalit. In this book, the term Dalit has been used only in exclusive sense.
6. Human Development Report 2001. United Nations Development Programme's (UNDP), Oxford University Press, 2001.
7. Christopher J. Fuller. Caste. In The Oxford India Companion to Sociology and Social Anthropology. (ed). Oxford University Press: New Delhi, 2001, pp. 477-501.
8. Louis Dumont. Homo Hierarchicus: The Caste System and its Implications. Weidenfeld and Nicolson: London, 1970.
9. Christopher J. Fuller. *Ibid.*
10. Quoted in Wilson, Indian Caste, I, p. 22.
11. Geetha B. Nambissan. Equity in Education? Schooling of Dalit children in India. Economic and Political Weekly, April 20-27, 1996, p. 1011.
12. *Ibid.*
13. Other backward castes are now divided into two categories: Upper Backward Castes and Most Bacward Castes.
14. A.N.Das. Agrarian Movements in India: Studies in 20th Century Bihar. Frank Cass: London. 1982, p. 50.
15. Hetukar Jha. Lower Caste Peasants and Upper Caste Zamindars in Bihar 1921-51: an Analysis of Sanskritization, and contradiction Between the Two Groups. Indian Economic and Social History Review 9, (4) 1977, p. 551.
16. Interestingly, Kallars are not one of those non-polluting upper castes but come from the backward castes. They were themselves treated

as polluting castes by the upper castes. This is akin to the pecking order. Since, the Kalars were ill-treated by the upper castes, they in turn imposed sanctions on the hapless lower castes. It is this type of mind set and behaviour pattern which is leading to crisis in Bihar, Uttar Pradesh, Punjab and Haryana, where the erstwhile other backward castes like the Yadavs, Kurmis, Jats and Gujjars who are equally oppressive towards the Dalits. This also reduces any scope for building a broader alliance between the lower segments of the caste order.

17. Adi Dravida refers to one of the sub-castes among the Dalits in Tamil Nadu.
18. Quoted in J.R. Kamble, Rise and Awakening of Depressed Classes in India. National Publishing House, Delhi, 1979, p. 9.
19. Dr. J.H. Hutton. Caste in India, Oxford, 1963, p. 79 as quoted in J.R. Kamble, Rise and Awakening of Depressed Classes in India. National Publishing House, Delhi, 1979, p. 7.
20. Report on the Census of British India taken on 17th February 1881, Vol. 1, as quoted in John Zavos, The Emergence of Hindu Nationalism in India, p. 14.
21. Palamu is a tribal region, which was made a district under the British rule in 1928 itself. Till the year 2001, it was part of Bihar State and now is under Jharkhand State. Palamu district was and is known for extremely oppressive feudal behaviour.
22. Gyan Prakash. Bonded Histories: Genealogies of Labour Servitude in Colonial India. Cambridge University Press: Cambridge. 1990, p. 153.
23. Refer to Prakash Louis. People Power: The Naxalite Movement in Central Bihar. Wordsmiths: New Delhi, 2002.
24. Javed Alam. Is Caste Appeal Casteism?; Oppressed Castes in Politics. In Community and Identities: Contemporary Discourses on Culture and Politics in India. Edited by Surinder S. Jodhka. Sage Publications: New Delhi, 2001, p. 99.
25. Jan Nederveen Pieterse (ed). Emancipation, Modern and Postmodern. Sage Publications, London, 1992, p. 6.
26. Message of the UN Secretary-General Kofi Annan on 21st March 2003.
27. Moses Seenarine. The Persistence of caste and anti-caste Resistance in India and in Diaspora, available in the Internet.
28. Naresh Puri. Caste Splits Earthquake Appeal, BBC News, February 26, 2001. For a detailed report on the discriminatory behaviour during

the earthquake relief operations, refer to 'Report of the Relief Activities in the Earthquake Affected Areas of Gujarat: The Perceptions of the Marginalised Communities'. Published by the Indian Social Institute, New Delhi, 2001.

29. Sat Pal Muman. Caste in Britain, available in internet. For more details refer to Human Rights Watch, Caste Discrimination: A Global Concern, August 2001.
30. Slavery. Collected Works of Mahatma Jotirao Phule Vol. I. Translated by P.G. Patil. Education Department: Government of Maharashtra, 1991, p. ix.
31. D. Keer and S.G. Malshe (eds). Jotirao Phule. The Collected Works of Mahatma Phule, Maharashtra State Society for Literature and Culture, Bombay 1969 (Marathi), p. 79. The ingenuity of the Brahmins is beyond limits. Recently, I was struck by the remarks of a teacher from Delhi University, who comes from a Dalit community. He commented 'Now I understand why the Brahmins have monopolized teaching as their individual and community profession. To begin with, teaching is the most non-crisis occupation. Further, the teacher builds a wide network, which is often used for pulling the strings'.
32. Taken from the Address to the Nation on the eve of Republic Day – 2001. President K.R. Narayanan has emerged as the conscious keeper of the country at this juncture when good governance seems to be on the decline.
33. Slavery. Collected Works of Mahatma Jotirao Phule Vol. II. Translated by P.G. Patil. Education Department: Government of Maharashtra, 1991, p. 47.

1

Dalits and Caste Discrimination

Dalits and caste discrimination go hand in hand. That the Dalits and the downtrodden are denied even the most basic and fundamental rights is a historical as well as contemporary reality. In the recent past efforts are made to eliminate discrimination. While this approach has become more pronounced, there is also the perception that as long as caste system exists, caste discrimination cannot be done away with. Thus, discrimination of the Dalits within the caste system is assuming gigantic proportion. Also, in the ensuing human rights discourse, discrimination of the Dalits has come to occupy centre stage. Since human rights basically deal with the right to be human, from the point of view of the Dalits, elimination of discrimination constitutes the central agenda than poverty eradication, special provisions etc. Thus, in the human rights discourse, upholding the rights of the Dalits means protecting them from any form of exclusion, segregation, exploitation and subjugation.

The Protection of Human Rights Act 1993 defines human rights in the following manner: "human rights" means the rights relating to life, liberty, equality and dignity of the individual guaranteed by the Constitution or embodied in the International Covenants and enforceable by courts in India.[1] Article 21 of the Constitution of India enjoins upon the state that it uphold the personal liberty of all the citizens. From legal point of view, Article 21 is of the widest amplitude and it covers a variety of rights, which go to constitute the personal liberty of man and some of them have been raised to the status of distinct fundamental rights and given additional protection under Article 19.

The Constitution of India also ensures for all the citizens a life with human dignity. Right to live with human dignity enshrined in Article 21, derives its life breath from the Directive Principles of State Policy and particularly clauses (e) and (f) of Article 39 and Articles 41 and 42. And at the least, therefore, it must include protection of the health and strength of workers, men and women, and of the tender age of children against abuse, opportunities and facilities for children to develop in a healthy manner and in conditions-of freedom and dignity, educational facilities, just and humane conditions of work and maternity relief. These are the minimum requirements, which must exist in order to enable a person to live with human dignity and no State — neither the Central Government nor any State Government — has the right to take any action, which will deprive a person of the enjoyment of these basic essentials.

Thus, the framers of the Constitution ensured that the State shall make provisions to right to work, right to education, right to public assistance etc. It also called for preferential security of health and strength of workers, men and women, children etc. The Directive Principles of State Policy goes further and demands equal justice for all and in the case of those who can not afford the lengthy legal procedure it proposes free legal aid. Above all, the constitution prescribes special provision for the advancement of any socially and educationally backward classes of citizens or for the Scheduled Castes and Scheduled Tribes.[2]

Discrimination

Discrimination has been usually considered to be part of every social order. The International Labour Organisation (ILO) Discrimination (Employment and Occupation) Convention, 1958 (no. 111) defines discrimination as any "distinction, exclusion or preference, which has the effect of nullifying or impairing equality of opportunity or treatments in employment or occupation as may be determined".[3] In this Convention, the grounds for non-discrimination include race,[4] colour, sex, religion, political opinion, national extraction or social origin. While the rhetoric of eliminating or reducing discrimination has become a global concern, the reality is that newer forms of discriminations can be seen at all levels and in all sectors.

In the recent past, non-discrimination also came to centre stage of debate at the national and international levels. 'The moral argument for non-discrimination carries a great deal of weight in both the international and the national domains. It stems from the basic human rights premise that all human beings are equal and deserve to be treated as such. Such principles are embedded in the Universal Declaration of Human Rights as well as in the ILO Declaration of Fundamental Principles and Rights to Work. The argument against discrimination is that society disintegrates under discrimination. Race riots, race-related arson attacks, racially motivated murders and the proliferation of neo-Nazi tendencies are all manifestations of the socially detrimental consequences of leaving discrimination unchecked. Equally, violent backlashes against inequality are also more likely to occur when discrimination is not addressed. Economically speaking, it is not only society but also the individual employer who pays the costs of discrimination. By discriminating, employers are failing to use the full potential of the human resources available to them and are therefore neither maximizing production nor minimizing costs.'[5]

The definition of discrimination according to the International Encyclopedia of Sociology *reads*, "Discrimination is the denial of opportunities and rights to certain groups on the basis of race, sex, ethnicity, age or disability'. In common parlance discrimination can be simply defined as prejudice transformed into action. Thinking of a group of people in a certain way and then promoting practices or conditions that support that thinking is discrimination.[6] Discrimination is learned behaviour and this is passed on to next generation.

Sociologically there are four categories of discrimination.

(1) Intentional individual discrimination. This refers to isolated act of discrimination performed by an individual on the basis of personal prejudice.

(2) Unintentional individual discrimination, which is an isolated act of discrimination performed unconsciously by an individual.

(3) Intentional institutional discrimination occurs when discrimination is based on the personal prejudices of the members of an institution.

(4) Unintentional institutional discrimination is discrimination that is part of routine behaviour of an institution that has unknowingly incorporated prejudicial practices into its operating procedures.

In the recent past, discussions on discrimination have focused on unintentional institutional discrimination by suggesting different measures for correcting this. Some people believe that this form of discrimination can be corrected by affirmative action programmes. But there are others who argue that the protective action only pretends to rectify the wrongs but protect the statusquo.[7]

In India, discrimination in general and discrimination based on caste was supposed to have been done away with after the introduction of Constitution. One social reformer and political leader who would be remembered for presenting scathing critique on caste discrimination is Dr. Ambedkar. In his work "On Annihilation of Caste" he argued that the untouchables were subjected to various forms of discrimination. "Under the rule of the Peshwas in the Maratha country the untouchable was not allowed to use the public streets if a Hindu was coming along lest he should pollute the Hindu by his shadow. The untouchable was required to prevent the Hindus from getting themselves polluted even by an accidental touch. The caste Hindus were intolerant to accept any token change in the daily routine of the lower castes, which they feared as change against the hierarchical order .In November 1935 in the village of Zanu in the Ahmedabad district of Gujarat, some untouchable women of well-to-do families started fetching water in metal pots. The Hindus looked upon the use of metal pots by untouchables as an affront to their dignity and assaulted the untouchable women for their impudence."[8] This is a clear case for the social and historical discrimination in the Indian society.

Discrimination in various forms and intensity seems to have coexisted with humanity. Apartheid based on race is usually considered to be one of the most exploitative forms of discrimination. In the recent past, with the efforts by Dalit activists and human rights activists, caste discrimination is considered to be equally if not more horrendous than racial discrimination. Caste discrimination, compared to many other forms of discrimination leads to more disadvantage, dispossession, dehumanization and degradation, and maintains and reinforces social segregation and exclusion.

Social Exclusion

Social exclusion is an institutionalised attempt to keep out or to 'outcast' a segment of the population from the social order. Here we do not deal with one particular individual who 'ill-treats' another person, but the social processes that are operative in general. Thus, social segregation is an institutionalized form of social distancing expressed in physical separation. It signifies the convergence of physical and social space and is to be distinguished from other social forms, which also structure social distance in spatial terms[9].

In course of human development, social exclusion has taken the form of segregating a group of people from the social, political, economic and cultural domains of societal life.[10] But the fundamental social reality that needs to be exposed here is that social exclusion does not limit itself to segregation and deprivation. Social seclusion and isolation provides base for a sense of superiority and inferiority among the citizens of the same society or country. Further, it also culminates into a system of domination and subjugation. All these processes ultimately lead to oppression and exploitation. The seminal social fact of segregation is that it is justified and legitimized by social or religious traditions.

Since social exclusion and segregation provide space for domination, discrimination and deprivation, those who benefit out of this social formation do not want to introduce any change in this structure. Significantly, this social system becomes highly resistant to change and transformation. Interestingly it is not only those who discriminate against those who are supposed to be 'inferior, incapable, less meritorious and lower' who resist change, even those who are victims of discrimination also do not want to alter the existing social system. This is not because they want to remain in the dehumanising social order. But because they fear that greater discrimination and repression may be heaped upon them if they resist discrimination. There is a strong unconscious want, across the generations of the oppressed to remain under the supremacy and hegemony of the dominant segment of the population. Thus, there is a socio-cultural agenda behind the perpetuation of caste system.

Hatred is one of the dominant sentiments that operate in the interaction between the Dalits and the non-Dalits. The Penguin Dictionary of Psychology defines hatred as follows, 'hatred is a deep, enduring, intense emotion expressing animosity, anger and hostility towards a person, or a group or an object. Social discrimination in due course of time culminates into hatred. Hatred usually assumed to be the desire to harm or cause pain to the object or the emotion and feelings of pleasure from the object's misfortune' (1985). According to the Chambers Dictionary, the term 'hate' means to dislike intensely, or extreme dislike or enmity. Thus, hatred could be defined as an intense dislike towards a person or a group of persons, which in course of time leads to objectifying the sentiment of hate. Thus, there develops an inimical attitude and behaviour towards the person hated.

Going further it can also be stated that the sentiment of hatred is transformed into destructive action. Here, the destruction is not limited to material universe but gets extended to social space and psychological arena. In this way hatred gets institutionalised and it becomes the regular form of reaction as well as special mode of counteraction towards the person or object of hate. When hatred gets institutional sanction it become much more brutal and barbaric. Moreover, violence inflicted on the 'victim' is not limited to physical alone but extends to all spheres of life. This leads to violence and counter violence.

From the point of view of the Dalits, caste hatred is an institutionalised form of discrimination and dehumanization. It has permeated all aspects of social life. In this process, caste hatred has deprived the lower castes of resources, power and human dignity and thus has reduced the Dalits to the most degrading social existence. Thus, caste segregation did not confine itself to individual realm but took hold of collective interaction too. And thus, the Dalits became the victims of socio-historical process of segregation, exclusion and discrimination.

Caste Discrimination

With regard to the Indian caste system there is a line of thinking, which holds and propagates the myth that the division of social units and placing them in a hierarchy based on caste is the basis for integration of social order. In extension, it is also argued here that this 'integrated caste system' is also the basis of non-disintegration of Indian social order. According to the Vedic texts, the *chaturvarna* or the caste system is supposed to have emerged from the sacrifice of the primeval being, the *Purusa Sukta*. But this religious myth was extended to justify the social stratification of society. An analogy was extended to real social grouping. Here, the legitimacy for social exclusion was derived from religious texts.

Among the writings of Hindu religious texts, the *Smrtis* preserve the traditions, precepts, customs and rules of conduct and rites in the Vedas. Manu Smriti falls under this category. It has been considered as the standard and the most authoritative work on Hindu law, and contains information about the social, cultural, religious, ethical, educational, political, and judicial aspects of life. Manu in Chapter I, verse 87 declares, " For the preservation of all his creation, He, of great, effulgence, laid down separate duties for those originate from his mouth (Brahminas), from His arms (Kshatriyas), from His thighs (Vaisyas) and from his feet (Sudras). The duties of the Brahmins/priests are study of Vedas, teaching, performance of sacrifices, officiating as priests, and gift making and acceptance of gift [88]. Protection of the people, gift making, performance of sacrifices, study of Vedas are the duties of the Kshatriyas [89]. The Vaisyas are to rear cattle, gift making, performance of sacrifices, study of Vedas, merchandize, money lending and agriculture [90]. Only one work the creator ordained for the Sudras, that is to ungrudgingly serve the above three [91]".[11] The above presented quote from Manusmriti unravels the fact that varna basically refers to a scheme of socially fixed positions and privileges.

Continuing the analysis in the same vein it becomes amply clear that the ideological basis of social exclusion is mostly found in major socio-cultural values. But most often than not they are expressed in religious terms. Thus in the caste order of India, the concept of pollution regulates contact and avoidance in a most extensive range of roles by supernatural sanctions and by sentiments of deep revulsion for defiling contacts. Social exclusion in principle defines boundaries between groups, locates the different groups in a hierarchy and regulates and guides their interaction. The cardinal principle is that there are also strict injunctions against those who do not adhere to these laws. The punishment is stricter and severe as one goes down the caste ladder. Thus, what one is left with is a rigid pyramidal structure with the higher echelon enjoying all the powers and privileges and subjected to nominal restrictions. The lower rung of the order is reduced to unlimited constrains. Above all, any of their behaviour that does not comply with the dominant castes' perception is liable for punishment.

Interestingly, today when the proponents of market economy are propagating the concept of a 'global village' and through this defending an ideology of monoculture as the way of existence and operation, human beings continue to be divided on the basis of caste, class, creed, colour, region, language, ethnicity etc. But among all the basis of social segregation and seclusion, it is caste, which is the most dehumanising, depriving and discriminating phenomenon of all ages, especially in this technological age. As stated above, if the barber from the most backward caste community who is socially just one step ahead of the Dalits in the caste order denies his service to the Dalits, it is a clear indication of the extent of social exclusion and 'untouchability' to which the Dalits are subjected to.

There are some who argue that the barber's behaviour is coloured by his fear of loosing the 'patronage' of the dominant castes. The barber may also have to face the wrath of the dominant castes for engaging in his traditional occupation. There is no denial of this phenomenon in a highly feudal society of Rajasthan. But this is only part of the story. The barber also operates on the principle of purity and pollution in conceptual level. It is also a manifestation of the depth and the intensity of caste discrimination and caste hatred that are inherent in Indian society.

Social exclusion and seclusion are part of every society. With regard to Indian society, Gail Omvedt argues 'wherever we look in the traditional Indian system, hierarchy and inequality among the exploited stands out clearly. Such inequality existed among all feudal societies (medieval Europe); but in India it was institutionalised in the caste system. Cultivating peasants with firm rights to the 'lower share' or to supervising the village distribution of the 'grain heap' were at the top of the village hierarchies; artisans and subordinate tenants had rights that were both institutionalised and secondary; herders and forest dwelling hunters and gatherers exchanged sometimes on a basis of inferiority, sometimes with more independence; but everywhere the lower castes of Dalits/ untouchables performed the most menial labour and were fundamentally differentiated form the others in being classed as 'impure'.[12]

Untouchability is ingrained in the behaviour, in the minds, in the beings, in the social psyche, in the mind-set and in the very existence of the Indian society and Indian State. Mind-set does not refer to thought alone but it denotes the thought pattern of an individual as well as a social collective. But this thought pattern or the mind-set does not get limited to attitudinal realm but gets converted into concrete behaviour. The twice-born or the so called upper castes retained itself as the purest, resource-full, capable, intelligent and superior and reduced the lower castes into an inferior state of existence. This social exclusion and isolation in course of history engrained in the untouchables a deprived and distorted mind-set. In other societies sources of discrimination are being done away with or at least brought under scrutiny. But in India the continuity of the consistency of the iron grip of caste system bears testimony to the ideological basis it provides to all forms of exploitation.

Ambedkar: Caste Discrimination

Dr. Ambedkar having examined the historical roots of untouchability in different societies argues that 'the non-Hindu societies only isolated the individuals affected by defilement. They did not segregate them in separate quarters. The Hindu society segregates the untouchables. The Hindus will not live in the quarters of the untouchables and will not allow the untouchables to live inside Hindu quarters. This is a fundamental feature of untouchability as it is practiced by the Hindus'. Dr. Ambedkar goes on to argue that

'Untouchability among the Hindus is a unique phenomenon, unknown to humanity in other parts of the world.... The debate on untouchability can be reduced to two investigations:

1. Why did the untouchables live outside the village?
2. What made their impurity permanent, and ineradicable?'[13]

Ambedkar engaged in a lengthy examination of this phenomenon of untouchability. He explained it in the following manner, 'the primitive society with the discovery of new wealth land became settled from being nomadic. But there were regular warfare among the tribes and the defeated tribes became 'Broken men'. Since these people were defeated and became broken people

(1) they could not live within the 'settled village community' and had to live outside the border of the 'settled village community'.
(2) By living at the border of the village they could also meet the raids of the hostile tribes'.[14]

Continuing with his argument, Ambedkar locates living facts about the reality of the untouchables as broken men.

(1) According to the 'divine creation' theory the terms like '*antya*', '*antyaja*' and '*antyavasin*' etc., signifies the end of creation, namely the untouchables. But Ambedkar differs from this view and states that according to the divine creation theory, the Shudras are the last[15] in the ladder of creation. For him, '*antya*' means the end of the Hindu village system. This has double significance:
   (a) that living in separate quarters was such a peculiar phenomenon that a new terminology had to be invented to give expression to it;
   (b) the word chosen express, the conditions of the people to whom they applied, namely, that they were aliens.
(2) The second set of facts, which shows that the untouchables were broken men, is seen in the lives of the Mahars of Maharashtra. The following facts shows the relationship that exist between the Mahars and upper castes:
   (a) the Mahars are found in every village;
   (b) every village has a wall around it and the Mahars live outside the wall;

(c) they do the watch and ward on behalf of the village;
(d) the Mahars claim fifty two rights against the villagers. They are:
   (i) the right to collect food from the villagers;
   (ii) the right to collect corn from each villagers at the harvest season;
   (iii) the right to appropriate dead animal belonging to the villagers.

These two evidences support the theory that the untouchables lived outside the Hindu village from the beginning, because they were broken men and belonged to different tribe. Ambedkar located similar practices in Ireland and Wales. But in those countries, the broken men could be absorbed into the main tribe but with the notion of untouchability the broken men of Indian society could not be assimilated with the village. And the system of separate quarters for the untouchables became a 'perpetual' and 'permanent' feature of Indian village.[16]

Ambedkar then presents two theories regarding the origin of untouchability.

(1) Contempt for Buddhism as the root of untouchability;
(2) Beef-eating as the root of untouchability.

Then he shows that how in the census operation itself there were elements, which showed that, the Brahmins shunned the untouchables but it did not bring out the fact as to how the untouchables also shunned the Brahmans. Some of these areas are: the untouchables do not receive mantra form the brahmana; that the untouchables are not served by good brahmana priest; that the untouchables have their own priests reared from themselves.[17]

To comprehend this reality, Ambedkar goes into historical investigation. He explains this phenomenon by saying that the 'broken men' were Buddhists and they did not show any respect to the brahmanas; they did not employ them as priests and considered them as impure. The brahmans also disliked the broken men because they were Buddhists and preached hatred against them with the result that the broken men came to be regarded as untouchables. Thus Ambedkar concludes his argument that one of the roots of untouchability lies in the hatred and contempt, which the Brahmans created against those who were Buddhists.

In addition to this reason, Ambedkar also proposes another reason. He stated that there was a time when every one irrespective of the group they belonged to ate beef. Animal sacrifice was part of religious ceremonies. But Buddhism created a strong feeling of reverence towards the animals and the broken men who embraced Buddhism avoided beef eating and thus they looked down upon the Brahmans who were eating beef. In reaction the Brahmans not only stopped eating beef but also made the cow to be a 'sacred animal'. By this they succeeded in snatching away from the broken men the social prestige acquired by becoming Buddhists. Thus by adopting vegetarianism they regained their lost prestige and power.[18]. Thus he argues that had there been no Buddhism and if the broken men had stopped eating beef and considered cow, as a sacred animal there would have been no broken-men in the form of untouchables.

The theory of untouchability can be summarised as follows:

(1) there is no racial differences between the Hindus and the untouchables;
(2) the original distinction was in the form of settled tribes men and the broken men and it is the broken men who came to be treated as untouchables;
(3) just as untouchability has no racial basis it has also no occupational basis;
(4) there are two roots from which untouchability must have sprang:
    (a) contempt and hatred for broken men as of Buddhists by brahmanas.
    (b) continuation of beef-eating by the broken men after it was given up by the brahmanas.

Dr. Ambedkar then takes some of the aspects presented as salient features of caste by different thinkers. He refutes Nesfield's view that the absence of commensality is the cause of caste. Opposed to this view, Ambedkar states that the absence of inter-dinning is the natural result of the caste mechanism that is 'exclusiveness' and not its cause[19]. For Ambedkar as argued by Dr. Ketkar, the absence of inter-marriage or endogamy seems to be the essence of the caste system. The penalty imposed upon the individual who breaks endogamous laws is excommunication from the main class. The excommunicated people formed another distinct group within the main class. Thus, for Ambedkar, caste is an artificial chopping off of the population into fixed and definite units, each one prevented from fusing into another group through the custom of endogamy.[20]

From the above debate it can be seen that Ambedkar became more and more dissatisfied with the Indian social order and wanted a radical change to take place in it. Radhkrishnan also admitted that, 'the Hindu social order degenerated into an instrument of exploitation, tyranny and oppression. It tended to perpetuate inequality and inhumanity and developed the spirit of separatism, hatred and enmity, low and high'.[21] Though the philosophers and intellectuals of India comprehended the real cause behind the ills of Indian social order, they did not dare to identify concrete and appropriate solutions to remedy the situation.

Most of them suggested change of heart hoping that change of heart would lead to change in the social structure. In this regard it needs to be stated here that even after decades of expectations that change of heart would lead to change in the deplorable condition of the Dalits the reality is opposite. Yet, upper caste intelligentsia would continue to suggest similar measures. Bharat Jhunjhunwala writing about 'Dalit Welfare' argues that 'for the betterment of the Dalits two things need to be done: first is to rely upon the law to undo inequality; second, is to create morality in the society and encourage the rich and the powerful to use their wealth for the common good'.[22] But Bharat Jhunjhunwala over looks the fact that the Dalits about whose welfare he has written were reduced to this state of affairs due to the so-called "superior morality " upheld by the dominant castes.

While most of the upper caste social thinkers suggested change of heart of the rich and the dominant castes towards the Dalits for the welfare of the Dalits, Dr. Ambedkar argued for the annihilation of caste for the emancipation of Dalits. He systematically demonstrated that the caste system was not just a religious system but also an economic system much worse than slavery. It excluded the Shudras and the untouchables from acquiring any property. It also segregated the Shudras and the Dalits from places of power. He also stated that 'the caste system is not just a 'division of labour' but also a "division of labourers". Civilised society undoubtedly needs division of labour. But in no civilised society is division of labour accompanied by this unnatural division of labourers into watertight compartments'.[23] He further argued that the division and segregation of labourers is not a spontaneous process but cleverly manipulated societal exercise.

Based on this reality, Ambedkar raised a fundamental question, why were there no social revolutions against this cruel order? He answered saying, 'the lower classes have been completely disabled for direct action on account of this wretched system of Chaturvarnya.[24] Hence, he suggested that, caste system should be abolished in totality. He ridiculed those who suggested inter-dining and inter-marrying as the means to do away with caste discrimination. In a pointed and perceptive manner he argued, 'To agitate for and to organise inter-caste dinners and inter-caste marriages is liked forced feeding brought by about artificial means. Make every man and woman free from the thralldom to the Shastras, cleanse their minds of the pernicious notions founded on the Shastras, and he or she will inter-dine and inter-marry, without your telling him or her to do so'.[25] Instead of these reformative measures, Ambedkar advocated the total annihilation of caste system itself.

Gandhi took note of the severe criticism presented by Ambedkar. Hence, he stated, that Dr. Ambedkar is the most uncompromising exponent and one of the ablest among the critics. He is certainly the most irreconcilable among them'.[26] Though Gandhi took note of the staunch criticism presented by Dr. Ambedkar, he goes on to argue that 'Caste had nothing to do with religion. It is a custom whose origin I do not know and do not need to know for satisfaction of my spiritual hunger. But I do know that it is harmful both to spiritual and national growth. ... The law of varna teaches us that we have each one of us to earn our bread by following the ancestral calling. It defines not our rights but our duties.... It also follows that there is no calling too low and none too high. All are good, lawful, and absolutely equal in status.[27] The calling of a Brahmin- spiritual teacher- and a scavenger are equal, and their due performance carries equal merit before God and at one time seems to have carried identical reward before man. Both were entitled to their livelihood and no more'.[28]

In this regard it needs to be stated here that Gandhi tried to brush aside the crucial subject by elevating varna system away from religious sphere. He also strove to reduce the religious sanctions behind caste system in general and caste discrimination in particular. Thus, he too like the major segment within the dominant caste refused to look into the root cause of malice that is affecting the Indian social order. Dr. Ambedkar on the other hand tried to attack the edifice of the caste system with its foundation the religious and political power. He argued that the root of untouchability is caste system, the root of the caste system is religion attached to varnashram and the root of varnashram is Brahminical religion, and the root of Brahminical religion is authoritarianism or political power. Untouchability is only an extended form of caste and, therefore, without abolition of caste there is no hope of abolition of untouchability.

Before proceeding with our debate, it is appropriate to pause for a brief comparative note about Ambedkar and Gandhi. Mahatma Gandhi advocated *antyodaya*, meaning 'let the last person rise up'. *Antyodaya* was presented by Gandhi as a progressive step from *sarvodaya*, that is, the wellbeing of all. This springs from this philosophy that the upliftment of the last person is the indication of well being of society. This was a bold attempt by Gandhi when the caste discrimination was taken for granted and the 'last persons' were doomed to discrimination. For Ambedkar, antyodaya means end of the village, settlement and habitat. From this it is clear that for Ambedkar it is not just any last and least person who needs to be brought into mainstream development, but the Dalits who are at the end of society in all respects who are the ones who need to be liberated from the clutches of caste order.

The entire process of systematization of caste system took years to emerge as one of the most rigid and rigged social stratification the universe has ever known. This social order was considered to be fixed and finalised by those who were at the top of the hierarchy. Within this hierarchy, as stated above there are certain occupations that were considered to be higher and pure than the others. Significantly, it is not the purity that was at stake of higher status but the power, privilege and the authority that went with 'superior position' that came into scrutiny. This in the ultimate analysis led to the questioning of the caste system itself.

Anticipating and pre-figuring the debate that is to ensue after his speech, Dr. Ambedkar argued, "The effect of caste on the ethics of the Hindus is simply deplorable. Caste has killed public spirit. Caste has destroyed the sense of public charity. Caste has made public opinion impossible. A Hindu's public is his caste. His responsibility is only to his caste. His loyalty is restricted only to his caste. Virtue has become caste-ridden and morality has become caste-bound. There is no sympathy to the deserving. There is no

Figure 1

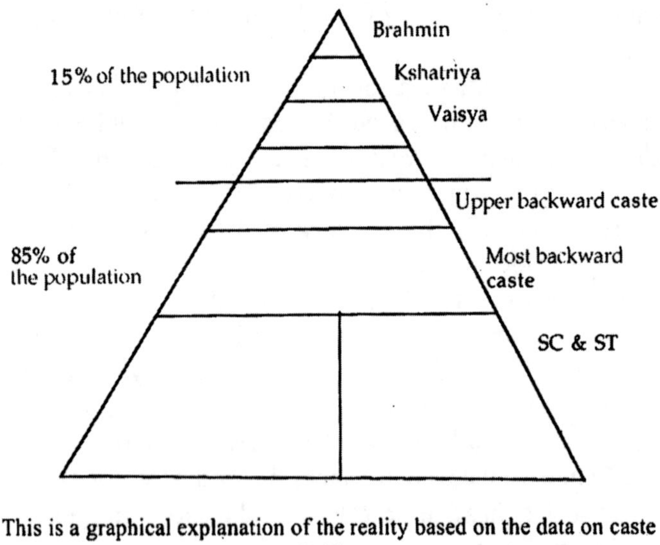

This is a graphical explanation of the reality based on the data on caste division

appreciation to the meritorious. There is no charity to the needy. Suffering as such calls for no response. There is charity but begins with caste and ends with caste. ... There is appreciation of virtue but only when the man is a fellow caste-man"[29]. Having exposed the hold of caste on Indian social order, Dr. Ambedkar raised a vital question, which is relevant even today. "Have not the Hindus committed treason against their country in the interests of their caste?"

As shown in Figure 1, the division of society was pyramidal in formation and operation. The figure is not based on any scientific assessment. But it provides a broad picture of the various social groups that are placed at the different layers of the ladder. The twice born, that is, the Brahmins, the Kshatriyas and the Vaisyas constitute a minority of the population. The Shudras are today known as the backward castes. There are two groups among them: the upper backward castes or what has come to be known as the creamy layer and the most backward castes. The Shudras formed part of the varna system but were placed at the lowest rung of the ladder. The erstwhile untouchables who are known, as Dalits today did not even form part of the varna system. Though the Tribals do not fall under the caste system nor form part of the Hindu socio-religious system they are placed at the same level with the Dalits, since they constitute the oppressed and exploited masses of the Indian socio-political order.

Based on the above philosophy the caste system came to acquire certain salient features:

1. A society based on hierarchical division;
2. Placement of a persons in the hierarchy based on birth;
3. Prohibition of marriage outside one's own caste;
4. The principle of purity and pollution to determine social interaction as well as daily life;
5. Hereditary occupation. These principles appear to be straightforward directives. But if one delves deeper into the reality as stated by Ambedkar, one realizes that this placement of persons in different castes also determines the power and privilege of individuals who are part of that caste.

All in all, the Dalits came to be placed at the lowest rung of the hierarchical caste order from where there was no scope for upward mobility. Since they were predestined to occupy the last step in the ladder, they also had become the foundation of the ladder without benefiting out of this edifice. Whenever these downtrodden made efforts to raise their voice against the heavy burden laid upon them, they were severely dealt with. Moreover, religious injunctions blunt even the limited scope for resistance. The entire process of systematization of caste took years and finally this is the picture we have at present [Figure 2].

Figure 2
Systematization of Caste Power

Board Classification	Caste	Aryan Birth	Twice born	Power over people	Ritual Performance
Chaturvarnal caste Hindus	Brahman	+	+	+ [Ritual]	+
	Kshatriya	+	+	+ [Political]	—
	Vaisya	+	+	+ [Economic]	—
	Shudra	—	—	—	—
Panchamas/ Outcastes	Avarnas	—	—	—	—

As stated above, it is common knowledge that caste system draws its sustenance from religious foundation. But it does not remain confined to religious or cultural sphere alone. Over the years, caste interacts with social, political and economic aspects of human life. In this historical process, it is the dominant castes who share among themselves the existing power and privileges. Among the dominant castes, it is the Brahmins who have appropriated monopoly over all the aspects of collective living. In terms of power equations, religious, political and economic power is shared among the three dominant castes.[31]

Caste in Existence

As already mentioned, the power and the privilege accorded to the upper castes in the varna social order in course of time resulted in the appropriation of wealth and resources. Since wealth, power and resources were under their disposal, they could acquire more resources and these resources could be converted into power and power ensured acquisition of resources. This cycle of enhancing power leading to agglomeration of wealth and intensification of resources in turn culminating in appropriation of greater power enabled them to become rulers, dispensers of law, owners, and ultimately *sarve sarva*, that is 'all in all' of the village, area, region, society and state.

Figure 3
Control over Resources

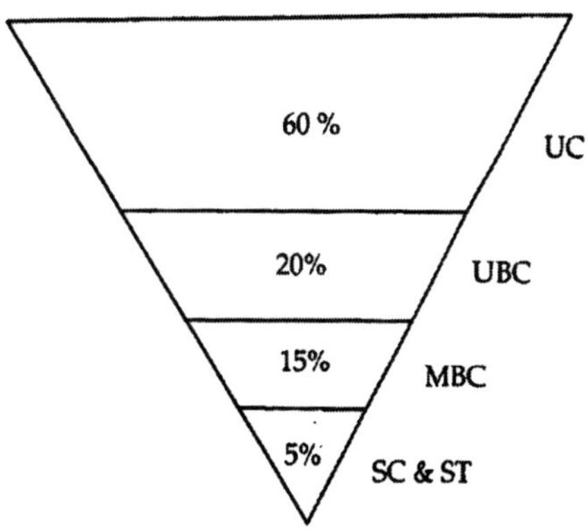

This is a graphic explanation of the reality based on the data on access over resources

In the ultimate analysis resources, wealth, power, position, privileges, higher status, authority, education, employment, services, land and labour got concentrated in the hands of the upper caste landed gentry (Figure 3). The Dalits and the downtrodden of the society on the other hand were denied any place in the society and were outcasted not only in terms of physical space, social distance but also from the mindset. Above all they were denied and deprived from economic resources, political participation, social interaction and cultural articulation. The depth of dehumanization is such that even cultural components like singing, drumming and dancing were performed for the enjoyment cf the dominant castes. Thus, the Dalits were reduced to a state of *sarvahara*, that is, denied of resources, assets, power, position and privilege.

Another crucial and central factor that needs to be raised here in the debate on ownership and control over resources is that ownership of material resources does not only provide economic power but it enhances ones bargaining power in political realm too. Devanathan in his analysis of the rural Bihar tires to capture this reality in a poignant manner. 'In the colonial period the *zamindars* had quasi-judicial powers to enforce revenue payments. These powers were backed by armed forces of retainers maintained at the revenue-collecting centres, the *kucheris* and *bhandars* (barns). They were backed by the colonial rulers for whom the zamindars collected rent. The zamindars were also themselves organised as organs of the state. British colonilaism initiated the process of separating the state machinery from the landlord class, but this separation was not carried through the end. Consequently, zamindars continued to be organised as quasi-state institution[32] right through the colonial period. In common language, the zamindar was not only '*malik*' (master) but also the '*sarkar*' (ruler).[33] The case of Bihar is presented here not from the perspective of the prophetic backwardness but to highlight the fact that this was the case in most of India where feudalism and casteism got integrated.

A cursory glance at the profile of the Dalits in India unravels this social fact that irrespective of colonial rule or democratic rule, the life of the Dalits continues to be deplorable and distressing. Though the Dalits constitute more than 16.48 per cent of the total Indian population, in terms of representation in various services or they are nowhere in the picture (Table 1). Compared to the Dalits, about 61.62 per cent of the non-Dalits are engaged in primary sector or in agricultural operation. Against this figure, more than 76.22 per cent of the Dalits are pursuing agricultural operations. But one should not be carried away by this data. If one ventures to examine the percentage of cultivators among the Dalits and the non-Dalits the difference is overwhelming. For instance there are only 25.44 per cent of Dalits who are cultivators while about 45 per cent of the non-Dalits are cultivators. Agricultural labour has been the mainstay of the economic survival of the Dalits. This subordinated absorption of the Dalits into agriculture has far reaching consequences of Dalit women becoming the main labour force of agriculture. The most incongruous aspect of this reality is that the Dalit women are only productive force of agriculture but are not owners of the means of production nor have control over their own labour power.

Further, the presence of Dalits in centres of power, economic resources etc, are abysmal. Whether it is in the area of literacy and education, safe drinking water and sanitation, employment and occupation they are totally discriminated against. While for the others, agriculture became the major source of economic, caste, political and social power, for the Dalits it provided them space for survival. In public sector the Dalits are legally sanctioned 16 per cent of reservation. But in the last five decades, the Dalits could not appropriate the space, and this goes to establish how difficult it is for them to utilize even those provisions that are constitutionally ensured in their favour.

If this is the case with public sector one can imagine what would be the situation in the private sector where the Dalits have no legal standing for any occupation. It needs to be stated here that the government should enact a law for earmarking some percentage of reservation for the Dalits in the private sector too. Interestingly, a group of delegates who had gone to Durban to represent the Dalit cause in the World Conference Against Racism demanded that the international body should impose sanction on the private sector, which does not recruit the Dalits.

From these general remarks let us briefly focus on some concrete cases. Among the Dalits most of those engaged in agricultural operation are landless agricultural labourers. In states like Bihar and Andhra Pradesh[34] over 70 per cent Dalits are returned as landless agricultural labourers in the 1991 census. The irony of some of these agrarian categories also needs to be exposed here. A few decades ago being counted as an agricultural labourer indicated the limited opening for the Dalits in economic sphere.

Table 1
A Profile of Dalits

S. No.	*Area*	*Representation (%)*
1.	Population	16.48
2.	Literacy	
	(i) Total	37.82
	(ii) Male	49.91
	(iii) Female	23.76
3.	Dropout by High school	79.88
4.	Central Government Jobs	
	(i) Class	10.14
	(ii) Class	12.67
	(iii) Class	16.15
	(iv) Class	21.26
5.	Public sector unit A grade	8.41
6.	Cultivators	25.44
7.	Agricultural Labourers	49.04
8.	Agriculture and Allied Activities	76.22
9.	Female Agricultural Labourers	68.00
10.	Household with drinking water, electricity, toilet facilities 19.83%	6.62
11.	Prime Minister	0
12.	Chief Justice	0
13.	Party Leadership[35]	10
14.	Teaching	9.49
15.	Below Poverty Line	56.00
16.	Manual Scavenging	100

Source: Census Reports 1991; 2001; Jean Dreze and Amartya Sen. India: Economic Development and Social Opportunity. Oxford University Press: Delhi, 1995.

Now the Dalits are struggling to retain themselves at least as agricultural labourers. With the slide in economic growth, employment opportunities are being restricted to Dalits. While on the one hand, no new recruitment is done in public sectors, on the other hand, they fear being victimised in the 'down sizing' policy of the present government. So the last resort is to hold on to the status of being agricultural labourer.

Hard data can be presented to highlight this social reality. One can observe from Table 1 that only about 7 per cent of the Dalit households can afford safe drinking water, electricity and toilets. Even after 53 years of Independence this most vulnerable and marginalised community cannot afford or is not provided with basic facilities, this is indicative of their deplorable social condition. Another distressing area is the drop out of Dalit students by the time they reach high school. Due to positive discrimination or reservation the educated Dalits are provided some space for obtaining employment. But if the students from the Dalit communities drop out, then there is no possibility of utilising the opportunities for jobs, restricting social mobility not only for individuals but also for the entire community.

In this regard Geetha Nambissan argues that early access to regular sources of income and opportunities for schooling, urbanisation, political mobilisation and enlightened leadership were among the socio-historical factors that were responsible for the initial, though meager, spread of education among some sections of the untouchable castes in pre-independent India.[36] Some of the sub-castes among the Dalit community understood that education could be utilised as a weapon for social mobility in a society, which is controlled by rigid stratification.

An overview of the literacy rate of various castes in India amplify the fact that there is a vast difference among the dominant castes and the Dalits [Table 2]. In the Bombay Presidency in 1931, the literacy rate of Brahmins was about 79 percent. Compared to this the literacy rate of Mahars who were more literate among all the Dalits was only 6 per cent. Even this is not the final picture. If we look at the literacy among the females of these two communities, they are 23.1 percent and 0.5 percent respectively. But if we move to what is at times derogatively called the 'cow belt' or the Gangetic belt or the Hindi belt, the literacy rate of the Dalits is much more deplorable.

Table 2
Literacy Among Castes in the Provinces (1931)[37]

Province	*1931*		*1921*	
	Male	*Female*	*Male*	*Female*
Bombay				
Brahman	78.8	23.1	65.2	14.4
Mahar, Dhed	6.3	0.5	2.3	0.1
Bhil		1.0		0.4
Madras (including Cochin and Travancore)				
Brahman	80.0	28.6	60.8	15.2
Nayar	60.4	27.6	49.1	21.5
Pallan,Paraiyan	5.6	0.6	3.7	0.3
Cherumar	1.3	0.3	0.8	0.1
Central Provinces and Bihar				
Baniya	59.8	7.4	43.0	4.1
Brahman	58.1	12.2	38.6	6.3
Chamar	1.6	0.1	0.8	0.1
Bihar and Orissa				
Kayastha	60.5	11.8	59.1	8.4
Brahman	35.6	2.8	30.4	1.9
Dhobi	2.9	0.2	2.0	0.1
Dosadh	1.2	0.1	0.8	0.1
Chamar	1.0	0.1	0.8	-
United Provinces				
Kayastha	70.2	19.1	52.3	9.0
Brahmin	29.3	2.5	19.1	1.3
Bhangi	1.0	0.1	0.5	-
Chamar	0.6	-	0.2	-

Source: Hutton (1933), Census of India 1931, India Part-1, Report.

In the last two decades, this fact has dawned on the social scientists, social activists and educationists, that literacy and education are not neutral entities. In a horrendous and heinous caste order, education does play the role of being the agent for social mobility or for social stagnation. It is argued that when the British colonial powers were spreading their tentacles in India, educated and skilled persons were employed as assistants to the foreigners. Those who had the facilities for education responded to this positively and benefited out of it. The old association of the higher castes with the skills of literacy gave them a much greater flexibility and readiness to exploit these new possibilities than was possessed by any of western India's agricultural or urban lower castes. The result of this disparity was the higher castes, and Brahmans in particular, came to occupy a proportion of clerical and professional positions at all levels of the British administration that was far in excess of their numerical proportions in the population as a whole.[38]

Table 3
Participation in Schooling (1981)[39]

Sector	Children (5-14 Years) Attending School (Per Cent)	
	Scheduled Caste	Total Population*
Rural	28.95 (17.39)**	38.80 (28.4)
Urban	49.70 (41.53)	65.17 (60.64)
Total	32.21 (21.22)	44.20 (34.8)

* Includes Scheduled Caste and Scheduled Tribe children.
** Percentage of girls attending school in the 5-14 year age group are given in parenthesis
Source: India (1989), Census of India 1981, Series – Part IV-A, VII (SC/ST)]

While the dominant castes due to their proximity to educational institutions profited immensely, the Dalits continued to be deprived of education. If one examines the participation of Dalit children in schooling, one comes across another social block against them. Table 3 indicates that barely 17.39 per cent of Dalit girls (aged 5-14 years) in rural areas participated in schooling in 1981.[40] Compared to Dalit children, children from the general category are more in number in schools. There is also another aspect to this reality. The students from the general category have the facility of enrolling themselves in private educational institutions, while the Dalits can afford to avail only the government facilities.

Education is usually considered to be one of the powerful tools, which would bring change in the lower castes. But the reality at the ground level is very different. On the one hand, rate of literacy and education among the Dalits continue to remain in a pitiably low level, on the other hand, innumerable programmes are 'envisaged for their upliftment'. This is the irony of Indian political and administrative system. Table 4 presents only a glimpse of the various educational programmes and projects undertaken by the ruling class for the benefit of the lower castes. Interestingly, not only national resources are supposed to have been used for this purpose, finance is borrowed from World Bank to make sure that the 'illiterate Dalits' are made literate by 2000 and now 2020. Slogans like 'Education for All by 2000' and now 'Education for All by 2020' are rampant within the corridors of power.[41]

Whether it is in the Total Literacy Mission or the National Literacy Campaign or the District Primary Education Programme, parents of Dalit children are accused of paying little attention to the educational aspirations of their wards. But empirical data seem to go counter to this perception. In this regard Geetha Nambisan argues that 'What is noteworthy but little acknowledged is the extent of support, material and moral, that Dalit parents (and relatives) extend to their children despite poverty, lack of educational exposure and quality of schooling they experience. In the ICSSR study,[42] 89 per cent of the Scheduled Caste high school respondents stated that they had to depend on parents and relatives for financial support. This is despite the fact that only 12 per cent of students came from financially 'stable' homes. Only 5 per cent of the pupils interviewed in the study said that the entire cost of their education was covered by freeship, etc. The study of Milind College reveals that the parents of 52 per cent of the Scheduled Caste students had to raise loans from village moneylenders at exorbitant rates of interest, to finalise the education of their wards'.[43]

Table 4
Financial Allocation For Important Programmes of Elementary Education

Item	*Budget Estimates (Plan)* 1991-92	1992- 93
INFE Centres		
(i) General	4.500(16.15)	4.080(14.6)
(ii) Centres for girls	3,000(10.77)	2,725(9.76)
(iii) Through Voluntary Agencies Total (1)	10,500(67.69)	9,010(32.29)
II Programme with NFE component		
(i) Shiksha karmi	230(0.83)	470(1.68)
(ii) Bihar Education Project	600(2.15)	1,200(4.30)
(iii) Improving learner achievement	-	200(0.72)
(iv) Lok Jumbish	-	200(-)
(v) World Bank Assisted project	-	2,090(7.49)
(vi) South Orissa Project - Total (II)	830(2.98)	2,090(7.49)
III Other Programmes		
(i) Operation Blackboard	10,000(35.90)	9,914(35.53)
(ii) Teacher education	6,424(23.06)	6,450(23.12)
(iii) Others Total III	16,524(59.67)	16,800(60.22)
IV Total for elementary education	27,854(100.00)	27,900(100.00)

Note: Figures in bracket denote percentages
Source: India (1993D), Annual Report 1991-92, Ministry of Human Resources Development 333-334.

A careful comparison between the rhetoric and reality of educational development among the Dalits and the downtrodden speaks volumes of truth about the real interest of the ruling elites of this country. The Central government with the sponsorship of World Bank had come out with a novel programme known as "Bihar Education Project" for educational development in Bihar, a state usually considered to be one of the most backward states in India. In spite of these projects, the literacy rate of this state has not seen any tangible growth. Table 5 pointedly depicts the inequality in education between the general population and the Scheduled Castes of Bihar. The literacy rate of the Scheduled caste women is very low. It is at least four times lower than the rate of Scheduled Castes men, while it is 7 times lower than the general male population of the state. Interestingly, Bihar is the place, where Buddha attained his nirvana that is, enlightenment.

Table 5
Literacy Rate of General and Scheduled Caste Population, Bihar

	General Population			*Scheduled Caste Population*		
Year	*Male*	*Female*	*Total*	*Male*	*Female*	*Total*
1961	29.8%	6.9%	18.4%	11.2%	0.9%	5.95%
1971	30.64%	8.72%	19.94%	11.9%	1.0%	6.53%
1981	38.11%	13.62%	26.20%	18.02%	2.51%	10.40%
1991	52.49%	22.89%	38.48%	30.64%	7.07%	19.49%

Source: Census Report 1991

Literacy rate in Bihar is a dismal 38.48 per cent, compared with the national average of 52.49. In female literacy rate, the Bihar average is only 22.89 per cent, compared with the national average of 39.42 per cent. There has been considerable improvement in the literacy rate of the Scheduled Castes from 1961 to 1991. But the situation is far from satisfactory. This distressing reality becomes all the more glaring if we observe the fact that the Scheduled Castes took many years to reach 30 per cent of literacy. Dalit women till date have not crossed the double figure. There is nothing to wonder about this because according to a government record out of 100 districts identified as the most backward districts, 38 are from Bihar.[44] In most of these districts, there is a high concentration of Dalit population.

Moving away from the sphere of education and literacy, it is pertinent that we examine the economic indicators like job opportunity for the Dalits and the downtrodden. With regard to employment of teachers from the weaker sections, the hiatus between rhetoric and reality is well evident [Table 6]. Only about 9 per cent among the Scheduled Castes and 6 per cent among the Scheduled Tribes are returned as teachers.

Table 6
Teachers Position in School

		All Communities	*SC*	*ST*
(i) Primary				
	Rural	1275218	159278(12.49%)	114933 (9.01%)
	Urban	348161	24592(7.06%)	9213(2.65%)
	Total	1623379	183860(11.32%)	124146(7.65%)
(ii) Upper Primary				
	Rural	790271	78063 (9.88%)	61921(7.84%)
	Urban	33946	23151(6.82%)	10805(3.18%)
	Total	1129747	101214(8.96%)	72726(6.44%)
(iii) Secondary				
	Rural	532328	38070(7.15%)	21794(4.09%)
	Urban	297077	15535(5.23%)	7839(2.64%)
	Total	829405	53608(6.46%)	29633(3.57%)
(iv) Higher Secondary				
	Rural	247584	18802(7.59%)	8013(3.24%)
	Urban	367440	19726(5.37%)	6552(1.78%)
	Total	615024	38531(6.26%)	14565(2.37%)
(v) Total				
	Rural	2845401	294186(10.34%)	206661(7.26%)
	Urban	1352154	83007(6.14%)	34409(2.54%)
	Total	4197555	377193(8.99%)	241070(5.74%)

Note: Figures in brackets indicates percentages
Source: National Commission for Scheduled Castes and Scheduled Tribes, Fifth Report, 1998-99, Volume-I.

Over the years, the educational environment has also come to play an important role in the planning for improving the educational system of the country. But when it comes to providing teachers from the weaker sections to teach children from the Scheduled Castes and the Scheduled Tribes, then there is a shortfall. Thus the absence of teachers from the weaker sections affects the community in many ways. The reservation quota provided constitutionally is denied to them on one pretext or the other so that others can benefit out of this. Secondly, if some one from the weaker sections had obtained this job he or she would have improved the economic situation of his or her household. Appointment of teachers from these communities would have led to an encouragement of the children from the marginalized communities. Thus, denial of access to basic amenities once again throttles the very aspirations of these communities for social mobility. In contrast to this, it is the job as 'Sweepers', which seems to be earmarked for the Dalits [Table 7]

Table 7
Representation of SCs/STs in Central Government Services –As on 1.1.1997

Group	Total	SC	%	ST	%
A	60,067	6,135	10.21	1,840	3.06
B	94,111	11,649	12.38	2,840	3.02
C	19,59,477	3,14,995	16.08	1,22,903	6.27
D (Excluding Sweepers)	8,18,748	1,76,368	21.54	54,931	6.71
Sweepers	15,51,137	61,149	39.42	12,812	8.26
Total (Excluding Sweepers)	29,32,403	5,09,149	17.36	1,82.524	6.22
Total (Including Sweepers)	30,87,540	5,70,296	18.47	1,95,326	6.33

Note: This information excludes information from 7 Ministries/Departments.
Source: Department of Personnel & Training. Quoted in National Commission for Scheduled Castes & Scheduled Tribes. Fifth Report 1998-99, p 130.

This anomaly is irrespective of the fact that the Union Department of Personnel and Training at regular intervals is supposed to send orders to various departments for the implementation of these safeguards. While the Scheduled Castes seem to have faired better, the Scheduled Tribes are at the deplorable stage. If this is the state of affairs with regard to public sector, there is no scope of entry even in private sector.[45] The moot question that needs to be raised at this juncture is, what is that which prevents the political establishment from enforcing policies and programmes enacted by itself. The only answer one can garner is that there is nothing sinister or intensely malicious about non-implementation of welfare schemes. The very caste edifice that this society has constructed has denied even the limited economic opportunity to the marginalized groups.

Let us not quibble about details but examine another area of denial of rights of the Dalits. The state and the central governments have introduced at regular intervals schemes like self-employment, wage employment and other programmes. Sukhdeo Thorat in his perceptive analysis of the introduction of social security schemes and the subsequent improvements in the lives of the Scheduled Castes gives the following as the indictors to evaluate the state of affairs: 1) The proportion of land owning self-employed cultivators should increase. Priority in the distribution of surplus land under the ceiling, government land and other land should bring a shift in the occupational status of a substantial proportion of the Scheduled Caste popualtion from wage labour to self-employed households. 2) Similarly, the proportion of self-employed households/persons in the rural non-form sector and in urban area should increase due to self-employment programmes under IRDP. 3) The expected increase in the proportion of self-employed, should lead to a corresponding decline in the proportion of wage labour households. 4) The wage employment programmes should reduce the unemployment among the Scheduled Castes wage labourers in rural areas. 5) With an increase in self-employed activities and wage employment, the incidence of poverty, both in rural and urban areas, among the Scheduled Castes household persons should decrease, and finally, in relative terms, the gap between the Scheduled Castes and others should reduce.[46]

Keeping these criterions in mind, if we scrutinize the lower castes access to agricultural land, the difference between rhetoric and reality becomes clear. As presented in Table 8 as on September 30, 1996, about 52.13 lakh acres had been distributed at the all-India level. Of these, about 18.08 lakh acres were distributed among 18.48 lakh persons among the Dalits. Out of the total area distributed about 34.67 percentage of land has been distributed among the Dalits.[47] This in fact appears to be an impressive figure. But on verifying the reality of this persuasive achievement, one may come up with something different. Even if the data is true, the amount of land distributed among the Dalits is not even an acre. This meager amount of land often becomes a burden to the lower castes and they are forced to sell out this land and join the army of agricultural laborers.[48]

Table 8
Distribution of Surplus Land to SCs as on September 1996

Total Area and Beneficiaries		Area Distributed and Number of SC Beneficiaries					
State	Area Distributed	Total No. of Beneficiaries	Area Distributed	No. of Beneficiaries	% share in area	% share in no. of beneficiaries	Average Area Distributed
A.P.	594352	521563	226890	216537	38.17	41.51	10.4
Assam	479878	441804	45746	43406	9.53	9.82	1.05
Bihar	303217	372529	179161	229832	59.08	61.69	0.779
Gujarat	133999	31376	83247	14584	62.12	46.48	5.20
Haryana	87259	27392	37623	11753	43.11	42.90	3.20
H.P.	3340	4400	2305	2934	69.01	66.68	0.785
J & K	45000	450000	0	0	0	0	0
Karnataka	117147	31415	71133	18953	60.72	60.33	3.75
Kerala	64283	145106	25197	62174	39.01	42.84	0.40
M.P.	185313	72131	49433	21528	26.67	29.84	2.29
Maharashtra	554870	14580	161715	41945	29.14	29.83	3.85
Orissa	154298	135219	49075	45561	31.80	33.69	1.077
Punjab	103487	28287	44015	11301	42.53	39.95	3.89
Rajasthan	452176	77899	145317	28453	32.13	36.52	5.10
Tamil Nadu	162369	135269	62096	59729	38.24	44.15	1.03
Uttar Pradesh	390501	346209	263815	236599	67.55	68.33	1.11
West Bengal	965293	2151632	359519	800870	37.24	37.22	0.44
Total	5213328	5120859	1807575	1848833	34.67	36.10	0.97

Source: Report of the Commission for SC/ST, 1995-1996, Delhi.

Table 9
Percentage of Landless and Near Landless Households among SCs

(Percentage to total rural households)

State	1982				1992					
	Landless	Less than half acre	Between half & one acre	Upto one acre	Landless and upto one acre	Landless	Less than half acre	Between half and ibe acre	Upto one acre	Landless and upto one acre
A.P.	13.58	44.34	7.95	52.29	65.87	12.49	49.95	9.91	59.86	72.35
Assam	5.02	36.98	17.27	54.25	59.27	5.52	37.10	7.94	45.04	50.56
Bihar	35.58	69.78	9.76	79.54	89.24	19.73	62.62	6.15	68.77	88.50
Gujarat	23.86	44.69	6.38	51.22	75.06	18.09	34.11	4.22	38.88	56.42
Haryana	10.09	87.52	0.97	88.49	98.58	7.95	73.10	3.63	76.73	84.68
H.P.	6.01	34.71	9.96	44.67	50.73	7.09	22.67	5.37	28.04	35.13
J & K	0.66	41 56	3.58	45.14	45.80	4.00	34.37	7.91	42.28	46.28
Karnataka	14.52	38.41	8.51	46.92	61.44	10.69	32.60	2.67	53.27	45.96
Kerala	16.56	77.33	5.35	82.68	99.24	14.33	79.32	-	79.32	93.65
M.P.	18.11	24.21	2.55	26.76	44.87	20.53	19.04	3.17	22.21	42.74
Maharashtra	26.39	33.42	3.38	36.80	63.19	24.31	32.13	2.99	35.12	59.43
Orissa	7.2	47.78	6.70	54.18	61.38	11.19	49.82	9.78	59.60	70.79
Punjab	6.01	56.84	2.96	89.50	95.81	6.7	85.57	1.43	87.00	93.78
Rajasthan	12.91	18.10	2.40	20.50	33.41	76.11	29.10	8.18	35.28	43.04
Tamil Nadu	14.5	61.66	7.48	69.14	83.64	19.21	57.4	9.82	67.03	86.24
U.P.	7.18	40.88	18.33	59.21	66.39	6.15	45.98	16.08	62.06	68.21
W.Bengal	19.13	42.74	11.05	53.79	72.92	12.02	47.66	11.64	59.30	71.32
India	12.62	47.97	9.53	57.50	70.12	13.34	47.50	8.89	56.39	69.73

Source: NSS Landholding Survey, 1982 and 1992

Any discussion on the access of agricultural land to the Dalits and the downtrodden has to take into account the various measures and instruments worked out by the central and state governments. From 1950 onwards, the state governments have been enacting different types of land reform legislations to improve the lot of the rural masses. Two stated objectives of the land reform policies were as follows: a) accelerate the agricultural production and b) control the growing rural agrarian tension and conflict. Thus economic development coupled with social justice was the slogan given by the ruling elite of this country.

Though land reform was a state subject, the central government of India at regular intervals organised meetings with the concerned officials to review and to enforce reform in land structure. The following pages present the various Conferences of Chief Ministers and Revenue Ministers held at National level to enact Land Reform laws and some of the acts and special committees appointed by the government to look into speedy enactment of land reform regulations.[49]

A. Conference of the Chief Ministers

1. July 23rd 1972. This conference drew up the Guidelines on the basis of the Conclusions of the Chief Ministers' Conference on Ceiling on Agricultural Holdings;
2. 11th –12th June 1990. Conference of the Chief Ministers;
3. 4-5th October 1991. Conference of the Chief Ministers;
4. 9th October 1992. Conference of the Chief Ministers.

B. Conference of the Revenue Ministers

1. 18th May 1985. Buta Singh who was the Agricultural Minister addressed the gathering;
2. 28th November 1986. Conference of the Revenue Ministers;
3. 19-20th December 1988.[50] Conference of the Revenue Ministers;
4. 14th March 1992. In this Conference the then Prime Minister Mr. Narasimha Rao stated that, "There is something seriously wrong. And it is nobody's credit that after 45 years we are

still having a conference on land reforms, which means that what has been promised to the people before independence, after independence, elections after elections, has not been done".

5. 27th December 1995. Conference of the Revenue Ministers;
6. 28th November 1997. Conference of the Revenue Ministers;
7. 17th September 1998. Conference of the Revenue Ministers.

C. Special Committees

1. As early as 1966 a Task Force Committee on Agrarian Relations was appointed by the Planning Commission of the Government of India to review the land reform enactment. It stated categorically that lack of political will is one of the major hindrances as far as the implementation of land reforms is concerned.
2. Another Special Committee was appointed to look into the agrarian situation. The Committee submitted the report titled, "The Causes and the Nature of Current Agrarian Tensions". Ministry of Human Affairs, 1969.
3. Many other committees constituted after massacres also came up with the conclusion that non-implementation of land reforms was one of the main reasons for agrarian tensions.

D. Few Important Programmes that were supposed to impact on Development

1. The Community Development Programme 1952.
2. The Intensive Agricultural District Programme 1964 [IADP].
3. The Command Area Development Authority 1966.
4. Small Farmers Development Agencies; The Draught Prone Area Programme; Hill Area Development Programme 1970.
5. Twenty Point Programme 1972.
6. Green Revolution.
7. Integrated Rural Development Programme [IRDP] 1980.
8. New Twenty Point Programme 1982.

E. Land Reform Laws : Bihar

In similar manner, the weaker sections of the State of Bihar were supposed to be protected by the following legislations enacted from 1947 to 1974:

1. The Bihar Abolition of *Zamindari* Bill 1947, which after five years of legal tangle took the form of The Bihar Land Reforms Act 1950 which came into effect only in 1952;
2. The Bihar Privileged Persons Homestead Tenancy Act, 1974;
3. The Minimum Wages Act, 1948;
4. The Bihar Land Reforms Act, 1950;
5. The *Bhoodan Yagna* Act, 1954;
6. The Bihar Consolidation of Holdings and Prevention of Fragmentation Act, 1956;
7. The Chota Nagpur Tenancy Rules, 1959 Allied Acts and Regulations;
8. The Bihar Land Reforms (Fixation of Ceiling Area and Acquisition of Surplus Land) Act, 1961;
9. The Bihar Scheduled Areas Regulations, 1969;
10. The Bihar Scheduled Castes, Scheduled Tribes, Backward Class and Denotified Tribes Debt Relief Act, 1974;
11. The Bihar Money Lenders Act, 1974.

Besides these, many other Acts and provisions, many more Bills and Ordinances have been framed from time to time for the benefit of the 'downtrodden'.

As already discussed, there were no dearth of legislations and ordinances to enforce restructuring of the agrarian sector. Also, there was no lack of public pronouncements about the good intensions of the various governments at the centre and at the state level. These public proclamations raised the hopes of the landless masses that their rulers are serious about bridging the gap between the landholders and the landless. But as time went on they were subjected to crude shock that these are only rhetorics and the reality is their continued proletarianisation and oppression. As shown in Table 9, at the state level, 13 out of 17 states show higher incidence of landlessness among the Scheduled Castes in 1992. Despite the distribution of ceiling-surplus land to about 18.5 lakh [Table 8] Scheduled Caste beneficiaries, the percentage of landless households among them has increased from 12.62 per cent in 1982 to 13.34 per cent in 1992.[51]

This caveat must be borne in mind while interpreting the data too. If we look at the data of landless and those who own just one acre [Table 9, column 2 & 3] about 69.73 per cent are landless among the Dalits. Another distressing fact that can be seen in Table 9 is that more than 93 per cent of the Dalits of Punjab fall under the category landless or own just one acre of land. Punjab is known for green revolution. While the agricultural production has increased to such an extent that the godowns overflow with grain, forced to Dalits are starve. It is also true for Kerala, which has become famous for highest literacy rate in the country. But here too, about 93.65 per cent of the Dalits continue to remain landless. All these make the point clear that there is no tangible change in the lives of the Dalits. In fact, their situation seems to be becoming from bad to worst.

Taken together, the alarming inequality and a skewed power relation, which form the basis of caste system, has reduced the lower castes to a state of nothingness. Even an ordinary scheme to locate the place and role of various segments of the *varna* system poignantly points to the enormity of inequality between the dominant castes and the exploited castes. As shown in Table 10, the Brahmins though form only 3.6% of the entire population, control 100% of the priestly services, they are the most educated population of the society, and hence they also have appropriated

Table 10
Caste in Real Life Situation [%]

Items	Brahmins	Kshatriya	Vaisya	Backward	S.C.
Population	3.6	6.6	6.0	55.79	16.73
Reservation	-	-	-	17.0	14.0
Priesthood	100.0	-	-	-	-
Party leadership	41.0	16.0	10.0	10.0	10.0
Business	10.0	20.0	60.0	7.08	0.02
Land ownership	6.0	70.0	8.0	14.0	1.0
Education	54.0	16.0	12.0	8.0	6.0
Govt. jobs	64.0	10.0	10.0	8.0	7.0

Source: From different reports

the highest number of jobs. Though they do not own vast tracts of land the very fact of having secured the most lucrative jobs has given them enough economic security. The Kshatriyas like the Brahmins also enjoy enormous power and authority in the society.

Contrast to this fact, the Dalits neither own land nor have access to other resources. Since they cannot afford to educate themselves even to a limited extent they cannot be gainfully employed in the government and non-government jobs. As stated above, the only source that is left open for them is social mobility through affirmative action. The Constitution of India has made provisions for reservation for them so that they may be able to acquire jobs. But since they are not educated or 'qualified' they loose out here too to the upper castes. All these have cumulative effects on their lives and their psyche. Even these reserved seats are taken over by others at times with fake caste names.

In this regard one should focus on the deeper malaise that is affecting Indian society and polity. The Dalits are reduced to poverty and penury in spite of the fact that innumerable plans and schemes have been introduced by the central and state governments for the benefit of the weaker sections. But the significant fact is that in most of these plans and schemes the real issues are relegated to the background. The Dalits have been the victims of an age-old practice of exclusion. Hence, any plan to change their living conditions should begin form this fundamental truth. The whole area of bestowing social dignity, or redistributing common property resources never figures even in the discussions and debates. All that is envisaged is some ameliorative measures, which in reality do not contribute in the transformation of the lives of the Dalits. It is a fact that some individuals who have become socially mobile do benefit out of these schemes but the entire Dalit community is 'untouched' by these schemes.

Atrocities Committed against the Dalits

At this juncture it is expedient to look at the magnitude and the depth of atrocities unleashed on the Dalits by the non-Dalits. Knowing well the inherent nature of caste exclusion and oppression the framers of the Indian Constitution had made specific provisions for the lower castes. Article 46 of the Constitution clearly and categorically spelt out that, ' The State shall promote with special care the educational and economic interests of the weaker sections of the people, and in particular, of the Scheduled Castes and the Scheduled Tribes, and shall protect them from social injustices and all forms of exploitation'.

Table 11
Crime and Atrocities Against Scheduled Castes (1981-1997)

Year	Murder	Grievous	Injuries	Rape	Arson	Others	Crime
under POA		Total					
1981	493	1492	604	1295	10434	14318	28636
1982	514	1429	635	1035	11441	15054	30108
1983	525	1351	640	993	11440	14949	29898
1984	541	1454	692	973	12327	15987	31974
1985	502	1367	700	980	11824	15373	30746
1986	564	1408	727	1002	11715	15416	30832
1995	571	4544	837	500	11056	13925	31433
1996	543	4585	949	464	13862	9620	30023
1997	504	3462	1002	384	12149	7831	25338

Source: Annual Reports of Commission for the Scheduled Caste and Tribe, Delhi.
POA: Prevention of Atrocities Act.

The Constitution of India has clearly demanded that weaker section should be protected from any form of oppression and injustice. But in reality, all forms of atrocities are unleashed on them everyday. Table 11 presents this reality powerfully. But another crucial point that needs to be kept in mind is that these are not the only atrocities committed on the Dalits. These are the ones that managed to be reported in the police stations. There are many more atrocities that go unreported since the victims fear further retaliation. Also the police administration more often does not register these cases and brushes them aside as insignificant. If one presses them further they are scared to register the case of atrocity, since they too fear the wrath of the upper castes or they feel that they may loose their favour.

The crisis of legitimacy not only of the social order which has given rise to caste system, but also of the bourgeoisie political system becomes all the more profound if one examines the implementation of special provisions. The Scheduled Caste and the Scheduled Tribe (Prevention of Atrocities) Act, 1989 had the following stated objectives: This Act is enacted to prevent the commission of atrocities against the members of the Scheduled Castes and the Scheduled Tribes and to provide special courts for the trial of such offences and for the relief and rehabilitation of the victims of such offences. But Acts of this type are enacted only to be violated by the dominant castes.

Caste atrocities are not a new phenomenon in India. But the structure and the methodology employed in carrying out murderous attacks on the Dalits is something different. In this regard, Jagjivan Ram a Dalit leader had assailed the entire caste oppression. 'The problem of the Scheduled Castes has already assumed menacing proportions. With the little awakening that has taken place among them, they are trying in a feeble and modest way, to resist the injustices and atrocities that have been heaped upon them in a most shameless manner. These oppressions and atrocities are such as can hardly be dreamt of in a civilized society and seem to be growing in number and intensity. It is strange that the Indian society is tolerating all these and in some respects it may even be charged with connivance. Guilty persons are hardly brought to book immediately and by the time they are punished people generally forget their crime – so tardy are the legal procedures and so lengthy and costly are their processes'.[52]

Significantly, even today the Dalits are treated as the cancerous segment of Indian society. While talking about the scavengers Bindeshwari Pathak stated, 'the scavengers, constitute an unprivileged social group treated as 'impure' and consequently ritually avoided. They are socially ostracized because of their ritual impurity. As outcasts and rejects of the Indian society, scavengers have suffered condemnable human indignities throughout the ages. They have been treated like dreaded contagious disease calling for a disdainful distance and the most minimal social contact. Besides social backwardness scavengers are economically backward too. Most scavenger families, therefore, live in a situation of abject poverty'.[53] But if one engages oneself in a serious analysis of the occupation they are engaged in one realises the fact that they are impure because they perform the purifying work for others.

Forced by these external forces every Dalit child grows with this sentiment that he is an inferior being or not a full being or not a human being at all. A Dalit is often perceived as incapable, illiterate, ignorant, impure and even as an 'illegitimate' child. This gets instilled, ingrained and institutionalised in the mind of every Dalit child and ultimately he or she grows up to be an inferior being. This sense of being inferior or being a worthless creature generates a paralysing fear and dread towards the dominant castes. This fear gets fed into any person with power and authority.

Against this backdrop, C.W. Briggs illustrates an altogether different story. 'A catalogue of the different kinds of work which the *Chamar*[54] performs, shows that he belongs to the great class of unskilled labourer. He is a grass-cutter, coolie, wood and bundle-carrier, doer of odd jobs, maker and repairer of thatch and of mud wall, field-labourer, house servant, peon, brick-maker, and even village watchman. He also makes musical instruments.'[55] This perceptive understanding of Briggs tells in vivid forms the various ways in which this community contributes to the betterment of society. This is in spite of the fact that after all these toil and drudgery they are neither paid adequately for their labour nor their contribution to the betterment of the society recognized by others.

Abolition of Untouchability

Abolition of untouchability has been brought under the jurisdiction of Constitutional injunctions. But untouchability is practiced in all the senses. Dalits who are the erstwhile untouchables have eternally been subjected to exploitation and injustice. It is estimated that the caste system is atleast 3,000 years old and discrimination and barbarity towards the Dalits are equally an age-old phenomenon. The dominant castes consider that it is their privilege and birth right to beat, bash up and butcher the Dalits and the downtrodden.

Since the Dalits in the past silently suffered every detestable and barbaric crimes committed against them the dominant castes did not engage in many physical aggression. But now the Dalits have become conscious of their legitimate place and role in the society and nation, and they have begun to raise their head against atrocities. Hence, the dominant upper castes are engaged in vicious repressive measures to silence any form of dissent erupting among the Dalits. Significantly it is not upper castes alone who abuse the Dalits, but the backward castes too engage in oppression and exploitation of the Dalits. In states like Bihar Haryana, and Uttar Pradesh where the backward castes have come to the centre stage after the implementation of Mandal Commission Report, these communities also have become equally ruthless towards the Dalits.

One can also cite another common practice in the electoral politics. Adult franchise has been guaranteed to all the citizens of India irrespective of the caste, class, creed, region or religion. To make political participation more broad-based, the age of the voter was reduced from 21 to 18. But even after 5 decades of independence, in many villages, Dalits are not allowed to vote. Their electoral right has been denied not constitutionally but conventionally.[56] For a major segment of the Dalits and the marginalised of Indian society, their survival and sustenance is much more important than fighting for their political rights.[57]

The recurrent atrocities heaped on the Dalits by the dominant castes have once again opened the discourse between the caste politics and electoral politics. Dalits have been subjected to brutal and cruel atrocities in the past are not the point for debate. But the manner and the method in which these atrocities are being carried out before the run up to the Assembly elections in Uttar Pradesh is the crucial fact here.[58] In the past, all the political parties have used the Dalits as vote bank. Now the Dalits are beginning to assert their political right and are forming their own parties and are putting up candidates from their own communities. These electoral equations have enraged the dominant castes, especially the Brahmins and the Thakurs in Uttar Pradesh.

There are reports, which indicate the fact that from 10th June to 17th June 2001 in a span of 7 days there were 5 atrocities that came to light. In most of these cases, the dominant caste persons with the tacit approval of the police and administration engaged in criminal assaults on the Dalits and in some cases either burnt men and women to death or shot them dead. In one incident, a pregnant woman was paraded naked by the powerful Brahmins of the area. The youth were asked to smear their houses with human excreta. When this barbaric act came to light, it is reported that the incident was squashed up because the wife of a Minster in the Union Government took side of the culprits.[59] In some of these massacres, the heads of small children were banged against stones and were done to death.[60]

Any conscious citizen today would raise question as to how come such atrocities are heaped upon another segment of the population even in an age, which claims to be modern and technically 'advanced'. One of the answers to this query is that as argued in this book, the dominant castes consider any assertion from below as a challenge to their hegemony and superiority. This explains the ruthlessness and cruelty of their repressive measures. But what is happening in Uttar Pradesh also should be read from the perspective of the ascent of the Brahminical and Bania forces to maintain status quo. The outrageous crimes committed against the Dalits go to demonstrate this social fact that the rightwing *Hindutva* forces perceive the eruption of counter forces among the Dalits as a potential threat to their very existence and hegemony.

A study team comprising of Dalit activists and human rights activists that toured these areas reported that quarrels that took place between small children were utilised to settle score with the Dalits who were raising their head and demanding their rights. It was also recorded that a whole family was wiped out because some of these families due to hard labour had become economically independent and refused to follow the dictates of the dominant castes. This infuriated the dominant castes beyond limits. But above all these the real issue at stake is that with the emergence of Bahujan Samaj Party (BSP) the Dalits today have stopped being the flag bearers of so called mainline parties which are in fact dominant caste parties. The ruling Bharatiya Janata Party (BJP) wanted to retain power after the elections and thus engaged in criminal assault on hapless people.

It is significant to note this fact that a section of the Indian population made itself to believe that the caste system is a passing phenomenon. But in reality caste atrocities and caste discriminations are not isolated phenomenon. Nor are caste atrocities a vanishing phenomenon. Caste practices and caste discriminations are ingrained in the very foundation of the Indian society, Indian culture, Indian political economy and finally in the very Indian mind-set. Any crime committed against the Dalits is not an act perpetrated by an 'anti-social element'. It is also not an aberration from the rule. Caste discrimination and caste-related violence are the logical outcome of the historical hatred and social abhorrence the upper castes and the upper class maintain for centuries towards the Dalits.

Going further, one can also state that discriminatory behaviour towards the lower castes is palpable in the very way the dominant castes address the Dalits. Even the most educated and the enlightened upper caste person has fundamental and fierce repugnance and repulsion towards the Dalits. This ancient animosity in the day to day life gets converted into anger and the anger takes the form of outrageous crimes. These horrendous crimes have deleterious and dreadful effects on the Dalits. When these crimes go unabated, the conservative elements among the Dalits take charge of the situation and resist any type of search for alternatives.

At this juncture it is expedient to examine the cultural discourse that has erupted between the dominating castes and the Dalits. I have tried to present this discourse in the form of a diagram [Diagram 1]. This diagram presents the perception of the dominant castes about the Dalits, which is inherently derogative, negating the reality, and ultimately destroying the very source of life of the Dalits. For instance, attributes like *petu* or *khau* referring to 'being glutton', is an indication of obscuring reality. The empirical data does not support this perception of the dominant castes. The starvation deaths whether it is in Rajasthan or in Orissa prove this point beyond any doubt that the Dalits, the tribals and the downtrodden are the labouring class of any society but they are the starving caste/class of Indian society.

Diagram 1—Cultural Discourse

Dominant Caste's Perception of Dalits	*Dalits perception about themselves*
Dirty—Filthy fellows	Capable—But no opportunities
Thieves/Robbers	Hardworking
Cunning	Honest
Lazy—*kam chor*	Assertive
Useless—Good for nothing	Straight forward/less cunning
Gluttons—*petu, Khau*	Culturally talented
Loose Morals	Sensitive/emotional
Dishonest	Self-sacrificing
Quarrelsome—Disunity	Sagacious—good judgment
Ungrateful	Collective

Source: Based on the discussion held during the Workshops conducted about the Reconstruction of Dalit Identity in six north Indian States.

In contrast, the perception of the Dalits about themselves involves denial, assertion and preservation of all that is untruth. It is denial of the culture of deprivation imposed upon them by the dominating castes. It is an assertion of their rightful place and role in society and ensuring a plural form of culture and finally it is preserving traditions, cultures and life itself not only for themselves but also for the entire society. An apparent appraisal of the lives of the Dalits may make one believe that the Dalits are endowed with all forms of vices, 'immoral behaviour',[61] and dexterous in their operations. This is the level of propaganda that goes on every day existence. The Dalits also have come to believe that they are persons with these 'immoral behaviour'.[62]

Taken together, the Dalits have been and are subjected to poverty, indignity, insult, humiliation, dishonour, terror tactics and trepidation. Within the inhuman caste system, right from the childhood a Dalit is made to feel that he is an inferior being, an outcasted person, a person of loose morals and a person whose life is worth only for the service and the betterment of the dominant caste men and women. Since the Dalits continue to work day in and day out in sun and rain their very structure as well as the stature has been marked different. Because they were forced to engage themselves in hereditary occupation, they were identified as occupationally inferior beings. Not only individuals but the entire community of the Dalits all over India were and are constantly and perpetually engaged in the service of the dominant castes and classes, they could never enroll themselves for education. Any attempt by the parents to send the children to school or to non-formal education centres are staunchly resisted and at times they were physically assaulted for this 'misbehaviour'.

The Dalit labourers could be extended and expanded at will of the upper caste landed gentry. They not only engage them in the agricultural occupations but after whole days toil, they force them to carry out the household chorus. In return the labourer would get the leftovers of the previous day. This cannot be counted as wages but as a measure to keep the workforce alive so that the cycle of activities is carried out.[63] Dalit women were also subjected to physical assault and sexual abuse. Whether at agricultural operations or during the household activities or while the women are collecting fuel or fodder they could be teased, insulted and injured. The magnitude and the enormity of assault on Dalit women by the dominant castes could be gauged from this fact that even during festivals and religious ceremonies, they were not spared from ill-treatment.[64] But the entire Dalit community has to bear all these without recourse to justice.

In addition, it could be stated that the Dalits are extremely violent today because they have been the victims of centuries old non-violent ideology and operation. Anyone who wants to understand the entire gamut of Dalit struggle should not approach it as violence unleashed by the Dalits but should perceive it as emerging Dalit assertion.[65] All the schemes, policies and amendments of the Constitution that were carried out in the name of empowering the Dalits were in reality to disempower them. Moreover, this was not a matter of accident but definitional of the very design of the caste system. These have once again pushed the Dalits and the downtrodden to the grip of cultural deprivation. Hence, any understanding of the Dalit culture has to be within the emerging broader socio-political, economic and religious milieu. Any attempt to comprehend this reality has to begin from the atrocities and the agonies that the Dalits are subjected to due tot the atrocities. The anger and the aggression are the logical conclusion of the atrocities that they undergo everyday.

References

1. The Protection of Human Rights Act 1993. This act was enacted on 28th day of September, 1993 by the Government of India.
2. Constitution of India. Article 16. It is significant to note that the Constitution while ensuring special provision for weaker sections, it clearly and categorically identifies the Scheduled Castes and Scheduled Tribes as in need of preferential treatment.
3. The ILO Discrimination (Employment and Occupation) Convention, 1958 (no. 111).
4. It is significant to note that while racial, sex-related discriminatory practices have been brought under the purview of discourse, caste continued to remain untouched. This is due to the fact that while racial discrimination was taken to be a global phenomenon, caste discrimination was confined to India at the most to South Asia. But this is not the entire story. Even though at regular intervals there were attempts to raise caste discrimination in the conferences against racism, this remained a feeble voice. All those who represented India in the United Nations came from the dominant castes and on no account would raise the issue of discrimination suffered by the dalits.
5. Roger Zegers de Beijl. (ed). Documenting Discrimination against Migrant Workers in the labour market. A Comparative Study of four European Countries. International Labour Office: Geneva, 1999, pp. 5-6.
6. International Encyclopedia of Sociology. Volume 1. Fitzroy Dearborn Publishers: London, 1995, p. 373.
7. International Encyclopedia of Sociology. *Ibid.*
8. Dr. Ambdekar Writings and Speeches. Vol. 1. Education Department, Government of Maharashtra, 1990, pp. 39-40.
9. International Encyclopedia of Social Sciences. Vol. 13, The Macmillan Company, New York, 1968, p. 144.

10. For more details on this issue refer to forthcoming article, Prakash Louis, Social Exclusion of the Dalits, in the book to be edited by Dr. A.K. Lal, A.N.Sinha Institute of Social Sciences, Patna.
11. R.N. Sharma (ed). Manu Smriti, Chaukhamba Sanskrit Prakashan: Delhi, 1998.
12. Gail Omvedt. Dalits and the Democratic Revolution: Dr. Ambedkar and the Dalit Movement in Colonial India. Sage Publications, New Delhi, 1994, p. 47.
13. Dr. Ambdekar Writings and Speeches. *Ibid.*, pp. 266-267.
14. *Ibid.*, pp. 278-280.
15. The statement 'last in the ladder of creation' is indicative of being last both spatially and temporally. That is to say, the erstwhile untouchables are least in the order in terms of material possession. They are also the last of all segments both in spatial terms and time wise. In the ultimate analysis, what these expressions try to expose are that there is a cumulative effect on the Dalits and the downtrodden due to the heinous inequality of caste order.
16. *Ibid.*, pp. 281-285.
17. *Ibid.* pp. 311-320.
18. *Ibid.*
19. Dr. Ambedkar. *Writings and Speeches, Ibid.*, Vol. I, p. 8.
20. *Ibid.* Those who propagate inter-caste marriage and inter-caste dining as one of the possible means of bridging the caste differences should examine the barbarity and brutality exhibited in annihilating the youngsters who are supposed to have 'fallen in love' and got married. It is not limited to inter-caste marriage in which the lowest caste youth are involved; the intensity of assault on the young men and women of higher caste also indicates the same reality.
21. Radhakrishnan. The Hindu View of Life, 1949, p. 93.
22. Bharat Jhunjhunwala. Dalit Welfare: Moral Duty of the Rich and Powerful, The Statesman, 30.6.2001, p. 6.
23. B.R. Ambedkar. Annihilaion of Caste. Bheem Patrika Publications, Jullundur, 1936, p. 49.
24. B.R. Ambedkar. Ranade, Gandhi and Jinnah. Thacker and Co. Ltd., Bombay, 1943.
25. B.R. Ambedkar, Annihilation of Caste, *Ibid*, p. 85.
26. Harijan. Weekly, July 11, 1936 and July 18. Quoted in B.R. Ambedkar. Annihilation of Caste. Bheem Patrika Publications, Jullundur, 1936
27. Interestingly, during the World Conference Against Racism some of

the delegates from India made the following perceptive comments about Gandhi's experience of racism in Africa: Gandhi's experience of being thrown away from the first class compartment of the train in which he was travelling infact turned his career from being a barrister to a freedom fighter. This experience also moved him from being an ordinary human being to a "Mahatma", that is 'great being'. One dehumanising experience of Gandhi could turn the tides in his favour to become the Mahatma of not only India but also of the entire world. But for the Dalits and the downtrodden of India who go through degrading and distressing atrocities, there is no escape. The discriminatory behaviour shown to Gandhi by the white men in Africa was only related to colour, but for the Dalits the discrimination is economic, social, political, and cultural. It is this cumulative effect of deprivation and discrimination, which forced Dr. Ambedkar to present pointed criticism to caste system and to the extent of programming for its annihilation.

28. *Ibid.*
29. Dr. Ambdekar Writings and Speeches. *Ibid.,* Vol. 1. 1990, pp. 56-57.
30. The term *Panchamas* is usually translated as the fifth caste. In reality this term refers to that segment of the population within the Hindu social order who are outside the social system.
31. After the ascent of Hindutva forces in the Indian political scene, there is a stream of thinking which states that the emergence of right wing forces are due to the combination of the 3 Bs. Brahmins, Babusahebs or the Rajputs and the Banias. While the Brahmins are supposed to control the mind, the Rajputs are supposed to control administration and the Banias the market economy. This is the height of caste systematisation. This is also expressed in the statement "The *tilak*, *talwar* and *taraju* are the three sources of Hindutva forces. Tilak is the symbol of priesthood, talwar is the symbol of warrior and taraju is the symbol of business."
32. The quasi-state institution denotes two interconnected advantageous to the landed gentry. Though they functioned as agent of the state, they themselves were not the state and thus they were free from the responsibilities of managing the state. At the same time since they were part of the power structure at the local and at the regional levels, they reaped all the fruits of being power agents. This can social phenomenon can be called 'the shrouded dominance'. This could be discerned from many historical writings

about the zamindari system in Bengal Presidency.

33. Devanathan. Landlords as extensions of state. Economic and Political Weekly, 28th January, 1989, p. 179.
34. In the recent past the media has been trying to project this image that Andhra Pradesh is the "Most Happening State". The ruling dispensation there has been announcing one scheme after another. But what does all these mean to the common masses is a mute question.
35. The presence of the Dalits in most of the sectors is extremely lower than their strength. In party leadership, their presence is substantially high can be explained only by the scope provided by the reservation in political arena. That is, by virtue of Dalits being elected to the legislature bodies in a way forces the political parties to give some representation to the Dalits in party leadership. For example, Jagjivan Ram remained one of the front rank leaders in the Congress party. Bangaru Laxaman became the Party President of Bharatiya Janata Party, though for a short time.
36. Geetha B. Nambissan. *Ibid.*, p. 1014.
37. Quoted in Geetha B. Nambissan. *Ibid.*, p. 1014.
38. Rosalind O'Hanlon. Caste, Conflict and Ideology: Mahatma Jotirao Phule and Low Caste Protest in Nineteenth-Century Western India. Orient Longman, Bombay, 1985, p. 7.
39. Quoted in Geetha B. Nambissan, *Ibid.*, p. 1016.
40. Geetha Nambisan, *Ibid.*, p. 1016.
41. The ruling establishment is known for creating slogans. This is true for the health sector too and the slogan was 'health for all by 2000' and thus slogan has been put in the back burner and new slogans are already worked out.
42. Quoted in Suma Chitnis. A Long Way to Go. Allied Publishers: New Delhi, 1981.
43. Geetha Nambisan, *Ibid.*, p. 1020.
44. Hindustan Times, Patna, 26th December 1998.
45. As stated above, human rights and Dalit activists who participated in the World Conference Against Racism demanded that the Scheduled Castes and the Scheduled Tribes should be given reservation in private sector too.
46. Sukhdeo Thorat. Social Security for Scheduled Castes in Unorganised Sector, in S. Mahendra Dev edited "Social and Economic Security in India". Institute of Human Development: New Delhi, 2001, p. 370.

47. *Ibid.*
48. For more details on the reason why the lower castes sell out their land, refer to a study made by Prakash Louis, 'People's Perception of Land Reform Policies and Practices: A Comparative Study of Eastern, Western and Central Regions of Uttar Pradesh. Sponsored by Ministry of Rural Development, Government of India, June 2001.
49. Collected from various reports.
50. This data indicates the fact that in 1980s alone there were 3 conferences of the Revenue Ministers of the states to review the implementation of land reform policies and to plan out new programmes. But the irony of all these meetings, conferences etc., was that these got limited to only paper work and at the most they moved one step ahead and decided to 'computerise the entire land records'.
51. S. K. Thorat, *Ibid.*
52. Jagjivan Ram. Caste Challenges in India. Vision Books, New Delhi, 1980, p. 6.
53. Bindeshwari Pathak. The Psycho-Social Scenario of Scavengers and the Role of Sulabh International. In N. Hasnain edited, Weaker Sections: The Psycho-Social Perspective. Gyan Publishing House, New Delhi, 1998, p. 51.
54. The term *chamar* refers to one of the most dominant Dalit sub-caste among the Dalits of northern India. Since they work on *chamda* or skin, they were addressed as *chamars*. Thus, caste refers to descent based occupation. To address any one as *chamar* is considered offensive today.
55. C.W. Briggs. The *Chamars*. Low Price Publication. Delhi. Reprinted 1990, p. 56.
56. Various exercises have been carried out for electoral reforms. Most of these exercises are legal in nature. They fail to take into account the social and cultural specificity of Indian society. If the weaker section of society is continuously denied of their political right, the Indian democracy will be under serious threat.
57. No one should be dismayed by this perception of a deprived community. Those who are paying attention to the media hype on Indo-Pak Peace Process would regularly hear the people of Kashmir stating that 'for us the ground reality is more important. We want self-determination, freedom and political participation. But along with these and more important than these our economic needs are also equally important'. It is not that the common masses are disinterested in taking part in politics but since the ruling

dispensation do not make necessary provisions for their well being, they have to utilise all their energy in their struggle for food and other provisions.

58. The then Chief Minister of Uttar Pradesh, Mr. Rajnath Singh has accelerated the caste equations by announcing reservation within reservation for what he calls the 'Dalits among the Dalits' and the 'most backward castes among the backward castes'. This public pronouncement in itself sounds very pro-poor but in the ultimate analysis, it is a ploy to continue in power by 'divide and rule policy'.

59. Anand Swarup Varma, *Hindutva ki Rajniti ka Sawarna prakar*. Jansatta, 1.7.2001, p. 6.

60. Those who followed the different massacres that took place in Bihar in the course of agrarian movements would realise the barbaric and brutal nature of murders there. Whether it is in Lakshmanpur-Bathe or Shankarbigha or in Narayanpur, children were special targets for cruel attacks. It appeared that the Ranvir sena specialised on these forms of cruel massacres of the innocent. For more details refer to Prakash Louis, 'Bihar: Class War Spreads to New Areas'. Economic and Political Weekly, June 24, 2000, p. 2206-2211.

61. Today more than ever, this fundamental question has arisen 'who defines what as morality' and what 'moral authority' a person has to present something as 'moral' to others. At the level of the caste interaction, if a person from the dominant caste points out something as a 'moral value' to the person from the dominated caste, the person from the exploited caste today raises questions about the very legitimacy of this perception. Similarly, when the sangh parivar is trying to project the urgency of 'value education' for Indian society serious questions are raised about the legitimacy that this social category has to do so. Or in today's context, when the imperialist force the United States projects that its was on Afghanistan is a call for 'War Against Terrorism' because of what 'terrorist' did to America on the 11th of September 2001, it has tried to appropriate moral authority to decide what is terrorism and what is war.

62. Prakash Louis. The Cultural Deprivation of the Dalits of North India: Pointers for Counter-Culture, forthcoming article in the book to be edited by S. Arockiasamy for the CBCI.

63. For further reading refer to Prakash Louis, People Power, *Ibid.*

64. For more detailed discussion on this aspect refer to Devnathan in Satyamurthy edited, 'Agricultural Labour and the Poor Peasant Movements in Bihar: Class Formation and Political Transformation in Post-Colonial India", Oxford University Press, Vol. IV, 1996, p. 155.
65. Refer to the following articles that appeared after the vandalisation of statue of Ambedkar in Mumbai: J.V. Deshpande. Behind Dalit Anger. EPW, August 16-23 1997. P 2090-91. A.K.J ha. Dalit Ascendancy. The Times of India, 26.7.97, p. 8.

2

Dalits and Constitutional Provisions

No citizen shall, on grounds only of religion, race, caste, sex, place of birth or any of them, be subjected to any disability, liability, restriction or condition with regard—

(a) access to shops, public restaurants, hotels and places of public entertainment; or

(b) the use of wells, tanks, bathing ghats, roads and places of public resort maintained wholly or partly out of State funds or dedicated to the uses of general public – Article 15 [2]

The State shall promote with special care the educational and economic interests of the weaker sections of the people, and in particular, of the Scheduled Castes and the Scheduled Tribes, and shall protect them from social injustice and all forms of exploitation – Article 46.

The Indian Constitution is considered to be one of the most comprehensive and carefully framed Constitutions in the world. One of the fundamental objectives of Indian Constitution is to protect the rights of all the citizens but in a special way it ensures social justice to the marginalized and weaker sections. It was expected that this would set in a process of democratisation in the political arena, and lead to socio-economic welfare of the weaker sections. Further, it was hoped that these processes would ensure social mobility of the under-privileged, which in turn would affect the caste system. The Constitution broadened the horizon of the Dalits and the downtrodden by providing space for the economic upliftment and social justice to the weaker sections.[1]

The murder and mayhem that are perpetrated on the Dalits are irrespective of the fact that there are innumerable Constitutional and legal provisions enacted even before Independence. The post-independence period also has witnessed policies and programmes formulated for the wellbeing and the upliftment of the Dalits. The heart of the matter is that even after five decades of democratic rule, not even an iota of change has been initiated in the caste discrimination and caste violence. Further, there are positive actions or affirmative actions that are envisaged for the upliftment and well-being of the Dalits. On the other hand, there are also penal provisions against those who violate the rights of the Dalits and the downtrodden in this country.

The framers of the Constitution in general and Dr. Ambedkar[2] in a special way were acutely aware of the fact that India is a multi-faceted country and society. Hence, they kept the framework of caste, class, creed, colour, language, region and religion as the main markers while framing the Constitution. They were also aware of the fact that though caste was only a south-Asian phenomenon it should get central place in the Constitution because of its overwhelming significance in the Indian context. They equated the caste discrimination with every other forms of discrimination which humanity knew about and tried to make provisions for those afflicted by caste discrimination.

Some of the Constitutional provisions need to be spelt out here. As stated above, Article 15 denounces any form of discrimination. In the same vein, Article 16 [2] of the Constitution guarantees 'No citizen shall, on grounds of only religion, race, caste, sex, descent, place of birth, residence or any of them, be ineligible for, or discriminated against in respect of, any employment or office under the State'. Having made this general provision for all the citizens, Constitution makes special provisions for the weaker sections 16 [4 A]. 'Nothing in this article shall prevent the state from making any provision for the reservation in matter so promotion to any class or classes of posts in the services under the state in favour of the Scheduled Castes and Scheduled Tribes which in the opinion of the state are adequately represented in the services under the state'. This provision is usually known as protective action or affirmative action in favour of the discriminated and deprived communities of India.

Among all the Constitutional provisions, Article 17 is of seminal significance in terms of the discourse about caste and racial discrimination. The Constitution in clear and categorical terms declares that untouchability, which is the core of caste discrimination, should be abolished. This is something similar to the abolition of apartheid. 'Untouchability is abolished and its practice in any form is forbidden. The enforcement of any disability arising out of "Untouchability" shall be an offence punishable in accordance with the law'. The struggle against racial discrimination and the protracted movement against apartheid culminated in elimination of racial discrimination. The Constitutional provision to abolish untouchability could be seen as a step towards doing away with caste system.

Further, Articles 330 to 332 clearly delineate special provisions for reservation for the Scheduled Castes and Scheduled Tribes. This is another way of considering caste based discrimination and making specific provisions for the elimination of political discrimination. Article 340 demands that "the President may by order appoint a Commission consisting of such persons as he thinks fit to investigate the conditions of socially and educationally backward classes within the territory of India and the difficulties under which they labour and to make recommendations as to the steps that should be taken by the Union or any State to remove such difficulties and to improve their condition...". Based on this provision the National Commission for Scheduled Castes and Scheduled Tribes was constituted in the year 1990.

The Constitution (First Amendment) Act 1951, enjoined upon the ruling dispensation the following positive discrimination. "Nothing shall prevent the State from making any special provision for the advancement of any socially and educationally backward classes of citizens or for the Scheduled Castes and Scheduled Tribes". Historically speaking, the framers of the Constitution were well aware of the socio-historical root of the caste oppression and exploitation in India. Hence, they on the one hand formulated legal provisions for the protection of the rights of the Dalits and on the other hand enforced special provisions for the development of the Dalits and the Tribals. The ruling caste and class went one step further and enacted the Protection of Civil Rights Act, 1955.[3]

The Protection of Civil Rights Act, 1955 was an Act to prescribe punishment for the preaching and practice of "Untouchability" and for the enforcement of any disability arising from caste related behaviour. The Indian Parliament understanding the seriousness of the issue not only defined the various acts that could be termed as restrictions on the basis of untouchability but also prescribed punishment in the following manner, 'shall be punishable with imprisonment for a term of not less than one month and not more than six months and also with fine which shall be not less than one hundred rupees and not more than five hundred rupees'.

In spite of the fact that various Acts were promulgated and amendments were brought to the existing legislations, the plight of the Dalits continued unchanged and unchallenged. The Dalits have not been liberated from the servitude and bondage they are chained to under the caste system. Instead they continue to be subjected to ruthless repression and subjugation. While there is no change in the lives of the Dalits, the legal provisions have undergone amendments and have attained newer nomenclature. The Protection of Civil Rights Act, 1955 was rechristened in 1976 as the Untouchability (Offences) Act 1955. These Acts and ordinances gave a ray of hope that normalcy is returning in a society which is structurally skewed and discriminative.

In 1986 the political establishment introduced the Scheduled Castes and Scheduled Tribes (Prevention of Atrocities) Act 1989. The seminal significance of this Act is that it was devised to prevent if not eliminate criminal assaults on the Dalits. The Statement of Objects and Reasons declare, 'Despite various measures to improve the socio-economic conditions of the Scheduled Castes and the Scheduled Tribes, they remain vulnerable. They are denied number of civil rights. They are subjected to various offences, indignities, humiliations and harassment. They have, in several brutal incidents, been deprived of their life, and property. Serious crimes are committed against them for various historical, social and economic reasons'[4].

Though the political establishment was and continues to be brazenly pro-non-Dalit, yet the Scheduled Castes and Scheduled Tribes (Prevention of Atrocities) Act 1989 squarely took into account the existing reality, as well as recommended both punitive and protective measures. The Preamble of this Act spells out this clearly. "An Act to prevent the commission of offences of atrocities against the members of the Scheduled Castes and the Scheduled Tribes, to provide for Special Courts for the trial of such offences and for the relief and rehabilitation of the victims of such offences and for matters connected therewith or incidental thereto". The Act defined the nature of atrocities, prescribed punishment not only for the offender but also to any government agent for neglect of duties and further confers authority on officials to prevent atrocities committed on the Scheduled Castes and the Scheduled Tribes.[5]

The ruling dispensation went one step further and formulated the Scheduled Castes and the Scheduled Tribes (Prevention of Atrocities) Rules, 1995. These rules were supposed to function as precautionary and preventive measures. "With a view to prevent atrocities on the Scheduled Castes and Scheduled Tribes the State Governments shall i) identify the area where it has reason to believe that atrocity may take place or there is an apprehension of re-occurrence of an offence under the Act; ii) order the District Magistrate and Superindent of Police or any other officer to visit the identified area and review the law and order situation; iii) if deem necessary, in the identified area cancel the arms licenses of the persons, not being member of the Scheduled Castes or Scheduled Tribes, their near relations, servants or employees and family friends and get such arms deposited in the Government Armoury; iv) deploy special police force in the identified area; etc.[6]

It was hoped that a new beginning would be made with the introduction of the National Commission for Scheduled Castes and Scheduled Tribes. This was done under the 'Special Provisions Relating to Certain Classes'. Article 338 prescribed, "There shall be a Commission for the Scheduled Castes and Scheduled Tribes to be known as the National Commission for the Scheduled Castes and Scheduled Tribes. It shall be the duty of the Commission a) to investigate and monitor all matters relating to the safeguards provided for the Scheduled Castes and Scheduled Tribes under this Constitution or under any other law of the time being in force or under any order of the Government and to evaluate the working of such safeguards; b) to inquire into specific complaints with respect to the deprivation of rights and the safeguards of Scheduled Castes and Scheduled Tribes; c) to present to the President, annually and at such other times as the Commission may deem fit, reports upon the working of those safeguards; d) to discharge such other functions in relation to the protection, welfare and development and advancement of the Scheduled Castes and Scheduled Tribes as the President may, subject to the provisions of any law made by the Parliament, by rule specify.[7]

Among all the provisions, the Scheduled Castes and Scheduled Tribes Commission has far reaching consequences for the weaker sections. The Commission is vested with the following constitutional power: a) summoning and enforcing the attendance of any person from any part of India and examining him on oath; b) requiring the discovery and production of any documents; c) requisitioning any public record or copy thereof from any court or office; issuing commission for the examination of witnesses and documents, etc. But the examination of the reality bears testimony to this fact that these powerful provisions proved to be paper tigers at the most. It would be unrealistic to expect that these provisions would contribute in obliterating any signs of caste discrimination. But what remains the minimal role is that the Commission would provide space for the Scheduled Castes and Scheduled Tribes, to register their complaints and seek justice.

Interestingly, while the Commission for the Scheduled Castes and Scheduled Tribes continued to 'exist' as a national Constitutional body, vituperative assaults on the Dalits and the Tribals continued unabated, and the experience prove that the Commission did not engage in any major task to alleviate the sufferings of the weaker sections. But the most disappointing fact is that the Commission did not even deem it necessary or courteous to acknowledge the innumerable complaints sent to it by the distressed Scheduled Castes and Scheduled Tribes. This has added fuel to the fire, from the point of view of the Scheduled Castes and Scheduled Tribes.

The above mentioned fact could be verified from the following illustration: On 27th November 1999, over 500 Hati Darbars of Pankhan village of Junagadh district of Gujarat carried out a ghastly attack on the Dalits of the village.[8] Among the 100 Dalits who were clearing the thorny bushes to make the land cultivable, 40 were seriously assaulted.[9] Even seven months after the incidence, about 10 of the victims of this ghastly attack needed assistance to move about in their huts. Most of the seriously injured were above 60 years of age. Many young men and women managed to escape to nearby villages and thus were saved from the attack. But all of them were not lucky enough to escape the wrath of the upper caste Darbars. Jayaben Sondarva was gang raped by thirteen men and she was thoroughly bashed up. The impact of the atrocity was so serious that even for days she continued to scream with pain and agony. The marks of the wound inflicted with a crow bar and an axe were still there on her body. Even after seven months from the event she was not able to move about without the help of her children. The Darbars were armed to the teeth. It was reported that they not only carried conventional weapons like spears, woodcutters, swords, choppers, and axes but also modem firearms with them. This not withstanding, the dominant caste Darbars imposed 'social sanction' on the Dalits and thus denied them even the access to public places like schools or shops.

In January 2000 a group of social activists took up this matter with the National Commission for Scheduled Castes and the Scheduled Tribes as well as with the National Commission for Human Rights [NCHR]. The NCHR within a week sent a show cause notice to the Gujarat Government asking for explanation as well as the action taken report. The Gujarat Government in response sent a communication to the NCHR that these are allegations and there are no facts to substantiate. The social activists in collaboration with the local activist groups like the *Dalit Yuva Sanghatan*, Junagarh and the BAMCEF Junagarh once again visited the area and prepared a report and submitted it to the NCHR , which took up the matter once again with the Gujarat Government and ensured that the 125 of acres of *gairmazrua* land or government land, which was the bone of contention between the Dalits and the non-Dalits be distributed without delay among the Dalit families. After much delaying tactics, the Gujarat Government complied with this order of the NHRC. In contrast to the stand taken by the NHRC, the Scheduled Castes and the Scheduled Tribes Commission has not even acknowledged the complaint filed by the social activists.

Now one can make a speculative move to raise a fundamental question: What are the factors behind the mal-functioning or even dysfunction of the National Commission for the Scheduled Castes and the Scheduled Tribes. It is irrefutable that the Commission is a Constitutional body and it has been invested with powers and functions to carry out its job and infrastructure is made available for the same. But since the appointment to this commission is political in nature, those who are appointed to head this commission are more inclined to toe the line of the political party or the political establishment, which has provided them with the power and the privilege. Also, many of those who are appointed are persons who lost their elections and are to be accommodated in the corridors of power somehow. Hence, most of them bend backwards to follow the dictates of the political parties, which are of the dominant castes, by the dominant castes and for the dominant castes. It is this shrouded dominance of the upper castes and the cooption of the Dalit leadership which is highlighted here. Moreover, this discriminatory behaviour from the part of the dominant caste leadership as well as the Dalit leadership is not a matter of accident but definitional to the very design of the caste structure.

Affirmative Action

The concept of reservation did not emerge out of blue. The framers of the Constitution realised that if the Indian independence has to succeed, enhancing the social and economic power of the marginalised communities is imperative. Article 46 of the Constitution of India ensures, "The State shall promote with special care the educational and economic interests of the weaker sections of the people and, in particular, of the Scheduled Castes and the Scheduled Tribes, and shall protect them from social injustice and all forms of exploitation". While the Indian Constitution upholds the right of all for equal treatment before the law, it makes protective discrimination towards the Scheduled Castes and the Scheduled Tribes.

Providing reservation to the weaker section has not been without its controversies. There are some who would consider reservation as reparation for locational and institutional disadvantages. They would argue that the policies and programmes geared towards reserved preferences are in the line of distributive justice. Against this view there are others who would argue that reservation would only perpetuate the caste system. They would also pose the problem that reservation reduces the importance of merit.[10] The National Front Government on 7th August 1990 announced its intention to implement the Mandal Commission recommendations, which accorded 27 per cent reservations to the Other Backward Castes.[11] With this announcement the reservation issue came to the centre stage of discourse once again. This move not only raised bitter controversies among different sections of people but also become a grave law and order problem. Interestingly, the anti-Mandal agitations were more pronounced in northern India, especially in Gujarat, Bihar and Uttar Pradesh than in other parts of the country. While the upper castes formed a broader alliance to counter the move of the National Front Government, the other backward castes also aligned together to meet the challenges.[12]

Reservation per se was envisaged to build an egalitarian society instead of the maintenance of a stratified caste social order, as argued by few. The Constitutional provisions conceived in favour of the wellbeing of the Scheduled Castes and Scheduled Tribes[13] can be grouped under three areas:

(a) Developmental measures;
(b) Protective measures;
(c) Positive discrimination measures.

Developmental Measures

The Centrally Sponsored Post-Matric Scholarship to Students belonging to Scheduled Castes is the most important scheme to begin with. This was introduced in 1944-45 to help the Scheduled Castes, the provisions of which were extended to the benefit of the students from Scheduled Tribes in 1948-49. In the beginning this scheme had coverage of 114 students but at present over 20 lakh students are beneficiaries of this scheme.

National Overseas Scholarship for Scheduled Caste Students for Higher Studies was established as early as 1954-55. This scholarship was exclusively planed to provide financial assistance to such students who wish to pursue higher studies in highly technical fields abroad. Thus this scheme moved beyond any boundaries to open up newer avenues for the downtrodden.

The Centrally sponsored scheme of Pre-Matric Scholarship to Students belonging to Scheduled Castes is another scheme that came into being in 1977-78. The basic objective of the scheme was to provide financial assistance to children of scavengers, sweepers, tanners etc., to pursue pre-matric education. This scholarship is provided for 10 months in a year. Besides this a sum of Rs. 50/- is given per annum. It is estimated that 2.05 lakh students would benefit out of this scheme.

The concept of Special Component Plan (SCP) was adopted from 1979-80 onwards for the development and welfare of the Scheduled Castes. The SCP was designed to channelise the flow of outlays and benefits from the general sectors in the plans of the State and the Central Ministries for the development of Scheduled Castes. The State Governments look after the welfare and development of Scheduled Castes through their respective Special Component Plan with the support of Special Central Assistance provided by the Central Government.

The Scheduled Castes Development Corporations (SCDCs) was established in March 1979. The SCDCs are envisaged to interface between the poor Scheduled Caste entrepreneurs and the financial institutions in respect of bankable schemes of economic development. To avoid undue delay, from 1994 onwards it has been decided that the central share will be released directly to the SCDCs instead of through State Governments.

The Central Government also contributes in the Share Capital Investment of the States, which act as guarantors, promoters and catalysts for generating credit from financial institutions providing missing inputs by way of margin money loans and subsidy to target groups. SCDC Centrally Sponsored Scheme of Upgradation of Merit of SC Students was launched in 1987-88 under the Human Resources Development Ministry but transferred to the Ministry of Welfare in 1993-94.[14]

The National Scheduled Castes and Scheduled Tribes Finance and Development Corporation (NSFDC) was established on 8th February 1989 to play a major role in promoting self-employment and to develop entrepreneurial and skilled abilities among the Scheduled Castes and Scheduled Tribes. According to the Report of the Ministry of Social Justice and Empowerment financial assistance is provided for the following: agriculture and allied activities; horticulture; animal husbandry and dairying; minor irrigation; small industries; trade services and transport. It also states that disbursements have risen substantially from Rs. 35 lakh in 1989-90 to Rs. 409.15 crores as on 31st March 1998.[15]

The National Scheme of Liberation and Rehabilitation of Scavengers and their dependants, which was launched in March 1992, has been extended up to the end of the Eleventh Plan period. This scheme was launched in pursuance of Government's commitment to eliminate the inhuman practice of manual handling of night soil and filth by the end of the VIII Plan period. This scheme has three components: a) a rapid survey to identify scavengers and their dependents and their aptitude for alternative trades and professions; b) training of scavengers and their dependents in what all categories; c) rehabilitation of scavengers through projects with a prescribed funding pattern.

Dr. Baba Saheb Ambedkar Foundation was established on March 24, 1992 in the context of his birth Centenary Celebrations. Some of the activities undertaken at this juncture were: Establishing a National Public Library, Dr. Ambedkar's Chairs in Universities and Institutions, and Dr. Ambedkar Overseas Fellowship etc.

In June 1996, a new central scheme for establishing free Residential Schools for Scheduled Castes girls below the poverty line was launched through the *Zilla Parishad* in 48 districts[16] in which the Scheduled Castes female literacy rate was less than 2 per cent. This was a way of distancing removing them from their social surroundings, which are not conducive for formal education. By placing the girls in the residential schools, the government wanted to ensure the all round development of these children.

The National Safai Karmacharis Finance and Development Corporation (NSKFDC) has been made operative on 24.1.1997 to promote economic development/self-employment for the economic rehabilitation of Safai Karmacharis, besides providing training in technical and entrepreneurial skills and extending loans to students from the Safai Karmachari community for pursuing higher education.[17] The above presented developmental measures are representative in nature. There were and are many other projects and schemes introduced in course of time for the upliftment of the weaker sections.

Legal Measures

One can identify at least three most important legal measures envisaged by the state for the protection of the rights of the Scheduled Castes and Scheduled Tribes. The Protection of Civil Rights Act, 1955 [formerly known as Untouchability (Offences) Act, 1955] was enacted in line with the Article 17 of the Constitution is the first to begin with. By this Act, 'untouchability' was abolished and its practice in any form was forbidden under the threat of punishment.[18] This Act clearly and categorically states that denial of entry to members of Scheduled Castes into places for public utility and gathering is an offence and calls for punishment.

Going beyond the provisions of the Protection of Civil Rights Act, the political establishment of this country enacted the Scheduled Castes and Scheduled Tribes (Prevention of Atrocities) Act 1989 , which came into force from January 1990. Interestingly, the statement of objectives spells out the reasons behind the introduction of this Act. "Despite various measures to improve the socio-economic conditions of the Scheduled Castes and Scheduled Tribes, they remain vulnerable. They are denied number of civil rights. They are subjected to various offences, indignities, humiliation and harassment. They have, in several brutal incidents, been deprived of their life, and property. Serious crimes are committed against them for various historical, social and economic reasons".[19]

Further, the National Commission for Scheduled Castes and Scheduled Tribes was established in 1990, with wide ranging powers and functions. Some of the functions of the Commission are a) to investigate and monitor all matters relating to the safeguards provided for Scheduled Castes and Scheduled Tribes under the Constitution or under any order of the Government and to evaluate the working of such safeguards; b) to enquire into specific complaints with respect to the deprivation of rights and safeguards of the Scheduled Castes and Scheduled Tribes, etc.[20]

Positive Discrimination Measures

The positive discrimination measures or what is usually known as the provision of reservation is seen as the mainstay of Indian democracy. There are three types of provisions in this: a) reservation in the educational institutions; b) reservation of services and posts in the government services; c) reservation of seats in the legislatures. There is inter-connectedness between these three areas where reservation has been provided. Reservation of services and posts can be utilised only if the Scheduled Castes and Tribes who were denied access to education can be provided with the opportunity to educate themselves. Only when there are representatives from these communities in the legislatures a demand for reservation will be seriously put forth. Thus, the positive discrimination provisions were aimed at bridging the gap between the Scheduled Caste-Tribe population and non-Scheduled Caste-Tribe population.

The vision to provide representation to the Scheduled Castes and Scheduled Tribes in the educational, professional and political institutions was clearly spelt out by Dr. Ambedkar. "There shall be no disabilities attaching to anyone on the ground of his being a member of the Depressed Classes in regard to any elections to local bodies or appointment to Public Services. Every endeavour shall be made to secure fair representation of the Depressed Classes in these respects subject to such educational qualifications as may be laid down for appointment to the Public Services".[21]

The immediacy of reservation for the marginalised communities is clearly spelt out by the Constitutional provisions. According to Article 16 (4) "Nothing in this article shall prevent the State from making any provision for the reservation of appointments or posts in favour of any backward class of citizens which in the opinion of the State, is not adequately represented in the services under the state". Article 335 declares, "The claims of the members of the Scheduled Castes and the Scheduled Tribes shall be taken into consideration, consistently with the maintenance of efficiency of administration in the making of appointments to services and posts in connection with the affairs of the Union of a State". These provisions are made with the objective of right to equality, right to equality before the law, and right to equal protection of the laws. Keeping this reality in mind, on 21.9.1947 just after independence, instructions were issued to enforce reservations.[22]

Taken together, the above mentioned measures were supposed to usher in change in the living conditions of the weaker section of Indian society. But an examination of the various schemes envisaged by the rulers of this country unravel this fact that there was no dearth of projects and programmes that were supposed to alleviate the misery of the Scheduled Castes and Scheduled Tribes. But what in reality the 'affirmative action' or the 'positive discrimination programme' or reservation for weaker section achieved is far from the objectives behind introducing these measures. This is not only form the point of view of social mobility obtained by the Scheduled Castes and the Scheduled Tribes but also the manner in which allocations are made also present a tardy picture. For instance the allocation for SCP in the 6th Plan was 7.67 per cent and in the 7th plan it was 8.31 per cent against the total state plan outlay. While this is normally the case, the Ministry of Social Justice and Empowerment has consistently insisted that allocation of funds should be in proportion to Scheduled Caste population; the Ministry has demanded that a separate budget head for SCP be opened to prevent diversion, underutilisation, and misutilization of funds earmarked for Scheduled Castes; that the allocation of funds be in accordance with specific needs and priorities of Scheduled Castes.[23]

Education is considered both by the policy makers and the weaker sections to be the key for social mobility. Hence, many policy perspectives have been introduced during the last five decades. The 1986 National Policy on Education (NPE) aimed at universal enrollment of all Dalit children in the 6-11 age group and 75 per cent enrollment in the 11-14 age group as well as the successful completion by them of primary and middle school stages by 1990. The targets have been reiterated in the revised Programme of Action in 1992. The educational scene in the 1990s has been dominated by the District Primary Education Programme (DPEP), which placed special emphasis upon improved access, participation, and achievement in children from marginalised groups. In addition, the '*Sarva Shiksha Abhiyan*' announced in the year 2000 emphasizes the involvement of dalit communities in the ownership of school committees, setting up of alternative schooling facilities in unserved habitations, using community teachers, monitoring attendance and retention of Dalit children, and so on.

Strategies laid down to universalise primary/elementary education among Dalits are concerned with:

- Expanding school provisioning at primary and middle stages. In predominantly Dalit habitations, distance norms are relaxed so as to facilitate easy access to elementary education. Hostel facilities are also recommended to facilitate learning.
- Subsidized costs and providing incentives. Abolishing tuition fees and providing incentives such as free books, uniforms, school bags and midday meals. Scholarship to children from unclean castes, financial assistance for children of indigent groups and attendance scholarships for girls.
- Recruitment of teachers from within these communities by relaxing qualifications if necessary.
- Providing non-formal and alternative/innovative programmes for children who are seen as unable to access formal schooling.[24]

The basic objective in these exercises undertaken by various political parties was but to keep the electorate in good humour. While all these policies and programmes promised heaven to the electorate, it consistently and consciously denied the Dalits of their basic rights in reality. Even a cursory glance at the implementation of policies by both the state and central governments, amplify the fact that many of the policy documents begin with an acknowledgement of the depraved state of non-implementation of policies and preventive measures that are related to the Dalits. But this public confession seems to be only another ploy to sidestep the issue.

All these data go to establish the social fact that caste discrimination and atrocities are the logical outcome of the very caste edifice on which the Indian society is construed. The dominant caste is hell-bent on upholding its hegemony and monopoly by unleashing a rein of terror and repression on the Dalits. With the introduction of universal education, electoral politics, reservation policy etc., the Dalits are beginning to voice their protest against caste atrocities and caste system itself. This has created panic among the dominant castes who were the beneficiaries of caste and class domination. Hence, they want to throttle any attempt by the Dalits to raise the issue of violation of their rights both in the national and international forums. It is in the fitness of things to state here that this once again reveals the deep-seated caste discrimination in the Indian society.

Dr. Ambedkar understood the depth and the deleterious effects of the caste discrimination to which the Dalits were subjected to historically. Hence, he argued for emancipation of the Dalits as the first priority in the freedom struggle even before the nation could be liberated from the colonial rulers. In the 1930-31 Round Table Conference in London, he powerfully and profoundly argued, "The Depressed Classes can not consent to subject themselves to majority rule in their present state of hereditary bondsmen. Before majority rule is established their emancipation from the system of untouchability must be an accomplished fact. It must not be left to the will of the majority. The Depressed Classes must be made free citizens entitled to all the rights of citizenship in common with other citizens of the State".[25] But this lone voice got drowned in the sea of '*swadeshi* slogan' propagated by the upper caste and upper class politicians.

The Approach Paper to Tenth Five year plan[26] was released on the 7th of May 2001. On 29th June the Prime Minister of India gave official sanction to the Approach paper.[27] The issues, which according to him cause concern to the nation, were Power Sector and Railways. By stating this the Prime Minister once again has brought to centre stage the 'non-issues' and has in a sinister manner relegated to the background some real issues affecting the common masses and in a special way the Dalits, the Tribals and the women. There are a few fundamental issues that need to be highlighted about the Approach Paper.

In the entire document there is not even a mention of the Dalits. There is a small paragraph about the Tribals. In the previous plans, there used to be a separate section on the weaker sections. But in this paper there is no mention of the deprived weaker sections. Though the Approach paper speaks of "Growth, Equity and Sustenance" in reality the objective of the planning commission is to double the Per Capita Income. This is irrespective of the fact that the report accepts the truth that in the early nineties there was an expectation that employment opportunities will increase and income will go up. But in reality, the expected growth in economy did not take place and there is severe constrains on the economy of the nation. Moreover, the paper speaks volumes about high technology[28] and scientific invention. In this scheme the Dalits will be further outcasted and ostracised.

Another equally detrimental process to the Dalits is the Constitutional Review that is being carried out under the reactionary Hindutva force. There has been a debate in the political arena of India that electoral reform should be carried out to make Indian democracy work. But from the time the Hindu reactionary forces under the Sangh Parivar assumed power at the centre they have been making assiduous attempt to review of the Constitution. The stated objective of this move is to amend the Constitution in such a manner that improves the working of the Constitution. But there is another side of the story. This attempt is seen as a move to consolidate the supremacy and authority of the dominant castes and classes in India.

The Constitution has been in operation for the last 50 years. Hence, on the face value it appears that a review of the Constitution is in place. Further, there have been many amendments done in the Constitution in course of time. They all need to be incorporated and given an integrated picture. But the heart of the matter is that whether the ruling dispensation even tried to put the Constitution in practice? Have they made serious efforts to enforce laws and provisions that are specially enacted for the betterment and wellbeing of the Dalits, Tribals, women and the downtrodden. These are the questions that remain unanswered.

Noted Supreme Court lawyer, Rajeev Dhavan argues that 'the entire attempt to review the Constitution is a political gimmick. The real intent of the ruling party, the BJP is to establish its monopoly over the Constitution too. Hence, this process needs to be carefully monitored but one cannot avoid the review. The Commission appointed to review the Constitution is raising the same issue which have been raised already'.[29] The debate continues in favour or against the review. What would a review of this nature entail to the common masses is a million rupee question.

From the perspective of the Dalits and the downtrodden, the review of the Constitution needs to be examined from some fundamental aspects of Indian society and polity. The Hindu reactionary forces in the name of upholding the rights of the Hindu majority have taken the country to ransom. To succeed in their sinister plan, they have already worked out another Constitution for India.[30] They are measuring the ground reality for the time being by initiating the process of change in the existing Constitution. But once the Indian democracy is weakened and when internal and external forces taken hold of the country, the Constitution of the so-called 'Bharat' will be imposed on the masses.

Another salient feature of the move to review the Constitution is to delete once for all from the annals of history, the name of Dr. Ambedkar as the principle force behind the framing of the

Constitution. The upper caste and upper class could not digest this fact that a Dalit could be acclaimed all over the globe as the architect of the Indian Constitution. This has given them nightmare. Hence, they want to eliminate the Constitution and thus erase the name of Baba Saheb from historical records.

Going further one also need to view the entire exercise from the perspective of the assertions of the Dalits, the Tribals and the women. The downtrodden masses of India have from ages protested and resisted the authority and the hegemony of the dominant castes. The framing of the Constitution as well as Indian independence provided some more space for them to demand their legitimate rights. In the last five decades,[31] these deprived and dehumanised communities have registered their protest as well as raised their issues through innumerable people's movements. This has sent shock waves to the dominant castes and classes. Hence they are trying to hold on to the age-old caste stratification and discrimination.

The Consultation Papers prepared by the Review Commission are indicative of this trend.[32] The very understanding of the Commission about caste is faulty and hence, their recommendations are also redundant. According to the Commission, caste is a social vulnerability impairing its nationhood. Thus, nationhood and unity of the nation is the agenda of the Review Commission and the entire caste discrimination and deprivation is thrown in the winds. This is how the Commission presents the aspect 'how far India fared with developing countries is one of the criterion to measure the success of the operation of the Constitution'.[33] But it has failed to raise the more important question, 'how far India has faired with the liberation and emancipation of the Dalits, Tribals and women'.

Taken together, the Consultation Papers of the Constitutional Review Commission once again reiterated the resolve of the ruling caste and class that they are hell bent on carrying out their hegemony and monopoly over the downtrodden masses of India. This is amply demonstrated by the fact that the Papers have identified right diagnosis but have suggested defective remedies. In some places, they have projected wrong diagnosis and have ended up prescribing wrong remedies. Above all the Commission rightly has raised some fundamental questions for debate but has slipped away from giving appropriate answers.

There are few danger signals that need to be exposed here. On page 88 of the report, there is a clear and categorical mandate to the rulers that coercion and authoritarian approach will lead to population stabilization. But the members of the Constitutional Review Commission have forgotten the barbaric enforcement of forced sterilization during the emergency. Since the common masses are the victims of these authoritarian policies the ruling dispensation will enact the same policy in a disguised form. On the other hand, similar mandate is not given in enforcement of land reform policies, elimination of caste atrocities, violation of the rights of Dalit, Tribals and women.

Another issue, which has once again exposed the caste biased mindset of the dominant castes or the exploiter caste is the recent report published by the Madhya Pradesh Human Rights Commission (MPHRC). It is reported that MPHRC had undertaken a study of HIV/AIDS in some villages of Madhya Pradesh with the financial support from the UNICEF. But the study ultimately ended up branding 3 Dalit communities as being engaged in prostitution. The title of the report itself is revealing, "Caste Based Prostitution in Madhya Pradesh".[34] Any one who goes through the report will be baffled by the objectives of the study, the methodology followed, the outcome envisaged etc. When some concerned citizens and human rights activists registered their protest against this derogatory, anti-Dalit, anti-women report the UNICEF who funded the study denied having any direct responsibility of the report. But the MPHRC has gone ahead and has distributed the report and thus has done irremediable harm to these communities.

If one ventures into explore the factors behind publishing this detestable and nefarious report, one is struck by the fact that the real intent of the MPHRC is to reinstate a contrived notion of the lost glory of the Madhya Pradesh state. According to the commission, Madhya Pradesh has lost its name because these 3 communities have been involved in 'prostitution'. But by engaging in this exercise, the MPHRC has once and for all has stigmatized these castes. In the skewed and superstitious Indian society, if a group is branded then no girl from that community could be married outside nor can these communities take girls from outside. If they are working or living outside the territory then they will be subjected to social boycott.

The methodological flaw in this report is beyond comprehension. In page 1 it is stated that prostitution is the hallmark of this caste but in the same page in another place it is stated that not every unmarried girl of age is a prostitute. In page 58 it is reported that there are only 32 girls upto the age of 14 in the village and hence it appears that all of them are prostitutes. Moreover, the report bemoans the fact that state government treats these castes as 'special *harijans*'. The term *harijan* is legally considered to be derogative and contemptuous. Legally speaking one can not use this word which is offensive to a segment of the population. But the fact that a human rights commission has used this term is a point that needs to be registered here and condemned.[35] Moreover, the report unhesitatingly uses the term prostitutes 145 times in the report.

Any conscious citizen would be outraged by the insensitivity of the commission in bringing out a discriminatory report of this type. But if one delves deep into the dominant caste mindset one would not be baffled by the report. First and foremost the dominant castes claim that they never come under the purview of similar social evils. It has to always portray that the Dalits and the downtrodden are immoral, insensitive to their women, and illegitimate in their living. It is this social fact that the report brings out though latently. Also, this report has once again established the fact that the Dalits can be branded, stigmatised and stamped by the dominant castes and get away with it. If Dalits refuse to obey the dictates of the dominant castes or resists the abuses of the upper castes they can be severely dealt with. Further, this report has been published in English and thus the outcome of the study has not gone back to the very people who are stigmatized. These aspects once again depict the dominant caste frame of mind.

Historically speaking, anti-caste movements have been part of the narrative of Indian history. In the 1950s, the upsurge from the backward castes and in the 1970s the assertion from the Dalits have once again brought to centre stage the discourse on caste system and caste discrimination as it takes place in everyday plane. Hence, a brief understanding of the Mandal discourse and Dalit discourse is relevant here.

Shiv Vishwanathan in his critical appraisal of my work, "Casteism is more Horrendous than Racism"[36] throws light on the issue. As politics, as economics, as justice the Dalits don't figure except as acts of protest. Even protest is seen as intrusion and not a legitimate act of politics. Within the normalcy of current political discourse, there is little place for Dalit as discourse or tactics. It is true that Dalits in many ways are not given true status as citizens in India. But does caste work the same way for middle class or other backward castes? Or is there an emerging split-level view of caste with Dalits feeling oppressed and Mandalism and its reforms leaving one with a feel good feeling about India? Maybe what Dalit discourse needs to do is distinguish between a Dalit and a Mandalist perspective on caste exploring similarities but more importantly differences. One is forced to maneuver for international attention because only external politics might be able to leverage current paradigms. Dalit discourse is therefore a challenge to the current paradigms of constitutionality, rights and democracy indicating there is little space for maneuver within the current definitions of politics. The lack of space stems from two factors. It emerges from the lack of political will among the elite and the sheer marginalization and impoverishment of Dalits in everyday life. Democracy and development work only for those above the Dalit domain. In fact, it is not just part of academic sociology that Dalit politics challenges but Mandalist politics. Dalit discourse is an unconscious sparring with Mandalist worldviews. At the risk of being provocative let me formalize tactics and strategies.[37]

One has to be clear that the Durban conference is a rite of passage, a transition from one kind of politics of another. At one level, Durban and the months of preparation before it are like a thought experiment, an attempt to create what appears like outrageous hypothesis to rework the problem of caste. At another level, Dalit politics seems like a sideshow to the great celebration of condemning race at Durban. The Indian activists have to return to the everyday drama of caste oppression. But here Dalit activists must apply more critical rules for self-reflection and self-criticism. They could hold open seminars explaining their strategy, its possibilities, the extent of networking done. This also tempers down the ugly backlash that will follow from those who felt left out of the Durban Crusade, realizing one faction's possible failure might be another faction's opportunity. But there is a wider learning process

Figure 1
Political Discourse[38]

Dalit discourse	*Mandalism*
• universalist discourse	• regional discourse
• a theory of freedom	• affirmative action
• a critique of state	• committed to statistic action
• globalized	• within national politics
• anti-caste	• uses the politics of caste as vertical groups
• combination of isms	• generally within a socialist framework
• easy alliance of tribals, Dalits, Feminism	• uneasy relationship with tribalism and feminism
• based more on politics of humiliationexploitation or relative deprivation	• focuses more on politics of
• current public spaces appear constricting	• uses current public spaces
• resistance to vote-bank politics, move to autonomous articulation	• content with vote-bank politics
• mix of Hindu+Christian and Buddhist and secular enlightenment ideologies	• within a Hindu or secular frame
• challenges current frames of politics	• sees itself as a paradigmatic part of current politics

involved here. One needs to understand how NGOs or other groups in civil society can insert themselves into global politics. More critically one need to gauge how adept the Dalits were as a lobby in UN backroom politics and also ask whether Dalit activism might become a prey to donor driven politics of foundations and other international agencies. For a Dalit discourse and a Dalit politics, autonomy at every level is a crucial apriori.

Before we conclude this section it is in the fitness of things to reinstate this historical fact that there are Constitutional provisions for the protection as well as the promotion of the rights of the Dalits. But in day-to-day life these laws are more for violation than enforcement. The most detesting truth is that those individuals, agents and commissions who are supposed to uphold the rights of the Dalits are in the forefront transgressing their rights. It is not that the Dalits are unaware of their Constitutional safeguards and rights. But often they do not retaliate to the cruel oppression and suppression heaped upon them. This is because they do not want to enter into a long drawn-out legal battle since the judiciary itself is caste based and biased. Moreover they are exceedingly aware of this fact that their struggle for emancipation is protracted, multi-pronged and holistic. While they try to utilise the constitutional provisions they are engaged in an exercise of building up their armor for a decisive fight to the finish. The attempt to raise the issue at the international forum like the World Conference Against Racism was only one such exercise.

S.L. Gaikward based on sample study of 200 respondents, maintains that the respondents both employees and students who are beneficiaries of reservation policy were of the view that they were subjected to discriminatory treatment [Table 4]. More than 58.5 per cent of the respondents stated that they have to face discriminatory behaviour from the non-Dalits. If the teachers or the educational system operates in a partial manner, then the future of the students would be at jeopardy. It is consoling that at least about 8 per cent of the respondents were of the opinion that they receive encouraging and equal treatment from their colleagues. Thus, a debate on reservation policy should underscore the attitude and behaviour of dominant castes towards the weaker sections.

Richard Pais based on the study he made of the Scheduled Caste employees in government jobs in Mangalore district in Karnataka makes the following observation: the general attitude in any work organization regarding the employment status of Scheduled Castes is that they occupy the present positions because of their

Table 4
Perception of Beneficiaries about Treatment of Caste Hindus Towards Them[39]

S.No.	Treatment	Frequencies			
		Employees	Students	Total	%
1	Discriminatory	23	18	41	20.5
2	Caste hatred	2	9	11	5.5
3	Non-cooperation	5	5	5	2.5
4	Humiliatory	1	6	7	3.5
5	Partiality in Examination	3	16	19	9.5
6	Discriminatory along with one or more other treatment [S.No. 2-5]	55	21	76	38.0
7	All (from S.No. 1-5)	13	3	16	8.0
8	Equal and encouraging	1	16	17	8.5
9	Do not have personal experience	2	2	4	2.0
10	Not mentioned		4	4	2.0
Total		100	100	200	100

caste status and the policy of reservation. While this was the perception of the non-Scheduled Castes, the majority of the Scheduled Castes (about 73%) on their part also attributed their present employment status to the fact that their caste was a Scheduled Caste, and that they were eligible for reservation. They were of the view that they would not have go the job under the prevailing circumstances of caste discrimination in Hindu society.[40]

Marc Galanter further points out that there is intense resentment of the reservation policies among government servants, epitomized in the mocking reference to the Scheduled Caste officer as a "son-in-law of the government" or a "Government Brahmin". The term son-in-law is used to connote a person whose every whim is indulged, indiscriminately.[41] These terms are constantly employed by the dominant castes in the presence of the

Dalit and Tribal employees that they would be humiliated beyond recovery.

Historically speaking one can discern two different perceptions among the leaders of this country about reservation. Dr. Ambekdar argued, "Supposing, for instance, reservations were made for a community or a collection of coummunities, the total of which came to something like 70 per cent of the total posts under the state and only 30 per cent are retained as the unreserved, could any body sat that the reservation of 30 per cent as open to general competition would be satisfactory from the point of view of the ... namely that there shall be equality of opportunity. It cannot be in my judgment. Therefore, the seats to be reserved, if the reservation is to be consistent with clause (1) of Article 10 (now 16), must be confined to majority of seats... we have to safeguard two things, namely the principle of equality of opportunity and at the same time satisfy the demand of the communities which have not had so far representation in the State, then".[42]

Nehru was of the opinion, "There is a great danger, whether you deal with an individual, group or community, of giving certain propos to that community which give a false sense of strength which does not belong to it. The props are external to it, and when they are removed, suddenly make the community weak. A nation ultimately ought to stand on its own feet. So long as it relied on some external prop, it is not strong. It is weak. So these external props, as I might call them, that is reservation of seats and the rest-may possibly be helpful occasionally in the case of the backward groups, but they produce a false sense of the political relation, a false sense of strength, and ultimately, therefore, they are not so nearly as important as real educational, cultural and economic advance which gives them inner strength to face any difficulty or any opponent.

Pandit Nehru went on to state that in the present context of affairs, in regard to these unfortunate countrymen of ours who have not had these opportunities in the past, special attempts should be made, of course, in the educational and economic field and even in the political field to see that they have a proper place till they find their own legs to stand upon without the external aid".[43] Nehru's terming the weaker sections as 'unfortunate countrymen' itself goes to state that being reduced to the state of untouchability and suffering all forms of discrimination is just an unfortunate event for the so called liberal secularists, and not socio-historical manipulation of the dominant castes.

Here it is expedient to present the perception of former American President Lyndon Johnson, who at the Commencement Address at Howard University in 1965 declared, 'We seek...equality as a fact and equality as a result... equal opportunity is essential, but not enough... You do not take a person, who for years has been hobbled by chains and liberate him, bring him up to the starting line of the race and then say, "Your are free to compete with all others," and still believe that you have been completely fair.'[44]

The Discourse on Reservation

Prof. Sachchidananda while delineating the debate that ensued after the pronouncement about implementation of Mandal Commission Report asserts, "The higher castes, particularly the higher caste elites, feel their monopoly slipping out of their hands. The elite has only been able to maintain its life-style by an inordinate presence in the government, which enables it, through better salary and corruption, to provide for its extravagances. The elite's commitment to the equality of status and of opportunity enshrined in the Constitution is highly dubious, and it has been exposed in its true colours as self-serving and selfish. It sheds crocodile tears for Scheduled Castes and Scheduled Tribes reservations but feels insecure on account of the growing political clout of the backward castes and their quest for accelerated vertical mobility. The elite uses merit as a euphemism for privilege".[45]

Affirmative action is directed to provide opportunities for education and through that employment and thus lead to upliftment. Affirmative action also may be seen as 'making up for the past discrimination'. But protective discrimination has to move towards providing space and scope for rights of the weaker sections. Late A.N. Das remarked, 'the protection of merit is a manipulative plutocracy of the privileged. Such is the moral and intellectual degeneration of the Indian elite that it feels insecure when reservations threaten this privilege. It raises the bogey of merit being swamped by the multitude because it is not sure of its own competence'.[46]

There are some fundamental issues about reservation, which have continued to haunt the political sociology of India, and some newer issues have also come to the fore. 1) The legitimacy of reservation policy: Should there be reservation at all for what the Constitution terms as weaker sections, namely the Scheduled Castes, the Scheduled Tribes and the Other Backward Castes? 2) Prolonged preferential policies: Should the policy of reservation continue since the stipulated time of implementation of reservation policy has come to an end? 3) The determining factors of backwardness: if reservation has to be continued, what should be the criterion to determine backwardness? 4) The question of the creamy layer: should the provisions of the reservation policy accrue to members from the weaker sections who have attained social mobility? 5) The hierarchy and compartment: There is hierarchy and compartment within the Schedule Castes and Scheduled Tribes. How to ensure that the most backward people within the weaker sections also benefit from the provisions of affirmative action? 6) In the present context should not the preferential option be extended to other groups currently handicapped? 7) Reservation and Private sector: Should reservation policy be extended to private sector too?

It is frequently asked whether preferential policies are necessary in countries, which have laws against, discrimination or which have attained formal equality. Nesiah is of the view, "Laws against untouchability, segregation and discrimination are essential, but they cannot possibly eliminate the impact of prejudice, or compensate for group disabilities caused by environmental or historical circumstances, or otherwise ensure the achievement of equal opportunity as between individuals. The structural obstacles to mobility may be most formidable where there has been a long history of prejudice, discrimination and exclusion sanctioned by law or religion as in the case of Blacks and Native Americans in the USA, Dalits and Tribals in India, and women everywhere. Even if the legal and ideological basis of discrimination and exclusion can be overcome, prejudice and psychological conditioning may continue to hinder progress for a long period."[47]

Upendra Baxi in his perceptive analysis states, "Violence against untouchables, who constitute 15 per cent of Indian population, is on increase not just in levels of brutality. The period 1973 to 1978 according to one estimate, witnessed 62,295 violent incidents commonly called 'atrocities' against untouchables life and property. In 1977-78, 12,746 atrocities were registered involving 354 killings and 306 registered cases of rape. The very names – Kilvennmani, Belchi, Dharmapur, Villupuram, Pantnagar, Marathwada, Pipra- evoke a cluster of images of inhuman violence: huts set ablaze, people tied to trees and burned alive, people shot at point range or hacked to pieces, women raped and brutally killed, children bayoneted or buried alive. The gruesome story of genocidal violence against untouchables is not yet fully told. But what we know is already enough to strip away every pretence to tolerance and no violence from the face of India and to reveal instead, a brutalized and brutalising society".[48]

Dr. B.R. Ambedkar in an eloquent assertion of identity and claim to autonomy argued, "The right of representation and the right to hold office under the state are the two most important rights that make up citizenship. But the untouchability of the untouchables puts these rights far beyond their reach. In a few places they do not even posses such insignificant rights as personal liberty and personal security. These are the interests of the untouchables. And as can be easily seen, they can be represented by the untouchables alone."[49]

One can draw lessons from Gunnar Myrdal who identifies the central 'American Dilemma' as, 'the sharp contradiction between the egalitarian ideals upheld by many Americans and the deep-seated racism of their society'. This is the central focus of reservation policy today. There are many well-meaning persons from dominant castes, social scientists and social thinkers who would raise the issue that they do not practice discrimination both in word and deed and the weaker sections should respect and respond to this. But the discourse of reservation or affirmative action is not hinged on individual merit of non-discrimination but collective mindset of discrimination.

Future Course of Action

From the perspective of the more discriminated and disadvantaged segment of the population among the Scheduled Castes and the Scheduled Tribes, one need to unravel and explore the multifaceted aspects of affirmative action. Would the reservation policy as presented in the Constitution provide space and scope for access to knowledge, employment, political participation and resources to the weaker sections? Would it also open up avenues for an egalitarian and integrated society?

Affirmative action in favour of women has not surfaced as a major political issue in India. This is due to the fact that women from the 30 per cent upper echelon are not deprived or discriminated against. Now when women from the weaker sections are coming to the fore, they are demanding preferential treatment. This once again is a *divide-at-empera* policy of the ruling elite.

Goldman's views "Affirmative action programme seeks to rectify the consequences of social discrimination. It involves, among other things, discrimination in favour of communities that have been victimized by society and in law. Although policies involving reservations and quotas for members of disadvantaged communities has been the most widely used, and also the most hotly contested, policy within the affirmative action programme, it is by no means the only way of remedying the socially victimized communities. Under the affirmative action programme, governments have sought to supplement positive discrimination in jobs with special economic packages, social facilities and preferential spending".[50] Reservation pegged the quantum at 15 per cent for the Scheduled Castes and 7.5 per cent for the Scheduled Tribes. But having seen the tardy manner in which these policies are implemented, one should raise the supplementary question, would it be appropriate to hold on to this principle eternally or more avenues need to be opened for the weaker sections.

The preferential treatment package as set down in the Constitution goes against the principle of formal equality, which demands absence of discrimination on any grounds. Formal equality in a sense is akin to status-quo adherence. The compensatory action or preferential treatment is aimed at leveling the inequality that is historical in nature. It is at this juncture that there is a demand for strong political will to enact what constitutionally provided for the upliftment and wellbeing of the weaker sections.

The political economy of the country and society would not allow any easy entry to the downtrodden in the service sector and even if they have managed to enter this sphere, they would not be allowed to remain there. Hence, it is essential to workout short-term and long-term measures to increase representation of Scheduled Castes and Scheduled Tribes. If this measure has to be successful, then the State has to enact measures for special training and coaching for candidates from the weaker sections.[51] The long standing demand for constituting SC/ST Development Liaison Cells be met so that this apex body could coordinate between various departments and monitor the recruitment and proper treatment of members from the Scheduled Castes and Scheduled Tribes.

Let us conclude this chapter with the historical words of Dr. Ambedkar who fought for enacting affirmative action for the weaker sections. Dr. Ambedkar had argued for universal suffrage for the depressed classes. He told the Round Table Conference, "I am not going to place myself under the thumb and authority of any majority government unless I am certain that I can exercise in the elections electoral power which was commensurate with my social power. Unless I know that every man and every women in the Depressed Class community will be able to exercise the vote and to determine the destiny of the candidate who is going to represent the mass of the people in the country, I am certainly not going to consent to a joint electorate".[52]

"We must make our political democracy a social democracy as well. Political democracy cannot last unless there lies at the base of it social democracy. What does social democracy mean? It means a way of life, which recognizes liberty, equality and fraternity as the principles of life... On the 26th of January 1950, we are going to enter into a life of contradictions. In politics we will have equality and in social and economic life we will have inequality...We must remove this contradiction at the earliest moment, or else those who suffer from inequality will blow up the structure of political democracy which this Assembly has so laboriously built up".[53]

Affirmative action package enacted in its letter and spirit would lead to emancipation of the weaker sections and would ensure their right to be human. But the dominant castes and the ruling class would like to perceive reservation policies only as an electoral tool for continuing in power and thus maintaining the status quo. A long drawn out struggle is important to make affirmative action work in favour of ensuring the rights of the weaker sections to be citizens and human beings. From the point of view of the weaker sections in India, the risk has to be run by maintaining the pressure on the ruling establishment to continue with affirmative action as envisaged by the Constitution as well as mobilize and organize the various segments of the weaker sections to fight for the right to be human.

References

1. Weaker Sections is the term used to refer to the Scheduled Castes and Scheduled Tribes. These two communities are called by different names. Scheduled Caste and Scheduled Tribe are administrative terms, while Dalits and *adivasis* are evolved at the course of identity formation.
2. While a section of Dalit and many non-Dalits acknowledge the contribution of Ambedkar in framing the Constitution of India, there is also another stream of debate which argues that Ambedkar was used as a prop to keep claiming that the caste Hindus are magnanimous and to point out that the dominant castes had "appointed" a Dalit to frame the Constitution of the country.
3. For more details see, 'The Protection of Civil Rights Act, 1955, formerly known as Untouchability (Offences) Act, 1955. Interestingly, the Act begins with bold statement, "An Act to prescribe punishment for the [preaching and practice of "Untouchability"] for the enforcement of any disability arising therefrom and for matters connected therewith.

4. The Scheduled Castes and the Scheduled Tribes (Prevention of Atrocities) Act, 1989, with Rules, 1995. Law Publishers, 1996, p. 1.
5. *Ibid.*
6. *Ibid.*
7. The Constitution of India [as on the 1st June, 1996]. Law and Justice Ministry. Government of India, 1996, p. 105.
8. "Tension Back in Junagarh Village", *Asian Age*, 26.12.1999.
9. Incidences of this type are not anything new to Gujarat. Neither are they confined to rural or agrarian scenario. On 20th January, 2000, the *Indian Express* reported that the attempt by the Gujarat Government to take a survey of Scheduled Castes and Scheduled Tribes officials sparked a row. Among other things, Class I and II and higher grade SC and ST officials in the government are being asked in the survey if they have been converted to Christianity, neo-Buddhims or Islam. For more details on the atrocities committed on the Dalits, refer to Prakash Louis, "Dalit Human Rights are for Violation", In *State of Human Rights*, New Delhi: Indian Social Institute, 2001.
10. For more discussion on this refer to Reservation, Seminar 268 December 1981; Reservation, Seminar 375 – November 1990; list of articles published in Economic and Political Weekly beginning from 1981; V.A. Pai Panandiker. The Politics of Backwardness: Reservation Policy in India. Konark Publishers, Delhi, 1997; and A.K. Lal (ed). Protective Discrimination: Ideology and Praxis. G.B. Pant Social Science Institute, Allahabad, 2002
11. Reservation for Backward Classes: Mandal Commission Report of the Backward Class Commission. Delhi: Alankar Publications, 1990.
12. For personal testimony about the benefit of reservation refer to Kancha Ilaiah. Reservation: Experience as Framework of Debate, Economic and Political Weekly, Vol. XXV, Issue 41, 1990, p. 2307.
13. Under the Reservation Scheme both the Scheduled Castes and Scheduled Tribes are counted. But here we deal only with scheduled castes since the is about Dalit assertion.
14. All the details about the above-presented schemes are taken from Annual Report 1992-93, 1994-95 and 1996-97 Ministry of Welfare, Government of India.
15. Annual Report 1997-98, Ministry of Social Justice and Empowerment, Government of India, p. 22.

16. According to the 1991 census, there were 32 districts out of 42 districts in Bihar, where the female literacy rate was less than 10 per cent.
17. Annual Report, 1996-97. Ministry of Welfare. Government of India, p. 21.
18. The Protection of Civil Rights Act, 1955, Social Justice Ministry, Government of India.
19. The Scheduled Castes and Scheduled Tribes (Prevention of Atrocities) Act 1989. Law Publishers, India, p. 1.
20. The Ministry of Law and Justice. Government of India, June 8, 1990.
21. B.R. Ambedkar. What Congress and Gandhi have done to the Untouchables? Thacker & Co. Bombay, 1946, p. 88.
22. Brochure on Reservation for Scheduled Castes and Scheduled Tribes in Services, Ministry of Personnel, Public Grievances and Pensions, Government of India, New Delhi, 1993.
23. Annual Report 1997-98, Ministry of Social Justice and Empowerment, Government of India, p. 11.
24. Geeta B. Nambissan and Mona Sedwal. Education for All: The Situation of Dalit Children in India, in R. Govinda. India Education Report: A Profile of Basic Education. National Institute of Educational Planning and Administration, Oxford University Press, 2002, p. 76.
25. This famous quotation forms part of the memorandum submitted by Dr. Ambedkar and R. Srinivasan to Sub-Committee under the title "A Scheme of Political Safeguards for the Protection of the Depressed Classes in the Future Constitution of a Self-Governing India. Refer to Dr. Babasaheb Ambedkar: Writings and Speeches. Vol. 2. Education Department, Government of Maharashtra, 1987, p. 546. Part III of Volume 2 deals with Dr. Ambedkar at the Round Table Conference which contains his deep sense of anguish about the plight of the depressed classes.
26. Tenth Five Year Plan (2002-2007): Approach Paper, Planning Commission, Government of India.
27. *Sankat mein Hain Bijli chetra – Vajpayee*, Jansatta, 30.6.2001, 1.
28. 'High technology' has become the 'pass word' for modern development. Most of the government documents have reference to high technology in someway or the other. Even, the recent "National Curriculum Framework for School Education" argues that 'The process of education can no longer ignore the social and psychological impacts of the technology that structures information and the possibilities that global information sharing opens up'. By

the National Council of Education Research and Training, New Delhi, November 2000, p. 113. But this document has no plan for the 60 per cent or more of the Dalits who are illiterate.

29. *Sanvidhan ki naiye viyakiya zaruri*, Jansatta, 14.4.2000, 6.
30. Draft of New Constitution of Bharat. Rashtriya Swayamsevak Sangh. This is supposed to be a 'confidential document' circulated among the members of the Sangh parivar for discussion and approval.
31. It needs to be stated here that it is not only the anti-caste movements in general or the Dalit movements in particular which raised the banner of revolt in the 5 decades in India, but movements like the Tribal movement, Jharkhand movement, women's movement, ecological movement to name a few which challenged the hegemony of the dominant castes and classes.
32. Consultation Paper on the Pace of Socio-Economic Change Under the Constitution, National Commission to review the working of the Constitution.
33. *Ibid.*, p. 15.
34. Caste Based Prostitution in Madhya Pradesh. MPHRC, August 15th 2000. Banchharas, Bedias and Sansias are the three communities who are termed by the MPHRC.
35. In the Ministry of Home Affairs Circular dated 10th February, 1982 addressed to all the State Governments and Union Territory Administrations it has been clarified that the certificate issuing authorities should not insert the word 'harijan' or 'girijan' in the Scheduled Caste/Scheduled Tribe Certificates. Later considering the opposition to and resentment against the use of the terms harijans and girijans, by the various Organisations/Associations working for the welfare for the welfare of the Scheduled Castes/Scheduled Tribes in official dealings and matters etc.. the Government of India, Ministry of Welfare by their O.M. dated 19th August, 1990 have directed that for all official transactions, matters, dealings, certificates etc. the Constitutional terms Scheduled Castes/Scheduled Tribes in English and their appropriate translation in other national languages should alone be used for denoting the persons belonging to Scheduled Caste and Scheduled Tribes included in the Presidential Orders. Quoted in Rajendra Prasad. The Law of Social Status. Hind Law House: Pune, 1998, p. 26.
36. Prakash Louis. Casteism is more Horrendous than Racism: Durban and Dalit Discourse. Indian Social Institute: New Delhi, 2001.This was the book I had written before the Durban Conference trying to

highlight the various issues that were forming part of the discourse then.

37. Shiv Vishwanathan. Durban and Dalit Discourse. Economic and Political Weekly, August 18, 2001, p. 3125.
38. Ibid. Shiv Vishwanathan has not given this title, but I have given this title to indicate the political discourse that is going on within the arena of caste system.
39. S.L. Gaikward. Protective Discrimination Policy and Social Change. Rawat Publications: Jaipur. 1999, p. 113.
40. Richard Pais. Scheduled Castes, Employment and Social Mobility. (In) S.M. Michael (ed). Dalits in Modern India: Vision and Values. Vistaar Publications: New Delhi, 1999, p. 327.
41. Marc Galanter. *Ibid.*, p. 77.
42. Dr. B.R. Ambedkar. Constituent Assembly Debate. Vol. VII, pp. 701-702, 1948-49.
43. Democracy and Unity, Speech, Constituent Assembly, New Delhi, April 3, 1948. Dorothy Norman (ed). Nehru: The First Sixty Years. Asia Publishing House, 1965, p. 401.
44. Quoted in Devanesan Nesiah. Discrimination with Reason? The Policy of Reservations in the United States, India and Malaysia. Oxford University Press: Delhi, 1997, p. 5.
45. Sachchidananda. Welcome Policy. Seminar 375, November 1990, p. 18.
46. Times of India, 5th September 1990.
47. Devanesan Nesiah, *Ibid.*, p. 277.
48. Upendra Baxi. Violence, Dissent and Development (in) Indian Law Institute, Law and Social Change—Indo-American Reflections. N.M.Tripathi: Bombay, 1988, p. 83.
49. Quoted in Gail Omvedt. Dalits and Democratic Revolution: Dr. Ambedkar and the Dalit Movement in Colonial India. Sage Publication: New Delhi. 1994, p. 146.
50. Quoted in Gurpreet Mahajan. Identities and Rights: Aspects of Liberal Democracy in India. Oxford University Press: Delhi. 1998, p. 143.
51. For more in the line of recommendations refer to National Commission for Scheduled Castes and Scheduled Tribes, Fifth Report, 1998-99, Volume-I.
52. Dr. Babasaheb Ambedkar. Writings and Speeches. Vol. II. Education Department, Government of Maharashtra, 1987, p. 563.
53. Speech by B.R. Ambedkar on 25th November 1949, in Constituent Assembly Debates, New Delhi, Lok Sabha Secretariat, 1989, Vol. IX, p. 979.

3

Dalit Identity and Dalit Assertion

Discrimination, deprivation, exclusion and exploitation are endemic to every society, which leads to frustration, anger, and aggression. Those who are subjected to injustice and oppression tend to rebel and revolt. These reactions culminate in assertions which give rise to people's movements. But social movements are not an everyday phenomenon. Discrimination and deprivation always do not lead to protest and aggression. Only when people become conscious of these inequalities and injustices and mobilize and organize themselves to struggle against those who subject them to servitude and bondage, people's movement takes place. Moreover, when the disadvantaged and the downtrodden see that another alternative is both possible and viable they try to overthrow the existing social order.[1]

Politicization of the subalterns or the underdog is an important ingredient of people's movement, with ideologies providing the rational underpinning. Politicization legitimizes the inchoate understanding of the oppressed that the society they live in is unequal, oppressive and hierarchical, and further that the skewed social order needs to be transformed. But transformation does not take place at random. When the cumulative effects of discrimination and deprivation leads to frustration that the deprived section raises its head. According to T.R. Gurr, 'deprivation leads people to frustration and the greater the frustration, the greater the quantity of aggression against the source of frustration'.[2]

It is also an established fact that deprivation is only one of the factors that lead to organized resistance and revolt. Other factors like leadership, organizational base, ideological formation, alternative to the present system etc., are equally necessary for the emergence of people's movements. M.S.A. Rao, based on his study of Izhava community in Kerala asserts that the Izhava community suffered from conditions of actual relative deprivation within the existing caste system, but dissent became irresistible only when the leaders of the community were awakened to alternative sources of identity.[3]

In the same vein, Y.B. Damle argues, 'the social sharing of deprivation and disprivilege can be said to be the starting point of protest. On the other hand, dissent becomes meaningful only when it has the backing of a group, i.e., social change can only be brought about through concerted action which is backed by both an ideology and an appropriate organisation'.[4] Thus collective action becomes the central and crucial aspect of people's movements. But collective action does not emerge out of the blue. Only when there are favourable conditions, peoples action takes place.

Various terms used to describe collective action carry different inflections. They include attitudinal terms such as dissent, opposition, resistance, protest, defiance; terms emphasizing methods of action such as riot, violence, *jacquerie*, rebellion, mutiny, revolution, petition, demonstration, consciousness raising; general terms with normative or political overtones such as class struggle, liberation, emancipation, participation, empowerment; and social science terminology such as collective behaviour, collective action, social movement.[5]

Collective action leading to people's movements results in social change. As stated above, social change also refers to beliefs and perceptions of what is wrong with the existing society, the culture, the institutions, the economic order, the power equations etc. Above all, social change also underscores the fact that what needs to be done to change the present order. But there are also cases where social movements are initiated to oppose what is identified for change by external forces. Thus, the sense of discrimination and deprivation as well as the power and potent of assertion lead to social movement.

The vast literature on social movements or people's movements reiterates the fact that movements are ultimately calculated to being about social change. P.N. Mukherji is of the view that 'the relationship between social movement and social change (or resistance to change) is incontrovertible'. He presents four basic premises to prove his hypothesis: 1) Social movements are essentially related to social change and, therefore, to the social structure, but they are not a necessary condition for social change. They may be change promoting and, equally, change resisting. 2) Sociai movements, being products of a social structure, emerge out of certain conditions in the social structure. 3) Social movements have a recognizable structure in terms of which they are rendered functional relative to their goals. 4) Social movements have consequences for the social structure of which they are the products.[6]

People's movements or social movements, thus, are collective social actions aimed at either demanding change or resisting change in any or total realms of social order. They emerge out of the existing social structure. Also, they propose and pursue particular objectives, which lead to mobilization and organization of those who are victims of the present order to change it. Movements also mobilize and organize those who resist change and want to maintain status quo. Further, people's movements seldom emerge spontaneously nor do they spring from vacuum. They require long periods of preparation both at the individual, collective and societal level.

Dalit Identity

Identity formation is a historical process. Further, identity formation[7] is based on the experience about oneself, experience in relation to others who are different from oneself. This experience about oneself and about the 'other' does not take place in vacuum but in the existing socio-economic, political, cultural milieu. In this regard, it can be stated that identity formation is an interactional process.

Dr. Fernando Franco based on an empirical study argues that to deal with the issue of a group's identity is to be engaged in the analysis of a group's process of becoming. There are two components that are interrelated in this process of identity formation. The first one is the ideological-symbolic component. This refers to the system of beliefs and practices that flow from the understanding of the position of oneself and one's own group vis-à-vis others.

This set of beliefs and its various cultural expressions provide the group with a shared meaning and understanding about who they are and what their role is in a given social context. The second is the material-productive component and it refers to material, ecological and economic conditions shaping and determining the primary livelihood activities of the group and productive relations among there from. In other words, it includes factors that determine the economic life of the group and consequently the relationships they enter into with each other and with other groups in the course of earning their livelihood.[8]

The emerging Dalit identity, especially after independence is multi-faceted, multi-layered and multi-pronged. Significantly, the term 'Dalit' itself is indicative of the revolutionary progression made within the Dalit community vis-à-vis the non-Dalits. To begin with, one can identify the potency and the power of the concept 'Dalit' which, when taken into account denotes the assertion of the erstwhile 'untouchables', that they are the outcastes, achuts, that is, untouchables, excluded segment of the Indian population. In extension it is also affirming and asserting the fact that 'we are broken people' and 'we are people crushed by oppression and exploitation'. While this sense of affirmation is only the starting point, the sense of negation is the culminating factor. This can be framed as a collective monologue of resistance: "Yes, we were the broken people, we were crushed, but now we will not allow ourselves to be broken or crushed by your. And we will not allow you –the dominant castes- to break us or crush us any more".

The emerging Dalit identity has been compelling the social scientists for an in-depth analysis of various issues that go to constitute Dalit identity. But the mainline social scientists had concentrated their efforts to examine caste as a social reality, kinship and village as sociological category to comprehend the Indian social reality. In course of time caste discrimination, Dalit assertion and Dalit identity formation was not brought under the purview of sociological exploration. Yet, Dalit discourse was kept alive by individuals and groups within the Dalit community and those who extended solidarity to it. Further, Dalit identity formation was a reality even before the term Dalit was broadly came to be used.

The World Conference Against Racism held in Durban, South Africa in August-September 2001, clearly and categorically brought the issue of caste discrimination to centre stage. Dalit discourse is as old as caste system itself. But at different intervals, it was brought to focus of discussion. But it is in the run up to Durban conference, that the Dalit discourse has engaged everyone at the local to national to the international level. In an unprecedented manner, the issue of caste atrocities and caste discrimination has drawn the attention of Dalit activists and intellectuals, voluntary action groups, human rights activists, and even the politicians. The emerging Dalit identity in this scenario would determine the direction of Dalit discourse in the future.

Revising the earlier positions upheld by the social scientists, some of the recent works have tried to highlight the salient features of the emerging Dalit identity.[9] However, the identity of the Dalits was formed in relation to the dominant castes. But that does not mean all inquiries stop there. The dominant castes were and continue to be the feudal landlords, headmen of the village panchayats, moneylender and the 'representative of the state apparatus'. The Dalits on the other hand were and still are the landless agricultural labourers, illiterate, bonded labourers, outcastes and the 'beneficiaries' or at the receiving end of the welfare schemes of the state. In this heinously unequal and undemocratic socio-political milieu where the dominant castes constantly and continuously enforced subjugation, domination and dehumanization, the Dalits developed a sense of being second grade citizens.

Though, the Dalits were victimised by the process of bondage and servitude, they continued to protest and resist every form of oppression. Especially, with the enactment of constitutional rights and privileges, the Dalits began to demand equality of rights for all. This has further enhanced the political consciousness of the Dalits. The social ostracism, economic deprivation, political marginalisation and cultural subjugation the Dalits suffered has augmented and expanded the resolve of the Dalits to counter all forms of discrimination. It is this eruption of Dalit determination, which has shaken the 'untouchable and unalterable' caste edifice. It is not argued here that the Dalits have attained total liberation or that they are very near to achieving emancipation. But it is an undeniable truth that the Dalits have made great strides in terms of forging a long drawn-out struggle against caste system and caste discrimination.

The discourse analysis that ensued about caste system, discrimination of the Dalits, etc., opened up an array of options for the social scientists to interpret the emerging Dalit identity. But for the Dalits, it has become clear like the day light that compared to the past, the Dalits as individuals and as a collectivity have become politically conscious and their social awareness is on the ascent. One can also discern a confident behaviour pattern among the Dalits. But this assertion had to encounter the repressive measures of the dominant castes as well as the state, which often functions as the agent of the dominant castes. The findings of many research studies about the response of the Dalits to repression also have pointed to the two interconnected realities. In some cases, the Dalits and their organisations submitted to the repressive operations of the dominant castes and the state. In many other cases, the attempt to stifle the organisational and mobilisational efforts of the Dalits was countered by much broader and long drawn-out struggles.

Upholding the dignity of their women is one arena where the Dalits have shown formidable determination and power. Compared to Dalit men the Dalit women suffer from triple discrimination that is caste, class and gender. Hence, initiating change in their social condition was a concurrent aspect of Dalit assertion and Dalit movements. But this is once again a partial script of the emerging Dalit identity. Over the years, the Dalit women themselves have constructed an identity about their lives and struggles. This identity deals about their multiple roles and problems faced as an individual, in the family, at work places, in the religious sphere and in the Dalit and wider society.

The predominant image of the Dalit women that emerges from many narratives about themselves is that they are strong persons, capable of handling diligently many deprivations and sufferings, and still are able to rise above these discrimination and deprivation and keep themselves, their families and their communities together.[10] There is every indication that the Dalit women are taking many strides to liberate themselves from innumerable clutches. But the central and crucial aspect of this liberation is that the Dalit women are envisioning their emancipation and liberation within the context of discrimination and deprivation they are subjected to as well as the opportunities and possibilities that are unfolding in front of them.

The question of Dalit women's issues to be represented by non-Dalit women has also been debated repeatedly. This debate did not limit itself to women's movements but also rendered it essential to be discussed in the wider people's movements. Gopal Guru is of the view that 'in order to understand the Dalit women's needs to talk differently it is necessary to delineate both the internal and external factors that have bearing on this phenomenon'. He further argues that the issue of representing Dalit women, both at the level of theory and politics, has erupted time and again in the discourse on Dalit women. Dalit women justify the case for talking differently on the basis of external factors, that is, non-Dalit forces homogenizing the issue of Dalit women and internal factors, that is, the patriarchal domination among the Dalits. In this context the formation of the National Federation of Dalit Women (NFDW) on August 11, 1995 in New Delhi can be viewed as one of the pioneering, independent and autonomous assertion of Dalit women's identity formation.[11]

It is also significant to note that at the local, regional and national levels, the economic condition of the Dalits has not improved. On the contrary, almost all of them do not have access or ownership over resources. This enforces upon them the necessity to depend upon the dominant castes, who in turn exploit them. It is important to note that it is this economic dependence, which inhibits every resolve of the Dalits to fight against the dominant castes. The anomaly of the Indian planning and development is such that this basic and central social fact is not taken into account when welfare measures are worked out for the Dalits.

At this juncture it is expedient to underscore the social fact that a perceptive comprehension of the consequences of untouchability and atrocities has become part of the Dalit discourse.

This is due to socio-political mobilization of the Dalits. But it would be foolhardy to assert that this awareness and assertion has been evenly spread throughout the Dalit community or that every Dalit perceives his or her oppression and has empowered oneself to resist these onslaughts. But what is argued here is that this is the general trend among the Dalits as a social category and if this trend continues, it will not too far before the Dalits engage in an extended struggle for total restructuring of the Indian social order.

Finally, it needs to be stated here that the identity formation among the Dalits followed various alternative processes in different states and within a state. This is due to the nature of the social milieu, the counteracting forces, the level of mobilisation and organisation, the social mobility that has been possible in the given historical context and finally the strategy followed. In the given productive relations, the ideological and material-productive components have contributed in the emergence of Dalit identity. Only in the course of time, it will be revealed as to which direction the present identity formation will take in the future. But it is a fact that anti-caste movements and Dalit struggles have come to stay. It is they who will alter the very structure of Indian society.

Dalit Assertion

Dalit assertion, Dalit liberation and Dalit emancipation are other themes that have come to centre stage of the current sociological discourse. With the emergence of Dalit assertion the social scientists are forced to take note of caste discrimination as an engaging exercise. In common parlance, to assert is to declare positively, to lay claim to, to insist upon and to affirm. In the same vein assertion is defined as 'the act of claiming one's rights' or 'a positive statement about oneself or one's intent'.[12] Thus, assertion could be defined as a positive declaration about oneself, one's past, one's present and one's future. This assertion while spelling out ones resolve to determine ones course of action, also informs the others of this resolve.

Due to the iron grip of caste system, the religious sanction to the caste system, and the added dimensions of feudal economic order, the Dalits would not raise their head even if they were reduced to sub-human existence. With regard to Dalit women, caste system, feudalism and the evil effects of patriarchy forced them to extended and eternal silence. But in favourable conditions, Dalit individuals and groups raised their voice and stated that exclusion, marginalisation and deprivation that they are subjected to will not be tolerated anymore. Moreover, they demand their rightful place and role in the society and polity as envisioned for them in the Constitution. Thus, this act of claiming their right to be human like any other human beings of Indian society has shaped up a major component in Dalit assertion. Further, asserting their rights to be human in the society and citizenship in the country has become an essential part of individual and collective enterprise. Especially for a group of people on whom a negative identity was imposed, self-determination and self-definition become the central and crucial factor of identity formation.

The foregoing sections demonstrate the social and historical fact that the Dalits were at the receiving end for centuries. But at regular intervals they raised their heads to speak against the system that disrobed them of everything. In course of history of their struggle, the Dalits raised dominant issues;*jan suvidhayen* – public amenities, *bhagidari* – use of public utilities, *mazduri* – wages and finally *zamin* – land, *izzat*,-dignity; *rajsatta* -power;. These issues have taken the centre stage of their search for identity. These issues have given them the strength and the power to assert their rights.

Historical documents bear testimony to the fact that the earlier reform movements had focused on improving the lot of the Dalit community. But the recent resistance and revolts have highlighted the centrality of these basic issues. In this regard it is expedient to take note of the anger and the assertion that is becoming a fact of Dalit society today. Any attempt to overlook or misunderstand this reality will lead to destructive consequences. A clear case of this Dalit anger and assertion was witnessed in Mumbai on July 11th, 1997.[13] The vandalization of the statue of Dr. Bhimrao Ambedkar in Ramabai Ambedkar Nagar in Mumbai sparked off violent protests and revolts by the Dalits. This led to police firing in which about 11 people were killed.

It is of seminal importance to note that this is not the first instance of desecration of a Ambedkar statue in Maharashtra. It is stated that in the last 5 years about 508 such incidents have been reported.[14] But the social fact that needs to be paid attention is that this incident like previous incidents had led to revolt, but this time the nature of the agitation was severe and violent than the earlier ones. The protest was also widespread. This incident immediately caught fire not only in Maharashtra but it also in Gujarat where the Bharatiya Dalit Panthers gave a call for a *bandh* in Gujarat.

The multiple injuries committed on the Dalits by the perpetrators of this incident needs to be paid attention to. On the one hand, the statue of Dr. Bhimrao Ambedkar the very symbol of Dalit identity and struggle was desecrated. On the other hand, when the Dalits protested against the vandalism, the administration took to repression culminating in the massacre of 11 people. By this repression the police has not only absolved the crimes of the culprits but it has given them a free hand to commit similar crimes in the future. By this the political establishment gave a warning to the Dalit community that they will be dealt with severely if they plan to protest against any atrocities committed on them. The Dalits on their part are not lying low but are resisting and revolting against every form of atrocities. Moreover, over the years many unorganized and organized protests and revolts have given a specific identity to the Dalits and have established their anger and assertion in the Indian scene. All the individual and collective efforts have contributed in the formation of a liberative Dalit identity which in turn has given definite direction to Dalit assertion.

The Trajectory of the term Dalit

The nomenclatures that the Dalits were bestowed with by the non-Dalits or took upon by the Dalits indicate the path that this excluded and subjugated community in India traversed so far. It is but natural to raise the question 'what is in a name?' The term 'Dalit', like the assertion that the Dalits have engaged in has become a crisis generating term. It is crisis bound for the non-Dalits, because this term is chosen by the Dalits themselves. This term like many other terms was not bestowed upon the Dalits by the non-Dalits.

Interestingly, this term is also creating crisis among the Dalits, because of the various interpretation that is given to the term. The term Dalit is subject to both inclusive and exclusive definition. Those who prefer inclusive definition include under the term Dalit any exploited social groups like the untouchables, the Tribals, the other backward castes and even. Some would go to the extent of including even the Muslims. For instance, the formation of BAMCEF, that is, Backward Scheduled Caste Scheduled Tribes and Minority Community Employees Federation itself is an indication of this inclusive definition. The others who limit to exclusive definition refer to only the untouchables when they speak about the Dalits.

In his perceptive and analytical presentation, Gopal Guru traces the evolution of the term Dalit. 'In the political arena, categories have a trajectory of their own. They travel along a path full of challenges, counter-challenges, contradictions and transformations. That is why these categories and their labels change their meaning, connotation and significance from time to time and place to place, depending upon the specific socio-economic and ideological context and the politics of the users who formulate them. It is this rootedness of categories in their specific contexts and therefore in the people's consciousness that decides their nature. Since this consciousness involves progress and regression, the categories cannot be thought to be concrete, permanent or infinite, exclusive or inclusive. Yet, in the domain of politics, these categories do not acquire an arbitrary character; they are not aimless or passive representation of the world out there but are conscious constructions with either a positive or negative agenda as chalked out by their users'.[15] Let us briefly examine the trajectory of categories associated with the Dalits.

1. *Achut*—Untouchable

A*chut* is the Hindi word for outcastes' or 'untouchables'. It is probable that *achut*, meaning, untouchable or outcaste might have been one of the first terms used to address the Dalits. It is generally taken for granted that the untouchables are polluted people and they are placed lowest in the Indian caste order. In terms of occupation they are supposed to remove human waste, skinning animal carcasses, tanning leather and making shoes, washing clothes etc.[16] These are considered to be polluting or impure jobs which the untouchables were supposed to do. In terms of geographical location they are supposed to reside outside the village. It is not only that they are restricted in terms of space but the type of houses is also supposed to be inferior in quality and devoid of any facilities.

According to Gandhi, 'untouchability means pollution by the touch of certain persons by reason of their birth in a particular family'.[17] Dr. Ambedkar is one of those persons who understood the debilitating effect of untouchability, and stated that 'Untouchability is the notion of defilement, pollution, contamination and the ways and means of getting rid of that defilement. It is a case of permanent, hereditary stain which nothing can cleanse.'[18]

In the Report of the Committee Headed by Elayaperumal on Untouchability, Economic and Educational Development of the Scheduled Castes and Connected Documents, 1969 description of untouchability is given as follows: 'Untouchability is a basic and unique feature of the Hindu social system and order. It is generally held these days that it emerges from the economic backwardness of the people concerned. But the simple fact is forgotten that while economic issues are present in all other countries, untouchability is a unique problem confronted in this country only. It does not require much research to realize that the phenomenon of untouchability in this country is fundamentally a religious and political origin. Untouchability is not a separate institution in itself, it is a corollary of the institutions of the caste system of Hindu society. It is an attitude on the part of whole group of people. It is a spirit of social aggression that underlines this attitude'.[19]

Marc Galanter in his analysis on the constitutional meaning of untouchability states that the Constitution does not define 'untouchability' nor is it clear what constitutes its practice in any form or a disability arising out of untouchability. The English term 'untouchability' is of relatively recent coinage; its first appearance in print was in 1909 and as it gained wide currency it did not gain clarity. 'In its broadest sense 'untouchability' might include all instances in which one person treated another as ritually unclean and a source of pollution. A second somewhat narrower sense of the term would include all instances in which a person was stigmatized as unclean or polluting or inferior because of his origin or membership in a particular group i.e., where he is subjected to invidious treatment because of difference in religion and membership in a lower or different caste. Thus, we arrive at the third and still narrower sense of the term untouchability as referring only to those practices concerned with the relegation of certain groups beyond the pale of the caste system that is confining it to those disabilities imposed on groups commonly regarded as untouchables. Untouchability then, as used in Article 17 of the Constitution is confined to invidious discrimination against certain not readily definable classes of persons'.[20]

Even as early as 1895 there were regulations to reduce caste discrimination. The Caste Disabilities Removal Act of 1850 facilitated mobility across the region and caste in Gujarat. But in 1856 there was an instance, a boy was denied admission in a school because of his lower caste origin. In 1923, the government issued a resolution that no grants would be paid to any aided educational institutions, which refused admission to the children of Depressed Classes.

In the same year, the Bombay Legislative Council adopted the following resolution moved by S.K. Bole on August 4th 1923, "The Council recommends that the untouchable classes be allowed to use all public water in places, wells and *dharmashalas* [a house for pilgrim, an inn, alms house] which are build and maintained out of public funds or administered by bodies appointed by government or created by statute, as well as public schools, courts, offices and dispensaries".[21] The Depressed Classes of Bombay were so much overwhelmed with feelings of gratitude that they held a congratulatory meeting in Bole's honour and awarded him a gold medal for his signal services to their cause.

Dr. Ambedkar and Gandhi understood the reality of untouchability in fundamentally contradictory manner and their response to this evil practice was also different. Refusing a message to the journal *Harijan* started with the help of devoted caste-Hindu followers doing ground-level work among the depressed classes, Ambedkar explained his point of view: 'The out-caste is a bye-product of the caste system. There will be outcastes as long as there are castes. And nothing can emancipate the outcaste except the destruction of the caste system'. Gandhi politely protested that while untouchability was the greatest blot on Hinduism, the excess should first be removed but if the efforts fails it will be time enough to consider how and by whom *varnashram* is to be fought.[22]

Since there was fundamental difference in the understanding of the reality of untouchability between Dr. Ambedkar and Gandhi, there was also difference in their engagement in doing away with untouchability. For example, Gandhi formed reformist organisations like *Harijan Sevak Sangh* to ameliorate the sufferings of the untouchables. Organizations of this nature were supposed to 'persuade caste Hindus to abolish untouchability'. Dr. Ambedkar on the other hand, formed political organisations like the Depressed Classes League, leading to Scheduled Caste Federation and finally the Republican Party of India.

2. Panchamas – Chandalas- Avarnas

Panchamas, Chandalas, Avarnas etc., are some of the terms that are interchangeably used for the untouchables. It is extremely difficult to ascertain the exact period in which these terms might have come into usage. But the meaning ascribed to each of these terms indicates the process of exclusion and segregation that the Dalits were subjected to.

Panchamas is a Sanskrit term suggesting that the untouchables are the 'fifth category' of the varna or caste order. Hence, the term came to mean the fifth caste or in Hindi known as *pancham varg*. *Chandala* is also a Sanskrit word translated as 'polluting' which in extension refers to untouchability.

Avarnas means 'those who do not belong to the *varna* or the caste order. This term was also defined as exterior castes. Here exterior signifies those groups or classes who were required to stay outside the village settlement. But in extension it also referred to the act of keeping the untouchables totally and fully away from all that is social, political, religious, cultural and economic.

With regard to the term *Panchamas* Gail Omvedt presents an important episode in the evolution of Dalit consciousness in

Andhra Pradesh in 1917. "At this time, the reformer Guduru Ramachandra Rao called a conference in Vijayawada which was labeled 'First Provincial *Panchama Mahajana Sabha'*. But on the evening of the first day, its president, a Dalit from Hyderabad named Bhagyareddy Varma, argued that the term '*Panchama*' was nowhere found in the *Puranas* or other Hindu scriptures and that 'the so called *Panchamas* were the original sons of the soil and they were the rulers of the country. The delegates then rejected this term and constituted themselves as the First *Adi-Andhra Mahajan Sabha*".[23]

Similarly, in 1920, the Indian Buddhists of Madras Presidency met at Madras and declared that the *Panchamas* are getting converted to Buddhism. They observed that these *Panchamas* are the descendants of the original inhabitants of India but now their position in Hinduism is very bad.[24] These episodes and explanations seem to state that the term *Panchama* may be a term given to the Dalits by the non-Dalits.

3. *Adi* or Original Settlers

The term *Adi*[25] refers to original and reflects the aspect of original settlers and in extension original owners. It also has in its latent sense if not in its manifest sense 'the sons of the soil'. In the case of the Dalits this term also refers to them being 'non-Aryans'. For example, the term 'Adi-Andhra' arose in the post-1917 period when Dalits all over the south, influenced by the 'non-Aryan' themes of the Dravidian movement, were identifying themselves as *Adi-Dravidians*, *Adi-Andhras* and *Adi-Kanadigas* etc.[26] This re-christening indicates the efforts of the Dalits to assert a social status from being colourless or casteless people to a collectivity which is the original settlers and owners but subordinated by the Aryan immigrants.

The argument presented by the Adi-Dravida Education League is indicative of the ideological formation that was taking place within some of the Dalit communities. 'Judged by the history, philosophy and civilization of the Adi-Dravidas, the real aborigines of the Deccan, the Depressed Classes are, as a community entirely separate and distinct from the followers of Vedic religion, called

Hinduism. It is contended that Hinduism is not the ancestral religion of the aborigines of Hindustan; that the non-Vedic communities of India object to being called 'Hindu' because of their inherited abhorrence of the doctrines of the Manusmruti and like scriptures.[27]

4. *Harijan*

Gandhi who is considered to be the champion for removing untouchability within the Hindu *Chaturvarna* framework, called the untouchables "*Harijans,*" man of God or in extension "Children of God'. The denominator was used in 1931 amid conflict between Gandhi and Ambedkar on the issue of political representation to Dalits on the basis of a separate community- distinct from Hindus. Gandhi borrowed the name from a Bhakti saint of the 17th century, Narsinh Mehta. It is reported that Narsinh Mehta violated caste customs and directives. He freely mixed with untouchables and taught them Bhakti. He was then excommunicated from his Nagar Brahmin caste. The story goes like, "the Lord came to the rescue of the *Bhakta,* and when the Nagars were sitting down to a caste dinner, they saw a *dhed* (untouchable) sitting next to everyone of them. This vision, however, vanished as soon as they rescinded the decree of excommunication which they had passed against the *bhakta*".[28]

Gandhi primarily appealed to caste Hindus to use the term *Harijan* instead of *Antyaja*. While giving currency to the word, he explained, "The 'untouchables' to me is, as compared to us (caste Hindus), really a *Harijan* – a man of God- and we are "*Durjana*' (men of evil). For while the untouchable has toiled and moiled and dirtied his hands so that we may live in comfort and cleanliness, we have delighted in suppressing him. We are solely responsible for all the shortcomings and faults that we may lay at the door of these untouchables. It is still open to us to be *Harijan* ourselves, but we can only do so by heartily repenting of our sin against them.

Gandhi hoped that "..probably, *Antyaja* brethren would lovingly accept that name and try to cultivate the virtues which it connotes... may the *Antyaja* become *Harijan* both in name and nature".[29] Gandhi went further, saying that it was his object to have all the Hindus become *harijans*. Only by removing untouchability could they deserve to be called God's children. And if Hinduism can purify itself of untouchability, he said, there will be only one caste, known by the beautiful name *Bhangi*, that is to say, the reformer or remover of all dirt'.[30]

Gandhi's ideas were also converted into some activities. He and his devotees who predominantly came from dominant castes formed All India Anti-Untouchability League in Bombay on September 30th, 1932. Pandit Madan Mohan Malaviya of the Hindu Mahasabha presided over the first meeting. This organization was re-christened as *Harijan Sevak Sangh*, that is, 'Servants of Untouchables Society'. The objectives of the Sangh was to use peaceful persuasion to secure access for the Depressed Classes to all the public wells, roads, schools, temples, and cremation grounds. Social reform activities like inter-dining and inter-marriage were admitted outside the scope of activities of this organization.[31]

Opposition to the term *Harijan*

Right from the time, Gandhi tried to popularize the term, there has been opposition to this term. The All India Depressed Classes Conference held in Lucknow from 22nd to 24th of May 1936 came out with 11 resolutions. The 8th resolution stated "This conference expresses its sense of strong abhorrence and insult at the term '*Harijan*' as it is applied to the Depressed Classes, and asks those who have no desire to insult the Depressed Classes not to use the term '*Harijan*' in reference to them. This conference further expresses its dissatisfaction with the *Harijan* Movement launched by Mahatma Gandhi.[32]

An agitation was initiated by the leaders to oppose the Bill using the word *Harijan* in the Bombay Legislative Assembly. Subsequently in 1938, the word *Harijan* was replaced by the word Scheduled Caste.[33] Thus from early 1930 onwards, the nomenclature *Harijan* has been rejected by the Dalits. But the government of India woke up to this reality only in 1982.

"In the Ministry of Home Affairs Circular dated 10th February, 1982 addressed to all the State Governments and Union Territory Administrations it has been clarified that the certificate issuing authorities should not insert the word 'harijan' or 'girijan' in the

Scheduled Caste/Scheduled Tribe Certificates. Later considering the opposition to and resentment against the use of the terms harijans and girijans, by the various Organisations/Associations working for the welfare of the Scheduled Castes/Scheduled Tribes in official dealings and matters etc. The Government of India, Ministry of Welfare by their O.M. dated 19th August, 1990 have directed that for all official transactions, matters, dealings, certificates etc. the Constitutional terms Scheduled Castes/Scheduled Tribes in English and their appropriate translation in other national languages should alone be used for denoting the persons belonging to Scheduled Caste and Scheduled Tribes included in the Presidential Orders".[34]

While contrasting the two categories, Gopal Guru states, 'the category of harijan cannot be encapsulated within the dalit category since it is entirely 'metaphysical'. It imputes an element of 'resigned fate' to the subject and therefore can render it inactive. Second, the term *harijan* is an ascribed one since it does not flow from the untouchables own experiences. It was artificially imposed on the untouchables by Gandhi and those upper caste people who could not genuinely integrate them within their social consciousness despite its divine association. Overall, the category of *harijan* lacks a discursive capacity'[35].

5. Depressed Classes

The term Depressed Classes was first used by social reformers and then used by government administration. The Depressed Classes included (a) Untouchables, (b) Aboriginal and Hill Tribes and (c) Criminal Tribes. Official figures of 1931 Census shows that these untouchable castes were shown as depressed classes in the record of British India. In 1928 the Depressed Classes Association was formed which functioned upto 1942.

In his note to the Indian Franchise Committee (Lothian Committee) on the Depressed Classes submitted on 1st May 1932, Dr. Ambedkar argued, "There is considerable objection on the part of the communities which are now called 'depressed classes' to the use of the term in describing them... Besides the term 'depressed classes' has led to a great deal of confusion in the census because it includes others who are not strictly untouchables. Secondly, it gives the impression that the depressed classes are a low and helpless community when as a matter of fact in every Province numbers of them are both well to do and well educated, and the whole community is acquiring consciousness of its needs, is charged with ambition for securing a respectable status in Indian society and is making stupendous efforts to achieve it. On all these grounds the term 'depressed classes' is inappropriate and unsuitable".[36] Dr. Ambedkar and the Committee that took up this matter with Lothian Committee instead preferred the term, 'Exterior Castes' or 'Excluded Castes' since there are more expressive and not offensive.

The leaders of Depressed Classes pleaded before the Montagu-Chelmsford Committee that the British must remain in power and continue to provide protection to the Depressed Classes and others instead of leaving them at the mercy of upper castes. Consequently in 1917, the Congress for the first time expressed its concern over the issue of untouchability. The Congress urged the people to understand the 'necessity, justice and righteousness of removing all disabilities imposed by custom upon the Depressed Classes. But the party did not articulate any concrete demand or programme to protect the interests of the Depressed Classes. On the other and, the Franchise Committee of 1918-19 recommended nomination from the Depressed Classes in Provincial Councils. The Act of 1919 accepted the recommendations, but leaders of the Depressed Classes demanded for separate electorate.

In its memorandum to the Simon Commission, the *Bahiskrit Hitkarini Sabha* from Bombay, under the leadership of Dr. Ambedkar, opposed nomination and strongly pleaded for the extension of the principle of election to the Depressed Classes. The demands for a separate electorate, reservation of seats in Legislative Councils and local bodies and reservations of posts in government gathered momentum in the late 1920s.

6. Scheduled Castes

The term Scheduled Castes has become in the last 50 years or more the official identifier of the erstwhile untouchables or the exterior castes. The expression Scheduled Caste was first coined by the Simon Commission and embodied in the Government of India Act, 1935. In 1936, for the first time the Government of British India published a list of Scheduled Castes. The so-called Schedule is a list of castes entitled to parliamentary seats, public employment and special educational benefits. Thus, the scheduling or placing under a list was taken into account for providing certain protection and framing schemes in the matter of reservations in service on community basis. Thus, the term Scheduled Caste is a British bureaucratic invention.

The term Scheduled Caste comes in the line of categories like Outcastes, Depressed Castes and Exterior Castes created by the British administrators. While the term has useful moral neutrality, it is essentially legal in nature: the people in question have been transformed into a special legal class of citizens for certain purpose of the state.[37]

The Scheduled Castes are castes identified by the President of India under Article 341 of the Constitution and are put under a Schedule. The Article 341 says, "The President may with respect to any State or Union Territory, after consultation with the Governor thereof, by public notification, specify the castes, races or tribes, or parts, or groups within castes, races, or tribes which shall for the purpose of this Constitution be deemed to be Scheduled Castes in relation to that State or Union Territory, as the case may be'.

"Parliament may by law include in or exclude from the list of Scheduled Castes specified in a notification issued under the clause (i) any caste, race or tribe, or part of, or group, within any caste, race or tribe, but save as aforesaid, a notification issued under the said clause shall not be varied by any subsequent notification".

7. Dalits

The term 'Dalit' is supposed to have been used first by Jotirao Phule (1827-1890) in his attempt to work for d*alituthan*, that is, upliftment of the Dalits. Dr. Ambedkar (1891-1956) is also supposed to have used the term. Though Ambedkar did not popularise the word 'Dalit' for untouchables, his philosophy has remained a key source in the emergence and popularity of the term Dalit. In a way, the word Dalit is of relatively recent origin-of the 1960s- in public discourse. Marathi literary figures and neo-Buddhists began to use the word Dalit in their writings and the contributions of the literary initiatives in replacing *Harijan and* Achut with Dalit may be located as the first case of public use of the term Dalit. They expressed their anger, protest and aspiration through this new word.

The term *Dalit* is a past passive participle of the Sanskrit root *dal* meaning to crack, split, open, etc. *Dalana* means tearing or causing to burst. Dalit means split, broken, destroyed, scattered, torn asunder. The *noun dala*, besides meaning the splitting, has also the positive connotation of something unfolding itself (*dala-komala*, a lotus, *dala-kosal, a* jasmine). Two inter-related processes can be identified with regard to the term evolution of the term Dalit. Firstly, the term denotes an affirmative action, that is, 'yes we are Dalits, we are crushed and broken people.' Secondly, it also indicates assertion, that is, 'no we will not allow ourselves to be crushed by you the dominant castes anymore.'

The word gained currency in public sphere during the Scheduled Caste - caste Hindu riots in Bombay in the early 1970s. Dalit Panthers used the term to assert their identity for rights and self-respect. Later the term came to be used to include all the oppressed and exploited sections of the society. It has essentially emerged as a political category. According to Gangadhar Pantawane, "Dalit is not a caste. Dalit is a symbol of change and revolution. The Dalit believes in humanism. He rejects existence of God, rebirth, soul, sacred books that teach discrimination, faith and heaven because these have made him a slave. He represents the exploited man in his country... Dalitness is essentially a means towards achieving a sense of cultural identity. The inferiority complex based on 'to be a dalit' has now disappeared. Now Dalitness is a source of confrontation. This change has its essence in the desire for justice for all mankind.[38]

According to Gopal Guru, the category Dalit has faced criticism, particularly by the urban, educated middleclass Dalits, as socially regressive, derogatory and undesirable.[39] These middle class Dalits argue that this category forces Dalits to carry the load of their historical past,[40] and hence offers a socially reactionary agenda.

There are others who argue that the category shares the same reactionary agenda as the one invoked by Manu, the Hindu law giver.[41] These opponents argue that the ontological basis of the category of Dalit is class, which is undesirable. Instead, they prefer to define the category on an individualistic basis and foreground the category Buddhist. Ultimately, these attempts posit the category Dalit in opposition to the category Buddhist.

It is interesting that the category Dalit was used by Ambedkar in his fortnightly *Bahishkruit Bharat*. He defined it comprehensively: 'Dalithood is a kind of life condition which characterizes the exploitation, suppression and marginalisation of Dalits by the social, economic, cultural and political domination of the upper caste Brahmin cal order.[42] Ambedkar, however, did not use this category often, preferring to deploy different terms depending upon the changing context. For example, when dealing with the imperial state he used the category of depressed classes.[43] When addressing high caste Hindus he used the category *bahishkruit* meaning totally outcaste.

In the arena of competitive politics, he preferred the term 'scheduled caste'. It was evident when he used this term for establishing the political party, Scheduled Caste Federation. However, he also tried to provide a class identity to the Dalits during the late 1940s. Finally, in an effort to politically radicalize his own social constituency, he used the term Dalit, meaning those who are crushed under the feet of the Hindu social order. In recent years the category Dalit was first comprehensively deployed by the Panthers, thereby combining the caste, class and gender dimensions which were also part of Ambedkar's mode of thinking and his revolutionary politics.

8. Dalit-Bahujan

In recent years the term Dalit has been discarded as a socially reactionary category by a section of the community who prefer *bahujan* over both the Buddhist as well as Dalit categories.[44]

Kanshi Ram, the founder leader of Bahujan Samaj Party (BSP) popularized the term, *Bahujan*. According to Kanshi Ram Bahujan Samaj consisted of the Scheduled Castes, the Scheduled Tribes, the Other Backward Castes and the minorities, who together constitute about 85 per cent of the population and about 6,000 sub-caste groups. Kanshi Ram further argued that such a coalition based upon caste did not mean that the Bahujans are casteist. Rather, they were the victims of the caste-based society created and perpetuated by the Brahmins.[45] The Bahujan Samaj Party is critical of the justice provided by the Indian state and promises to provide alternative forms of social justice for Dalit-Bahujan. The BSP says it will redress the historical wrongs perpetuated by the upper castes and establish a new social and political order – a Dalit-Bahujan State- in which the former will replace the *Manuvadi* social groups that have ruled the country since independence.

Kanshi Ram further reiterated the fact that there are two ways by which the political position of the Dalit-Bahujan can undergo transformation. The first is capturing power through mobilization and electoral victory from the Brahmins. He consistently pointed out that since the Brahmins comprise only 10-12 per cent of the population, if the more numerous Dalit-Bahujan vote for the BSP, they can seize the system 'from within', that is capture state power without social revolution. In the second stage with the use of state power the revolution can, under the leadership of the BSP, penetrate deeper into society, transforming it.[46]

In contrast to the definition provided by Kanshi Ram and BSP, Kancha Ilaiah perceives Dalit-Bahujan as a state of mind or a philosophy of life than referring to particular social categories. He counterposes between Dalitism, that is, Dalit-Bahujans thought and action process with Brahminism, that is, Hindu Brahminical thought and action process. Examining the difference in the epistemology of both these communities Kancha Ilaiah states, 'In India, the Dalit-Bahujans knowledge system is far more fundamental and superior and commands far greater number of people than the Brahminical written and codified knowledge system. The Dalit-Bahujans have their own theory of knowledge which produces and reproduces itself in the day to day interaction with land, water, air, seeds, trees, animals, birds and so on. In the process their consciousness produces its own world-view. On the contrary, the Brahminical interaction with nature is anti-production as the Brahminical forces interact with forces of nature only to consume them or destroy them. Thus, they produce and reproduce Brahminical being and self.[47]

In his interpretation of Dalit politics, Gajendran states, the invention of categories such as bahujan or dalit-bahujan, usher in the plausibility of a progressive agenda of transforming Indian society as a whole including Dalits. So far the political processes in the subcontinent, at least in the modern period, have sustained a political structure favouring the top rungs of the Hindu social order despite pretensions of adopting diverse ideological orientations. In such a setting the category bahujan sought to upset the applecart of pro-caste Hindu politics. It actualized in electoral politics what Phule began in 19th century Maharashtra as a social reform movement and what Ambedkar contemplated in his political experiments of the 1940s.[48]

The categories defining the Dalits that were evolved or emerged over the years indicate the interactive process between the Dalits and the non-Dalits. They also point to the emerging Dalit identity formation. On the one hand, there is an attempt to rebuff and reject the term as well as the meaning attached to some terminologies. On the other hand, it is an effort to carve out a definition to oneself by the Dalits. In this process, assertion of the Dalits to re-establish their dignity, rights and humanity contributed immensely. This was not an easy exercise, given the debilitating and devastating effect of casteism in general and untouchability in particular.

As stated in the foregoing pages, at one time, the Dalits functioned within the identity imposed on them by the dominant castes. This helped the dominant castes in two ways. On the one hand, it enabled them to maintain the hierarchical, skewed and exploitative caste system by imposing a fatalistic worldview. On the other hand, it also enhanced their privilege, position and power, which in turn enabled them to appropriate resources and wealth.

The Dalits in turn were left to suffer the stigma of being untouchables, broken men, outcasted from every aspect of society. This social seclusion was not limited to denial of right to interact with the dominant castes, inter-dining, inter-marriage, entry into temples as some social scientists would argue, but it also resulted in the denial of right to own and operate resources. Further, this oppressive social process deprived of the right to appropriate the fruits of one's labour. Thus, the Dalits were reduced to being just a producing class for the betterment, enjoyment, and development of the non-producing dominant castes. It is this deprivation, which ultimately leads to cultural deprivation and thus sealed their fate as the most discriminated beings on this sub-continent. The caste discourse that has been emerging over the years depicts this scenario in the most vivid form [Diagram 1].

Diagram 1—Caste Discourse

Dalit discourse	*DominantCaste discourse*
Dalits are considered to be impure and polluting but they are the ones who are engaged in purificatory services for the entire society.	Dominant castes are supposed to be pure and superior beings but their attitude and behaviour has constantly been one of impure and unclean towards the lower castes.
Dalit women compared to upper caste women enjoy greater freedom of movement, speech, decision-making power at home.	Women from the dominant castes are restricted by very many dos and don'ts.
The practice of dowry, the consequent dowry deaths are unheard of among the Dalits. Although the reality among the educated Dalits is different.	Giving and receiving exorbitant dowry and when the exchange turns unpleasant burning of women is somewhat a common practice.
Communitarian in nature and operation and thus are democratic.	The dominant castes are individualistic and hence are authoritarian.
Dalits enjoy leisure, love music, dance and gathering etc.	Restless and scheming all the time to be on the top of the ladder.
Dalits are critical of the social order, creative and are care-free.	The dominant castes are status-quo maintaining by nature.
By option the Dalits engage in liberative and emancipatory struggles.	Since they are the beneficiaries of the system they opt for inaction or reformative policies and programmes.
Dalits are the productive class/ caste of the Indian society.	Upper castes are the consumer class and strive to thrive on the labour of others.

Source: Culled out from various discourses that are prominent today

Eleanor Zelliot while deliberating upon Dalit movement identifies three facets in the folklore of Dalit consciousness. a) the idea that they are and were creators of culture[49]; b) the idea that they were the 'Lords of the Earth", the original inhabitants of their areas shunted aside by the Aryan invaders; corollary with this is a disbelief in hereditary pollution and purity, a disbelief in karmic rebirth; c) the idea that they were and are a militant people, with heroes who used their strength in a self-sacrificial way for their people.[50] Thus, one can notice that in the process of identity formation there could even be an element of over emphasis on certain issues, projection of a golden past, etc. All these provide a sense of direction to a social group, which has been at the receiving end for a long period in history.

Facets of Dalit Movement

The foregoing argument spells out this fact that Dalit Identity formation has led to the assertion of the Dalits. This in turn has accentuated their resolve to secure their rights against all odds and these have culminated in Dalit movements. As stated above, Dalit movement is to regain lost identity, recover access over resources and reformulate their history. It is a struggle for self-determination, self-definition and self-actualisation. It is a social fact that Dalit movement has obtained a definite direction and determination in the last three decades or so. But Dalit movement is as old as caste system, caste discrimination and deprivation and marginalisation of the Dalits. Hence, it is essential that one should highlight the important historical factors that contributed in the evolution and sharpening of Dalit movement.

Conversion

Conversion to Islam, Christianity, Sikhism and Buddhism proved to be one of the major factors that opened avenues for the Dalits to search for alternative forms of social order. The untouchables hoped to find a more democratic, egalitarian and liberal social order in these religions. For the outcastes religious conversion was not just moving into another religion, it was a powerful means to demonstrate that they are also human beings, equal in status to anyone else. It is this factor, which led to crisis within Hindu social order, which in turn forced the Hindu society to rethink its principles and practices. A close scrutiny of the process of conversion reveals the fact that conversion addressed to both the material needs as well as the demand for social dignity of both the individual and collectivity that resorted to religious conversion.

The ideological underpinnings of Dr. Ambedkar, who refused to continue to remain a Hindu and encouraged the lower castes to embrace other religions, which promised a different social order is pertinent pointer for discussion at this juncture. Dr. Ambedkar argued, 'To get human treatment, convert yourselves, convert for getting organized, convert for becoming strong, convert for securing equality, convert for getting liberty, convert so that your domestic life may be happy'.[51] Thus, from the historical experience of oppression and dehumanization and from years of attempt to work for emancipation of the Dalits, Dr. Ambedkar came to the fundamental and unalterable conclusion that the road for social mobility was closed for the Dalits within the Hindu fold. He was also of the opinion that the path of political participation was sealed for the untouchables forever. Also he was convinced of the fact that the economic opportunities had been snatched from the very beginning of the establishment of caste system. Moreover, he strongly believed that only the religious root is left open for the downtrodden of Indian society. And hence he advocated and urged the Dalits to take the path of conversion.

Historically speaking, the response to Ambedkar's plea to convert was positive, probably because the untouchable castes in Bombay region had just gone through some eight years of attempts to participate in Hindu festivals and to enter Hindu temples without success. The 1939 announcement was made near Nasik, and many in Ambedkar's audience had undoubtedly participated in five-year-long *satyagraha* to enter the famous Kala Ram Temple in Nasik, a pilgrimage city. Efforts to gain education, and efforts to secure political rights such as special representation in legislative bodies, had been fairly successful; however, efforts to claim religious rights had generally ended in failure. The idea of leaving Hinduism met with considerable approval among Ambedkar's own caste in western India and found echoes both in the south and north of India.[52]

G. Aloysius has argued that, 'there were several mass conversions to Christianity which could be termed as religious movements of the oppressed. Conversion to another, often well developed, hence powerful religio-meaning systems had always been an aspect of the local caste resistance struggles even in pre-modern times. The presence of large segment of Muslim population in the country bears testimony to this social fact. With the advent of the Europeans, the members of lower caste embraced Christianity. The missionaries' efforts to provide literacy, health care and material help answered many of the existential dimensions. Mass conversion started in different parts of the country'.[53] Thus, wherever group conversion took place it was to register the protest of those who were marginalized and oppressed in society. It was also a process of spiritual emancipation.

It is not argued here that conversion has made a sea change in the lives of those who are converted.[54] But it has surely made a lot of difference in their social, economic and cultural milieu. It is also significant to note that conversion is the consummation of various material, social, religious and psychological factors. Hence the consequence of conversion cannot be discerned at the apparent. One has to explore the various facets of the lives of the converted so as to highlight the changes that have taken place in their lives.

Martial Services

The caste system as practiced over the years did not permit the Dalits to engage in martial services. But both in day-to-day activities and in extra-ordinary circumstances, the bravery, valour, hard labour and the skills of the Dalits have been extensively used by the dominant castes. Yet they were denied entry into military services. Against this practice, during the Mughal rule they were recruited in the military. In extension, some of them got converted to Islam and this in turn enabled them to escape the stigma of being an untouchable and on the other hand enabled the process of social mobility. This further, provided space and scope for social mobility.

In this regard Kshirsagar states that 'the untouchables including Mahars had a bright history of martial services under the Muslim and Maratha kings. However, their military career came to prominence under the British rule. The East Indian Company raised two battalions, mainly consisting of Mahars on 4th August 1768. The marines battalion of the Bombay Army was also raise in 1777, in which the Mahars formed a larger part... Moreover, they were quite familiar with the Indian situation including forts, forests and strategic points'.[55]

Speaking about the martial history of the Dalits, Raja Sekhar Vundru states that references to the Anglo-Maratha wars usually conjure up images of a horde of White men fighting the native Marathas. But the truth is, the British conquered India with an army composed mostly of Indians. The men who fought for the British against the Maratha rulers were Mahars, a community of untouchables from present-day Maharashtra. Ambedkar was a Mahar and the son of a subedar major, the highest rank the Indians could hold those days in the East Indian Company's army. The Maharas were a vital component in Chhatrapati Shivaji's army. He deployed 'low caste' Ramoshis, Mahars and Mangs in his infantry and naval forces. They latter helped him establish his empire. After Shivaji's death in 1680, the Peshwa rulers oppressed the Mahars making them hang a pot around their neck to spit and tie broom around their waist to sweep away their 'impure footsteps'. But the military training and contact helped them in terms of acquiring English education and modern outlook and in turn, the desire to break free from social shackles.[56]

Martial services, obviously, proved to be a boon to the untouchables in those days when they were deliberately debarred from all walks of life by the Indian society especially the caste Hindus. They could improve their economic condition to great extent... The East India Company provided compulsory education for its Indian soldiers and their dependents. When they brought home the victory by exemplifying their bravery in various expeditions, their confidence was raised. After retirement from military service they could disseminate the new idea of discipline amongst their brethren.[57]

Reform Movements

An examination of reform movements brings to the fore the manner in which a society is constructed, its general orientation, the sources of conflict and crisis, the structures of domination and patterns of resistance. Thus, it needs to be stated here that the social and religious reform movements came into existence due to the subjective and objective conditions of the era. It is also pertinent to highlight the fact that the religious reform movements had an added dimension of spiritual equality; it had pointers for social equality as well. While these reform movements spoke about the anomalies that exist in the present social order, they also portrayed an order, which is egalitarian, pluralistic and democratic.

Historically speaking, in the 18th century, there ensued a debate among the radicals in India, which deliberated on the religious and social ideas of the enlightenment era. These were characterized by a concern with the natural and political rights of the individual in society. Prominent social reformers sought to reach a larger audience and to create a recognized arena for the discussion of what seemed to them issues of overwhelming importance for India's future. Also, the B*hakti* devotional cults contained a strong dislike of any rigid equivalence of spiritual merit with high caste status.[58] Though at the philosophical realm, the *Bhakti* movement spoke about equality both at the spiritual and social realm, a careful reading into the history of this period unravels that most of these social and religious reform movements did not have manifest socio-political agenda. But in a latent way they led to social consciousness among the Dalits and the downtrodden.

One can identify many religious reform movements like the *Prarthana Samaj*, *Brahma Samaj*, *Arya Samaj*, *Satyashodhak Samaj* etc. In Punjab alone one could identify Singh Sabha Movement, Arya Samaj Movement, Ghadar Movement, Gurudwara Reform Movement, Adi Dharm Movement etc. About Arya Samaj movement in Punjab, Satish Sharma argues that Arya Samaj movement not only carried out social reform but also generated religious controversies and conflicts. Some historians argue that the development of Arya Samaj signified collective efforts directed essentially at the solution of the common problem of material and psychological adjustment with the Raj, the rise of Hindu consciousness in Punjab. It also engaged in educational activities. The Arya Samaj opened a school for the benefit of Bhangi children in 1923 in Jodhpur. While some of these were directed to alleviate the sufferings of the untouchables, the real objective was to retain and reclaim them into the Hindu fold.[59]

The religious and social reform movements were not confined to dominant castes alone. But the *Satyashodhak Samaj*, the 'Truth-Seeking Society" was founded by Jotirao Phule and his colleagues in 1873 to work for the deprived section of society. The activities undertaken by the Samaj spells out the objectives of the Samaj. "Some wise gentlemen founded this Samaj on the 24th September 1873, in order to free the Shudra people from slavery to Brahmans, Bhats, Joshis, priests and others. For thousands of years, these people have needlessly despised and exploited the Shudras, with the aid of their cunningly devised books. This action was taken, therefore, so that through good advice and the spread of education, the Shudras might be got to understand their real rights, and freed both in religious and more general matters from the false and self-interested books of the Brahmans".[60]

In the course of time various religious reform movements too came into existence leading to change in the thoughts and actions of the Dalits as well as raising question to the caste system and to the Hindu social order itself. *Ramdeo Panth*, *Satnami Panth*, *Naval Dharma*, *Warkari Panth*, *Kabir Panth*, *Nasraiah Sect* to name few. *Panth* is usually defined as sect. But if one looks closely at the objective behind the formation of *panths*, the manner in which they come into existence, one would realize the fact that these are attempts to follow a different path of life. The Kabir panth was known as the tradition of non-caste Hinduism. Most of the *panths* would envisage a casteless, non-religious society and work towards equality. It is a fact that these *panths* have not had the expected outcome but they provided scope for escape from the drudgery of the caste system.

Political formation

A cursory glance at the impressive volumes of literature on Dalit political formation highlights that there are various factors that contributed for the emergence of political formation among the Dalits. Social segregation, exploitation and oppression form the basic foundations on which these political formations were constructed. But these political processes did not emerge only focusing on the degraded state of the Dalits, but they also took serious note of the potentials that were and are inherent in this exploited society. Gail Omvedt points out that, Phule sought to unite the *shudras* and *ati-shudras*. Phule argued that the latter were not only more oppressed but had been downgraded because of their earlier heroism in fighting Brahman domination. More importantly, he argued that the *shudras* and ati-*shudras* together represented an oppressed and exploited mass, and compared their subordination with that of the native Indians in the Americas and the Blacks. Phule's broadsides are, in fact, an expression of a theory not simply of religious domination and conquest, but of exploitation.[61]

Dr. Ambedkar himself tried to wrest space for Dalit emancipation at religious, social, economic and political realms. In 1936, he gave the political movement a specific focus by establishing the Independent Labour Party.[62] In July 1942, Dr. Ambedkar decided to consolidate and nationalize his leadership of the Scheduled Castes. Thus, he founded the All India Scheduled Castes Federation at the All India Depressed Classes Conference in Nagpur.[63] All India Scheduled Castes Federation contested the elections in the 1951 general elections, but did not make much electoral gains. In 1956 Dr. Ambedkar made an attempt to transform the Scheduled Castes Federation into a party which would speak for all the 'dispossessed', the Scheduled Castes, the Scheduled Tribes and Backward Classes. The move to create the Republican Party came about the same time as the conversion to Buddhism in Nagpur on 14-15 October 1956. Both were efforts to take the Scheduled Castes out of untouchability and into a larger group, one religious and the other political.[64]

At the youth and struggle front one can count the following organisations, formations or movements: Dalit Panther Movement, Dalit Liberation Army, Youth Republican, *Dalit Sangharsh Samiti*, *Dalit Shoshit Samaj Sangharsh Samaj* (DSS), *Dalit Sena*, *Bhim Sena*, to name few representative ones.

There are reasons nevertheless, of a substantial nature to underscore the point that the marginalized are breaking newer paths for their emancipation and liberation in their course of their struggle. Political participation is one of these avenues. Javed Alam makes an intuitive note on this aspect. 'The proportion of those voting is titling towards the oppressed in terms of their electoral participation. In 1996, as against 1971, there were more poor, illiterate, Dalits, OBC, rural based people, and Muslim sections of the population among the voters. In 1971, there were more upper castes, well to do classes, literates, urban dwellers among the voters, whereas in 1996 these same groups made up a much larger section of the non-voters. In other words, the proportion of those voting out of the total electorate has remained the same, but its inner composition has changed drastically.'[65]

One can also identify the formation of socio-political formation based on the provision of reservation. One of the dominant political formations of this type is the employees association under the banner of Backward Scheduled Caste Scheduled Tribes and Minority Community Employees Federation (BAMCEF). The BAMCEF provided the social, political and financial basis for the formation of the *Bahujan Samaj Party* (BSP). Here a brief note on the emergence and expansion of BSP would not be out of place.

Sudha Pai while examining the emergence, ideology and progress, mobilisational strategies and electoral progress of the BSP against the backdrop of Dalit assertion and a shift from single party system to a cleavage-based multi-party system in the post-Congress phase highlights the emergence of Dalit assertion and BSP.[66] Irrespective of the absence of anti-caste movement in Uttar Pradesh in comparison to southern and western regions of India, with the emergence of Bahujan Samaj Party there converged space for Dalit assertion in Uttar Pradesh. With the constraints that are part of any party that caters to the agenda of excluded community, the BSP has provided a sense of dignity and a scope for political participation. It is this fact, which has been taken note of by the Dalits at the pan-Indian political level.

Ambedkar as Ideologue of Dalit Movements

It is irrefutable that the Dalit liberation movements especially in the last three decades or so have been centered on Dr. Bhimrao Ambedkar. This allegiance became all the more essential for the Dalits because the life and the struggles of Dr. Ambedkar unleashed a new awareness among the Dalits. This awareness led to the search for a culture of freedom, a political agenda for emancipation, a social order devoid of exclusion, and non-dependent economic engagement. Hence, the writings and speeches of Dr. Ambedkar became the ideological underpinnings of Dalit liberation movement.

Eleanor Zelliot based on the study of Dalit movements, documents the symbolic relevance that the statue of Dr. Ambedkar represents: education, success, contribution to the political world of India, courage, empowerment through reservations, protection through a relationship to government, 'one of us' who was not only important personally but was important to India. This overpowering image of Dr. Ambedkar does not obliterate other 'roots of Dalit consciousness'. Rather it encourages Dalits to look for the abilities, the talents, the triumphs, both of the historic past and at the folklore of the village as well.[67]

In a special way, the writings and speeches of Dr. Ambedkar has become the rallying point of Dalit emancipation. Valerian Rodrigues writing about Dr. Ambedkar portrays him as 'Scholar, politician, constitutionalist, teacher, lawyer, parliamentarian, administrator, journalist, negotiator, agitationist and leader'. Dr. Ambedkar privileged the written word. The written word enabled him to reach out to a larger world, conferring some degree of permanence or immortality and allowing him to usurp some of the Brahminical authority. In his writings Dr. Ambedkar resorted to various modes of expression-dissertations, records, papers, documents, outlines, notes early drafts, statements, briefs, memoranda, disputations and investigations. There are also speeches delivered by Dr. Ambedkar for various occasions and different forum, from the Constituent Assembly to mobilisational gatherings. Born an 'untouchable', Dr. Ambedkar became India's foremost opponent of the evil of untouchability and formulated the basis of affirmative action through his advocacy of fair and equal terms of social association.[68]

Within the permeating influence of caste system, the Indian state operates more as the instrument of dominant castes. Yet due to its bourgeoisie liberal polity, it also tolerated the scathing attacks of Dr. Ambedkar. Going further, the Government of Maharashtra set up an Advisory Committee in 1976, with the Education Minister as Chairman and comprising political followers of Dr. Ambedkar, scholars and noted writers, to compile the thoughts and writings of Dr. Ambedkar and have them published. Over 17 volumes in English and 11 volumes in Hindi with second editions have been published under government auspices.[69] There are other publications undertaken by various Ambedkarite movements, organisations in English and vernacular languages. This is an indication of the increased relevance of Dr. Ambedkar's writings and speeches.

Dr. Anand Teltumbde in his study of Ambedkar and Post-Ambedkar Dalit Movements emphatically states that Dr. Ambedkar has undoubtedly been the central figure in the epistemology of the Dalit universe. It is difficult to imagine anything serious or important in their collective life that is totally untouched by Dr. Ambedkar. For the Dalit masses, he is everything together, a scholar par excellence in the realm of scholarship, a Moses or messiah who led his people out o bondage and ignominy on to the path of pride, and a Bodhisattva in the pantheon of Buddhism. He is always bedecked with superlatives, quite like God, whatever may be the context in Dalit circles.[70]

The Resilience of Dalit Women

Dalit women have provided the basic foundation for Dalit identity and emancipation. It is another matter that the non-Dalits as well as the Dalits have systematically overlooked this historical phenomenon. There is no dispute that Dalit women are twice disadvantaged or they are the Dalits among Dalits: Dalit women are subjected to discrimination due to the gender bias that is deep rooted in the Indian society as well as within the Dalit community. This twofold oppression and exploitation drives them to the periphery. But this is only one side of the story. The equally important aspect of Dalit women is the enormous resilience they have to continue to carry on their lives, the lives of their families, the struggles of their community, in spite of insurmountable hardships and hurdles. Over 90 per cent of the Dalit women are illiterate and uneducated, an equal percent of them are landless agricultural labourers, who are denied access to resources both by the non-Dalit and Dalit society. Further they are kept away from centers of power. Yet, irrespective of all these structural constraints they continue to struggle to liberate themselves.

It took long time for the Dalit women's' movements to carve out a space for themselves on their own merit. The women's movement as a new social movement in India gathered momentum in 1970s and it included different shades of feminist perspectives subsequently. In the first phase, the women's movement laid great stress on women's rights and in the second phase it emphasised more on women' liberation and autonomy. In the 1970s, Dalit movement as a 'New Social Movement' expressed itself through radical literature and action. But even this upsurge did not give vent to the mute voices of Dalit women.[71]

The interface between caste and gender has also raised some fundamental questions about Dalit movement, about the place and role of Dalit women in general and in Dalit society in particular. It is argued that by using the term Dalit women we are trying to say that if women from Dalit castes and if Dalit consciousness create a space for themselves for fearless expression i.e., if they become subjects or agents or self, they will provide a new leadership to Indian society, in general and to feminist and Dalit movements in particular.[72] This argument gains support from the fact that Dalit women constitute the dominant production force. It is this production force, which against all odds continue to maintain the social system from crumbling. Hence, restructuring of Indian social order could be undertaken only by them.

Sharmila Rege tries to examine the complex reformulation the Brahminical patriarchies undergo in order to counter collective

Dalit resistance. According to her, the increasing visibility of Dalit women in power structure as sarpanch, as members of panchayat and in the new knowledge-making processes has led to an increased backlash against Dalit women. The backlash is expressed through a range of humiliating practices and often culminates in rape or the killing of their kinsmen. Such incidents underline the need for a dialogue between Dalit and feminist activists, since inter-caste relations at the local level may be mediated through a redefinition of gendered spaces. The emancipatory agenda of the Dalit and women's movements will have to be sensitive to these issues and underline the complex interplay between caste and gender as structuring hierarchies in society.[73] The Dalit movement will have to take into account the rightful place and role of women in their struggles on their own merit. Otherwise they would further become marginalized and thus all their potential for initiating, leading and ensuring Dalit liberation movements would be co-opted by non-Dalits.

Dalit-Dominant Caste Worldview

Before we conclude this chapter, let us briefly look at the Dalit and dominant caste worldview. There is no meeting point between the Dalits and the non-Dalits at the level of control over economic resources, social capital, political power and social mobility. Even at the realm of worldview, these two social categories are diametrically opposed to each other [Diagram 2]. While the worldview of the Dalits is related to present and this worldly order, the worldview of Brahminism speaks about the spiritual realm but this is done to appropriate all the power, privilege and facilities of the present.

There is a segment of the Indian population which continues to argue that the Dalits have been from the beginning in a state of servitude. But this argument in many respects has been proved to be misconstrued if not mischievous. Looking at the attributes of the Dalits and the dominant castes, it is but natural to ask 'with these basic and fundamental potency and capability how did the Dalits get reduced to a life of drudgery and slavery?' A corollary to this or question is 'how does one comprehend the degraded, deprived and discriminated state of Dalits who were invested with immense prowess and power?'

The caste discrimination was constructed both in principles and in operation in such a way that it reduced a segment of the population to eternal bondage and to a sub-human subsistence. These were ploys at which the dominant castes, especially the Brahminical group was adept. Thus, it can be stated that this particular variant of social stratification is *sui generis*, a product fashioned by the clever, scheming and crafty dominant castes. But it is also the outcome of India's socio-economic, and cultural milieu. Hence, the need of the hour is to free ourselves from the shaky constructs of authority of caste system as a source of integration. Simultaneously, we should engage in an honest recording and mapping of the changes demanded and initiated by the Dalits and the downtrodden.

Diagram 2—Dalit-Dominant Caste Worldview[74]

Dalit Worldview	*Dominant Caste Worldview*
Bhulok—This worldly. In extension this also meant down to earth, being practical.	*Parlok, brahmalok* – the word Brahma was derived from the name of a leader of the Aryan invaders called Brahma who was said to have killed many Indus food producers and food gatherers.
Lokayatas = the earliest Dalit-Bahujans, the original settlers who fought against the Aryan invaders.	Brahmins = Aryan invaders who slowly established the Brahminical socio-political and economic system in India.
Lokayatas were termed by Brahmins—*Asura, Rakshasu, Mlecha, Dehvadi, Prakritian, nastik*, meaning inferior beings.	Brahmins were termed by *Lokayatas* as, *Paralok vadi* , that is, busy with other world in another sense parasites.
Engaged in theoretical argument in their interaction with the others.	The dominant castes took to physical assault in their interaction with the others.
Dalit-Bahujans constructed their dialectical discourse in relation to nature. This emphasised that the 'unseen and untouched' Brahman was unreal and the real could be seen and touched.	Brahma centered *Purushasukta*, that is the primeval being. By this theory they established the Brahminical patriarchal system.
The Dalits entered into dialectical discourse based on materialism.	The dominant castes on the other hand, constructed a divine theory.
Born from mother's womb, which is normal to any human beings.	But the dominant castes that they are born from *Purusa*. This is what they say and that is why others ridicule them.

Close to nature, birth-death reality and hence, egalitarian status to women. Brahmins are challenged by this worldview.	Spoke about the other world but established their hegemony. And also reduced the untouchables women to second grade citizens, made them slaves.
Discourse conducted in Pali, which had vast communicative base. Continued with oral traditions which was the form of expression of common persons and much later codified it.	All the discourses were conducted in Sanskrit, which had narrow confines. Brahimins wrote it and also codified it and thus did not become part of the masses.
Flexible in attitude and behaviour. Adjustable and accommodative.	Strictly organised social structure, militant and violent mode of thinking.
Labouring but property less class. Producing and reproducing class.	Non- productive but consuming class. Hence, developed well structured *yagya* and *yoga* to legitimise the extraction of material resources and to justify their leisure-bound non-productive life.
Tribal republicanism and federation. *Sabha, samiti, janapada* (various levels of governance) were evolved to regulate social interaction.	Monolithic and hierarchical state formation. This enforced social ostracism of the *shudras* and outcastes.
Lokneeti, pro-people policy was central to collective interaction. Democratic principles coloured the operations.	*Dandaneeti*, that is, punishment, becomes central to Brhaminical rule. This is counter-revolutionary in nature. Authoritarian in nature and function.
Janpad, jan kalyan. In terms of functioning people's rule and people's wellbeing took primacy of place.	*Rajatilak, rajabhishek*. Among the dominant castes, monarchy and coronation etc were given priority.
Karm, engage in action that is beneficial to all was central principle.	*Dharm*, that is, duty but in reality it is *varnasram dharm*, that is, caste based duty.
Emotional and hence sensitive to all that happens around and thus affected by pain and pleasure.	Legalistic and hence can only engage in violence. Pretend to be not affected by suffering and pain.
Becoming and nothing is preordained, predetermined.	Being and hence everything is static, predestined and thus rigid.
Follow the motto of *Bahujan hitaya aur Bahujan sukhaya*, that is, prosperity and wellbeing of all is most crucial. Here there is a broadening of worldview from selfishness to other-centeredness.	The dominant castes follow the motto, *Brahmin hitaya aur Brahmin sukhaya*, (the prosperity of Brahmins is important) now changed into *bahujan dukhaya aur parjan sukhaya* (Prosper at the expenses of others.
Bali raj refers to Jotirao Phule's Dalit-bahujan governance. Ambedkar spoke about 'Sangha Nirmana' or state socialism.	Ram rajya or Akhanda Hindu Rajya refers to continued rule of the dominant castes. Mahatma Gandhi also advocated ***Ram Rajya without disturbing caste system.***

Dalits are engaged in purifying occupations and hence are treated as polluting.	Engaged in polluting occupations but treat oneself as purifying agents.
Among the Dalits customary laws mediate social interactions.	Among the dominant castes superimposed religious precepts determine the pattern of interaction.

Source: Kancha Iliah. Dalitism vs. Brahminism: the Epistemological conflict in History and Gopal Guru. The Language of Dalit-Bahujan Political Discourse in Ghanshyam Shah (ed). Dalit Identity and Politics. Sage Publications: New Delhi. 2001.

The above presented facts and figures reveal that the Dalits in India have been subjected to sever and sinister apartheid than any other internationally known oppressed communities. They are forced to engage themselves in degrading traditional occupation for the betterment of the others; they are physically segregated from the main habitation of the village; they are also socially ostracised at the will and fancies of the dominant castes; the Dalits are denied entry into temples, schools, hospitals, hotels and other public places; in course of time they were robed of all the natural and human resources; their very sight has become detestable to the so called pure castes; their men, women and children could be beaten, bashed up and brutally assaulted but they have to bear all these silently blaming only themselves and their fate. All these are not individual in nature, but are collective, institutional and social in content and context. Thus caste discrimination is the foundation and the basis of Indian social order. In today's context, caste discrimination is more horrendous than racial discrimination.

It is not that the Dalits are asking for a total restructuring of society and hence the upper castes are letting loose a reign of terror. But their legitimate demand for a share in the cake had led to severe repression and oppression. By unleashing violence and atrocities the upper castes are sending warning signals that any attempt to raise their voice against them would be severely dealt with. Thus by resorting to violence they want to prevent any serious and systematic questioning of their hegemony and monopoly. Thus, the orgy of death and devastation is not an unplanned act as many people make themselves believe.

The social exclusion had pervasive and cumulative effect on the lower castes. There were poor people in all castes. At the level of poverty and deprivation they are all at the same level. But the most fascinating feature of the caste system was that the sentiment of caste purity and superiority did not allow the general poor to align with the oppressed to wage a united struggle against the exploiters in all the castes. Hence, 'poor' does not constitute a category for emancipatory agenda in Dalit discourse. From the perspective of the Dalits it is they and other weaker sections who are the exploited, segregated and discriminated population in India. Hence, it is their struggle, which would lead to liberation of the Dalits and the downtrodden as well as the restructuring of the social order.

Waman Nambalkar's poem spells out this resolve[75]

> On the horizon I will erect
> The rainbow arch of mankind
> I am conscious on my resolve
> The worth of the blood of Eklaya's broken finger
> I will not bastard my word
> I stand today at the very end
> Of the twentieth century.

References

1. Prakash Louis. People Power: The Naxalite Movement in Central Bihar. Wordsmiths: New Delhi, 2002, p. 27.
2. T.R. Gurr. Why Men Rebel? Princeton University Press: Princeton, 1970, p. 7.
3. M.S.A. Rao (ed). Social Movements in India. South Asia Books: New Delhi. 1978, p. 209.
4. S.C. Malik (ed). Dissent, Protest and Reform in Indian Civilisation. Indian Institute of Advanced Study: Shimla. 1977, p. 30.
5. Jan Nederveen Pieterse (ed). Emancipation, Modern and Postmodern.. Sage Publications: London, 1992, p. 6.
6. P.N. Mukherji. Social Movements and Social Change. Sociological Bulletin. 26 (1), 1977, p. 38.
7. Identity formation is a universal phenomenon cutting across all social categories. For example, the Jats who today claim upper caste

status and have become economically and politically mobile in the past had to invest in enforcing a different identity than they were subjected to. Rattan Singh pleaded from the Jat community in the *Jat Sudhar* in 1925, "Fame is greater than beauty, he who does not respect himself or his country; he is not a man, he is like an animal and his life a living corpse; he who sacrifices his life for the betterment of his community, he alone is immortal; Nobody attains fame through property'. Quoted in Nonica Datta. Forming an Identity; A Social History of the Jats. Oxford University Press: New Delhi, 1999, 167.

8. Fernando Franco (ed) Pain and Awakening: The Dynamics of Dalit Identity in Bihar, Gujarat and Uttar Pradesh. Indian Social Institute: New Delhi, 2002, p. 16.
9. In the recent past, there have been a plethora of studies specifically on dalit identity. The following works indicate this trend: Dr. Fernando Franco (ed). Pain and Awakening: The Emerging Dalit Identity in Bihar, Uttar Pradesh and Gujarat. Indian Social Institute: New Delhi, 2002; Ghanshyam Shah. Dalit Identity and Politics. New Delhi: Sage Publications, 2001; Badrinarayan. Documenting Dissent, Contesting Fables, Contested Memories and Dalit Political Discourse. Shimla: Indian Institute of Advanced Study, 2001; Gail Omvedt. Dalits and the Democratic Revolution. Sage Publications: New Delhi, 1994; Sudha Pai. Dalit Assertion and the Unfinished Democratic Revolution: The Bahujan Samaj Party in Uttar Pradesh. Sage Publications: New Delhi, 2002.
10. For similar narratives of Dalit women, refer to Pan On Fire: Eight Dalit women tell their story. Edited by Sumitra Bhave. Indian Social Institute: New Delhi, 1988.
11. Gopal Guru. Dalit Women Talk Differently. Economic and Political Weekly, October 14-21, 1995, p. 2549.
12. Chambers English Dictionary. New Edition. Allied Publishers: New Delhi, 1991.
13. J.V. Deshpande. Behind Dalit Anger. Economic and Political Weekly, August 16-23 1997, p. 2090-91.
14. A.K.Jha. Dalit Ascendancy. The Times of India, 26 July, 1997, p. 8.
15. Gopal Guru. The Language of Dalit-Bahujan Political Discourse. In Ghanshyam Shah. Dalit Identity and Politics. New Delhi: Sage Publications, 2001, p. 97-107.
16. Oliver Mendelsohn and Marika Vicziany. The Untouchables:

Subordination, Poverty and the State in Modern India. Cambridge University Press: Cambridge, 1998, p. 7.

17. A.T. Hingorani (ed). My Philosophy of Life by Mahatma Gandhi. Pearl Publications: Bombay, 1961 Edition, p. 146.
18. B.R. Ambedkar. The Untouchables: Who Were They and Whey They Became Untouchables? Bheem Patrika Publications: Jalandhar, n.d. p. 47.
19. The Report of the Committee Headed by Elayaperumal on Untouchability, Economic and Educational Development of the Scheduled Castes and Connected Documents, 1969 , p. 1.
20. Marc Galanter. The Abolition of Disabilities: Untouchability and the Law. In Michael Mahar (ed) The Untouchables in Contemporary India. Rawat Publications: Jaipur, 1998 pp. 227-314.
21. Dhananjay Keer. Dr. Ambedkar: Life and Mission. Popular Prakashan: Bombay, 1971, pp. 52-53.
22. H.N. Mukherjee. Gandhi, Ambedkar and the Extirpation of Untouchability. People's Publishing House: New Delhi, 1984, p. 21.
23. Gail Omvedt. Dalits and the Democratic Revolution: Dr. Ambedkar and the Dalit Movement in Colonial India. Sage Publications: New Delhi, 1991, p. 117-118
24. Quoted in Michael Mahar (ed). The Untouchable in Contemporary India. Rawat Publications: Jaipur. 1998, p. 116.
25. Pro. Virginius Xaxa while discussing the issue of the *adivasis* argues, that terms like *adivasis* and Tribals are interchangeably used. People in general however do not address these groups as tribes, far less the scheduled tribes. Such description of the people is more of a middle class conception. People rather address them as the *adivasis* (indigenous people), which is also the term the tribal people use to mark themselves off from the non-Tribals. Terms like *adivasis* and *moolnivasis* are used to refer to the Tribals and the Dalits being original settlers of India. This proposition is contested by the others. But among the Tribals and the Dalits there is a strong move to examine this phenomenon. For more details refer to Virginius Xaxa. The Adivasis in India. A draft paper. Delhi University: New Delhi 2003.
26. Gail Omvedt. *Ibid.*, 117.
27. Gail Omvedt. *Ibid.*, 123.
28. Ghanshyam Shah. Politics of Scheduled Castes and Tribes: Adivasi and Harijan Leaders in Gujarat. Bombay: Vora & Co. Publishers, 1975, p. 24.

29. Gandhi 1971: pp. 244-245
30. Harijan, July 7, 1946.
31. Quoted in Michael Mahar (ed). The Untouchable in Contemporary India. Rawat Publications: Jaipur. 1998, p. 86.
32. The Depressed Classes: A Chronological Document. Kurseong: St. Mary's College, 1936, p. 87.
33. B.D.Purohit and S.D. Purohit. Handbook of Reservation for Scheduled Castes and Scheduled Tribes: Employment-Education-Election. Jainsons Publications, New Delhi, 1990.
34. Quoted in Rajendra Prasad. The Law of Social Status. Hind Law House: Pune, 1998, p. 26.
35. Gopal Guru. The Politics of Naming. Seminar, 471, November 1998, pp. 14-18.
36. Dr. Babasaheb Ambedkar: Writings and Speeches. Vol. 2. Education Department, Government of Maharashtra, 1987, pp. 499-500.
37. Oliver Mendelsohn and Marika Vicziany. The Untouchables: Subordination, Poverty and the State in Modern India. Cambridge University Press: Cambridge, 1998, p. 4.
38. Barbara Joshi. Untouchable! Voice of the Dalit Liberation Movement. Selectbook Service: New Delhi, 1986, pp. 79-80
39. This is the general reaction that one comes across from the Dalit middle class all over the country. They look at the term Dalit with disdain.
40. The dalit middle class which is also criticised as the Dalit Brahmin expressed this reaction to the autobiography *Baluta* by the late Daya Pawar, one of the leading Dalit writers in the early 1980s in Maharashtra.
41. This comes up very frequently in the collection of R.D Gaikwad who collated Ambedkar's memoirs in Marathi. It was published by Sugawa Publication. Pune in 1996.
42. Dr. Babasaheh Ambedkar, *Yanche Bahishkruit Bharat ani Muknayak* (Marathi), [translated to mean the This is the Depressed India or Frontrunner].Education Department, Government of Maharashtra, 1990, pp. 194-98.
43. See Ambedkar's Writing and Speeches, *Ibid.*, Vol. 9, p. 304.
44. The term bahujan was floated by Kanshi Ram and also by Prakash Ambedkar and Makharam Pawar from Maharashtra.
45. Sudha Pai. Dalit Assertion and the Unfinished Democratic Revolution: The Bahujan Samaj Party in Uttar Pradesh. Sage

Publications: New Delhi, 2002, p. 121.

46. *Ibid.*, p. 123.
47. Ghanshyam Shah (ed). Dalit Identity and Politics. Sage Publications: New Delhi, 2001, p. 110.
48. A. Gajendran . Transforming dalit Politics. Seminar 471, November 1998, pp. 24-27.
49. This idea is expressed graphically "The Hindus wanted the Vedas and they sent for Vyasa who was not a caste Hindu. The Hindus wanted an Epic and they sent for Valmiki who was an Untouchable. The Hindus wanted a Constitution, and they sent for me". Ambedkar, Marathi, 1978, 25.
50. Eleanor Zelliot. From Untouchable to Dalit: Essays in the Ambedkar Movement. Manohar: New Delhi, 1996, p. 318.
51. B.R.Ambedkar. Why go For Conversion? Bangalore: Dalit Sahitya Academy, 1987, p. 16.
52. Eleanor Zelliot. From Untouchable to Dalit: Essays in the Ambedkar Movement. Manohar: New Delhi, 1996, p. 192.
53. G.Aloysius. Religion as Emancipatory Identity. New Delhi: New Age International Publishers: New Delhi, 1998, p. 18.
54. The hue and cry that is generated by the introduction of 'Freedom of Religion Bill' by the Tamil Nadu and Gujarat Governments is in the direction of upholding human rights. But to directly link this bill with the denial of rights of the Dalits to get converted is stretching the issue too far. Denial of the right to convert oneself or to propagate ones religion is against fundamental rights. But this is not limited to Dalit rights alone.
55. R.K. Kshirsagar. Dalit Movement in India and its Leaders. M.D. Publications: New Delhi, 1994, p. 38.
56. Dalit Battles. The Times of India, New Delhi, 1.4.2003
57. *Ibid.* p. 39.
58. Rosalind O'Hanlon. Caste, Conflict and Ideology: Mahatma Jotirao Phule and Low Caste Protest in Nineteenth-Century Western India. Cambridge University Press: Cambridge, 1985, pp. 52-68.
59. Harish K. Puri et.al. edited. Social and Political Movements. Rawat Publications: Jaipur, 2000, pp. 93-108.
60. Roaslind O'Hanlon. *Ibid*, p. 230.
61. Gail Omvedt. Dalit Visions. Orient Longman, 1996, p. 19.
62. Eleanor Zelliot. From Untouchable to Dalit: Essays in the Ambedkar Movement. Manohar: New Delhi, 1996, pp. 106-115

63. Owen M. Lynch. The Politics of Untouchability. Social Mobility and Social Change in a City of India. National: Delhi, 1974, pp. 135.
64. Eleanor Zelliot. From Untouchable to Dalit: Essays in the Ambedkar Movement. Manohar: New Delhi, 1996, pp. 106-115.
65. Javed Alam. Is Caste Appeal Casteism?; Oppressed Castes in Politics. In Community & Identities: Contemporary Discourses on Culture and Politics in India. Edited by Surinder S. Jodhka. Sage Publications: New Delhi, 2001, p 99.
66. Sudha Pai. Dalit Assertion and the Unfinished Democratic Revolution: The Bahujan Samaj Party. Sage Publications: New Delhi, 2002.
67. Eleanor Zelliot. The roots of dalit consciousness. Seminar 471, November 1998, p. 32.
68. Valerian Rodrigues. The Essential Writings of B.R. Ambedkar. Oxford University Press: New Delhi, 2002.
69. Dr. Babasaheb Ambedkar: Writings and Speeches. Vol.1- Vol. 17. Education Department: Government of Maharashtra, 1979 onwards.
70. Anand Teltumde. Ambedkar and Post-Ambedkar Dalit Movements. Sugawa Prakashan: Pune, 1997.
71. P.G. Jogdand. Dalit Women: Issues and Perspectives. Gyan Publishing House: New Delhi, 1995, p. xii.
72. V. Bhagwat. Dalit Women: Issues and Perspectives. In Jogdand edited, Gyan Publishing House: New Delhi, 1995, p. 2.
73. Sharmila Rege. A dalit feminist standpoint. Seminar 471, November 1998. p. 49.
74. This is a theoretical construct based on the discourse that is unfolding between the Dalits and the dominant castes.
75. Barbara R. Joshi (ed). Untouchable: Voice of the Dalit Liberation Movement. Selectbook Service: New Delhi, 1986, p. 80.

4

Durban and Dalit Discourse

The year 2001 witnessed an animated discussion among the social scientists and intellectuals 'whether caste is race' or 'is caste equal to race' and 'caste may not be race but share many things in common with race' etc. This debate which took place in India in a special way and in South Asia in general was amplified and augmented by the "World Conference Against Racism, Racial Discrimination, Xenophobia and Related Intolerance" (WCAR) held in Durban, South Africa from 31st August to September 7th 2001. The global community was conscious of the growing trends towards the discriminatory behaviour leading to conflict and violence. Durban Conference demanded a new look at the issue of racial discrimination and called for evolving national and international mechanisms to combat the menace of discrimination.

The selection of Durban in South Africa is logical and historical. The First and the Second World Conferences Against Racism were held in Geneva, Switzerland in 1978 and 1983 respectively. The choice of Durban, South Africa for the Third World Conference Against Racism is crucial because it is here that a massive movement was initiated for the defeat of apartheid.[1] Durban also represents the Indian presence in South Africa and it historically represents Gandhi's involvement in the battle against racism. Thus, Durban was an old theatre for recurrent battles and interpretations.[2] But as far as the Indian dominant caste rulers are concerned this conference was slated to deliberate upon the racial discrimination only, and nothing more. They point to those racial discriminatory practices in places like South Africa and demand their elimination at the earliest. But these protagonists of anti-apartheid struggle pretend to close their eyes and ears to the much more horrendous crimes committed on the Dalits and the downtrodden here in India.

Speaking on the need for the World Conference Against Racism, United Nations High Commissioner for Human Rights, Mary Robinson had observed, "Despite continuing efforts by the international community, racial discrimination, ethnic conflicts and widespread violence persist in various parts of the world. In recent years, the world has witnessed campaigns of 'ethnic cleansing'. Racial minorities, migrants, asylum seekers and indigenous peoples are persistent targets of intolerance. Millions of human beings continue to encounter discrimination solely due to the colour of their skin or other factors that indicate the race to which they belong. Effective and early action, as well as early warning measures, are required to prevent the growth of ethnic hatred and potential violence conflicts."[3]

Significantly, Mary Robinson while spelling out the objectives of the World Conference Against Racism, declared on March 31st 2001, "The World Conference is of the highest significance for the international community because the issues it will address are evils which we must combat with all power; because racism and xenophobia-manifesting themselves through discrimination and all forms of intolerance-are the wellsprings of many of the world's conflicts; because they are a key element of the vicious cycle of poverty and social exclusion; and because these forces run directly contrary to the fundamental message of human rights which is that every member of the human family has equal and inalienable rights".[4] Thus, on the one hand, the WCAR provided broader platform for the first time to examine other forms of intolerances. On the other hand, this conference called upon the universal community to unite their efforts to eliminate racial and other forms of discrimination.

This sense of repugnance and abhorrence towards racial and other forms of discrimination did not catch the attention of humanity all of a sudden. Struggle against every form of discrimination and deprivation is as ancient as human history. But after the pronouncement of Universal Declaration of Human Rights, in 1948 the international community has made some strides in trying to combat racism and all forms of intolerances. Both national and international mechanisms have been worked out one reinforcing the other to do away with all forms of deprivation and discrimination. It is common knowledge that one of the major success stories in terms of elimination of racial discrimination engaged collectively by the international community was the breakdown of apartheid in South Africa. This goes to state that one of the reasons for holding the WCAR in South Africa is to reiterate the resolve to do away with discriminatory principles and practices.

The five themes of the conference also reveal the direction the deliberations were supposed to take at Durban.

1. Sources, causes, forms and contemporary manifestations of racism, racial discrimination, xenophobia and related intolerance;
2. Victims of racism, racial discrimination, xenophobia and related intolerance;
3. Measures of prevention, education and protection aimed at the eradication of racism, racial discrimination, xenophobia and related intolerance at the national, regional and international levels;
4. Provision of effective remedies, recourse, redress, compensatory and other measures at the national, regional and international levels;
5. Strategies to achieve full and effective equality, including international cooperation and enhancement of United Nations and other international mechanisms in combating racism, racial discrimination, xenophobia and related intolerance, and follow-up.

During the WCAR, while addressing the delegates at United Nations Research Institute for Social Development (UNRISD)[5] United Nations High Commissioner for Human Rights declared, 'Durban has helped bring into sharper focus the linkages between inequality of treatment - in terms of status, identity, prejudice, and discrimination - and inequality of outcomes – in income, wealth, education, political power, health, housing, marriage and family formation, and other social goods. Durban has also made clear the critical need for improved policy responses and governance reforms to meet the challenges faced'. She noted the broad themes to address: a) the social construction of race and citizenship; b) the social dynamics of racism and inequalities; c) organised responses to cultural diversity; d) the impact of public policies on race relations. She went on to argue that, 'each of these themes provide opportunities to examine the linkages between inequality of treatment and inequality of outcomes, and to make recommendations on how reforms might be implemented. Take as an example the links between unemployment and heightened ethnic tensions. We all know that when jobs are scarce, minority and immigrant communities are often most affected. Immigrants may be accused of taking jobs away from others. This in turn can feed the politics of intolerance and racism. The question is: how can policy makers best address these complex issues?'[6]

The United Nations High Commissioner for Human Rights further reiterated the fact that, 'The segment of your conference, which focuses on the impact of public policies on race relations will address this question, among others. I have stressed repeatedly that this World Conference offers the opportunity to examine what is effective and what is not in rooting out discrimination and exclusion. Already these issues have been receiving attention at parallel events here. At the Global Compact seminar a few days ago there were useful inputs by business people on the pros and cons of affirmative action; a workshop is being organised jointly by my Office and the ILO to look at racism in the workplace; and an interesting panel discussion was arranged by UNDP on racism and development'.[7]

It is amply clear from the above statements that racial discrimination is a pan-world phenomenon. The documents that were circulated from the United Nations Commission for Human Rights had also made it clear that violation of dignity and equality of any person is paramount to violation of basic human rights itself. It had also pointed out that while racism is a universal phenomenon it is practiced in different ways in different regions of the universe. In this regard one also becomes acutely aware of the fact that all modern technology, development and education are a sham. Moreover, racial discrimination is only one form of discriminatory practice.

Run up to WCAR

The World Conferences organized under the aegis of the United Nations is usually seen as an unique opportunity to create a new world vision to fight against various evils that affect the global society. This is also kept in mind that those issues that are not adequately addressed at the local or the national levels could find some space at the international arena. Keeping this in mind, in 1997, the General Assembly of the United Nations decided in its resolution 52/111 to hold the World Conference Against Racism, Xenophobia and Related Intolerances not later than 2001. This decision reflects growing international concern for the rise in the incidents of racism, racial discrimination, xenophobia and related intolerance, and recognition of the challenges and opportunities in combating these phenomena in an increasingly global world.[8] Based on this decision, in 1998 the General Assembly designated United Nations High Commissioner for Human Rights, Mary Robinson, as Secretary General of the Conference.

The Objectives of the World Conference Against Racism as set forth by the General Assembly resolution 52/111 of 12 December 1997 are:

- To review progress made in the fight against racism and racial discrimination, in particular since the adoption of the Universal Declaration of Human Rights, and to reappraisal the obstacles to progress in the filed and identify ways to overcome them;
- To consider ways and means to better ensure the application of existing standards and the implementation of existing instruments to combat racism and racial discrimination;
- To increase the level of awareness about the scourge of racism and racial discrimination;
- To formulate concrete recommendations on ways to increase the effectiveness of the active and mechanism of the United Nations through programmes aimed at combating racism and racial discrimination;
- To review the political, historical, economic, social, cultural and other factors leading to racism and racial discrimination;

- To formulate concrete recommendations to further action-oriented national, regional and international measures aimed at combating all forms of racism and racial discrimination; and
- To draw up concrete recommendations to ensure that the United Nations has the necessary resources for its activities to combat racism and racial discrimination.[9]

As stated above, this WCAR was the third conference organized to deliberate upon the issues related to eradicating racism and other forms of intolerances. Meanwhile many international instruments have been worked out dealing with the issue. One can identify the following mechanisms that directly dealt with this issue: The International Convention on the Elimination of All Forms of Racial Discrimination, 1965 [ICERD]; The International Convention on the Suppression and Punishment of the Crime of Apartheid, 1973. In 1993, the United Nations Commission on Human Rights appointed a Special Rapporteur on Contemporary Forms of Racism, Racial Discrimination, Xenophobia and Related Intolerance. Thus, the decision to hold the Third World Conference Against Racism was a logical outcome of historical and international attempts to root out discrimination.

The preparation for the World Conference Against Racism was undertaken in the following manner:

1. The First Inter-Governmental Meeting was held in Geneva from 1st to 5th May 2000;
2. The Second Inter-Governmental Meeting was also held in Geneva from 21st May to 1st June 2001.

At the first meeting, governments took a number of organizational decisions, including the adoption of the provisional agenda for the conference and its draft rules of procedure.

From 1999 to 2000, Regional Experts Seminars were held in Geneva, Warsaw, Bangkok, Addis Ababa and Santiago de Chile. The objectives of each regional experts seminars was to discuss and identify the issues of priority concerns for that region, to advance the regional dialogue on racism, raise awareness, share information on the issues of racisms and intolerance and to share 'best practices' across the globe. In these seminars some issues specific to these regions came to focus, like: plight of refugees and migrants; trafficking of persons, socio-political conditions of multi-ethnic states, ethnic conflicts etc. These seminars also focused on the remedial measures like protection of minorities, social and economic measures for vulnerable groups and the remedies available for victims of discrimination.[10]

Further, regional intergovernmental meetings were also held to identify the issues and to look for alternative forms of responding to these issues. During October 2000, the European countries met in Strasbourg; the preparatory meeting of the American States took place in Santiago de Chile in December 2000; the African regional preparatory meeting was held in Dakar in January 2001 and in February same year, the Asian groups met in Tehran. The Dakar Declaration and Recommendations for a Programme of Action adopted by African Governments on 24th January 2001 recalls, "...the great importance African peoples attach to the values of solidarity, tolerance and multiculturalism, which constitute the moral ground and the inspiration for our struggle against racism, racial discrimination, xenophobia and related intolerance, inhuman tragedies which Africa has been suffering for too long".[11]

The Asian Preparatory Meeting for the World Conference that met in Tehran denounced racism and reiterated their resolve to do away with racism. "Reaffirm that all human beings are born free and equal in dignity and rights, and that any doctrine of racial superiority is, therefore, scientifically false, morally condemnable, socially unjust and dangerous, and has no justification whatsoever.... Also condemn past and current policies, practices, propaganda and organisations based on or theories of racial and national superiority, hatred discrimination and xenophobia, which are massive and flagrant violations of all human rights and fundamental freedoms, comprising civil, political, economic, social and cultural rights and the right to development".[12]

Member States also held informal consultations in January 2001 where they took stock of the recommendations of six experts seminars that took place from 1999 to 2000. They also discussed the Draft Declaration and Programme of Action that was to be presented, discussed and adopted by the Conference at Durban. Interestingly, the Non-Governmental Organisations also adopted similar process of preparation worldwide.

Elimination of Discrimination: International Scenario

At this juncture it is pertinent to examine the progress made with regard to safeguarding human rights in general and eliminating racial and other forms of discrimination in particular. One of the guiding principles of the United Nations is the principle of non-discrimination on the grounds of race. This principle was clearly stated in the preamble of the Charter of the United Nations, which reaffirms "faith in fundamental human rights, in dignity and worth of the human person". The death, devastation and the disaster that was wrought by the World Wars forced upon human collective sense to uphold and maintain this historical fact that basic human rights of all human beings can be ensured only when the rights of the individuals, social groups, and nations can be maintained. Any discriminatory and differentiating behaviour towards any human being or segment of population ultimately would result in the destruction of all human beings.

Since the adoption of the Universal Declaration of Human Rights in 1948, the international community has made considerable progress in the fight against racism, racial discrimination, xenophobia and related intolerance. Meanwhile, national and international laws have been enacted and numerous international human rights instruments, particularly a treaty to ban racial discrimination, have seen the light of the day. There have even been some spectacular successes, such as the defeat of apartheid in South Africa. Yet, the dream of a world free of racial hatred and bias remains only half fulfilled.

The United Nations Declaration on the Elimination of All Forms of Racial Discrimination (1963) clearly spells out the human endeavour to annihilate all forms of discrimination. "Discrimination between human beings on the ground of race, colour or ethnic origin is an offence to human dignity and shall be condemned as a denial of the principles of Charter of United Nations, as a violation of the human rights and fundamental freedoms proclaimed in the Universal Declaration of Human Rights, as an obstacle to friendly and peaceful relations among nations and as a fact capable of disturbing peace and security among peoples".[13] Thus the Universal Declaration not only takes note of the discriminatory behaviour but also condemns it in categorical terms.

The United Nations right from the beginning was engaged in a number of measures to combat racial discrimination and violence. Some of these efforts that had manifest and latent impact on racial discrimination are presented here below:[14]

- The Convention on the Prevention and Punishment of the Crime of Genocide, 1948;
- The Convention on the Political Rights of Women, 1952;
- Supplementary Convention on the Abolition of Slavery, the Slave Trade and Institutions and Practices Similar to Slavery, 1956;
- The Convention Concerning the Abolition of Forced Labour, 1956;
- The Convention Concerning Discrimination in Respect of Employment and Occupation, 1958;
- The Declaration on the Rights of the Child, 1959;
- The Convention Against Discrimination in Education, 1960;
- The Declaration on the Elimination of All Forms of Racial Discrimination, 1963;
- The International Convention on the Elimination of All Forms of Racial Discrimination, 1965;
- The International Covenant on Economic, Social and Cultural Rights, 1966;
- The International Covenant on Civil and Political Rights, 1966;
- The International Convention on the Suppression and Punishment of the Crime of Apartheid, 1973;
- The Universal Declaration on the Eradication of Hunger and Malnutrition, 1974;
- The Universal Declaration on the Protection of All Persons from Being Subjected to Torture and Other Cruel, Inhuman or Degrading Treatment or Punishment, 1975;

- The First World Conference to Combat Racism and Racial Discrimination, Geneva, 1978;
- The First Decade for Action to Combat Racism and Racial Discrimination, Geneva 1973-82;
- The Second World Conference to Combat Racism and Racial Discrimination, Geneva, 1983;
- The International Convention Against Apartheid in Sports, 1985;
- The Second Decade to Combat Racism and Racial Discrimination, 1983-1992;
- The Third Decade to Combat Racism and Racial Discrimination, 1994-2003;
- The World Conference against Racism, Racial Discrimination, Xenophobia and Related Intolerance, 2001[15]. Durban, South Africa.

These are the universal instruments envisaged by the global community to safeguard the rights of all in general and of the downtrodden in a special way. Moreover, the General Assembly in 1998 decided to proclaim 2001 as the International Year of 'Mobilization against Racism, Racial Discrimination, Xenophobia and Related Intolerance'. The explicit objective of this international exercise was to draw world attention to the objectives of the Conference and to provide a momentum for further political commitment to the elimination of racism and racial discrimination. These planned initiatives provided space for enhancing the awareness at the global level the various forms and levels of discriminations encountered today.

Elimination of Discrimination: Indian Scenario

In India too some serious attempts were made both by the state and the civil society in this direction. It is common knowledge that its course was marked by violations and resistance. Many legendary figures can be recounted who exerted both ideological and operational impact on the prevailing atmosphere to protest against violation of human rights. From the perspective of the Dalits and the Depressed Classes, Dr. Ambedkar was one of those persons who systematically waged a war against the transgression of Dalit human rights. As one of the main architect of framing of the Constitution Dr. Ambedkar fought for fundamental rights of all citizens of India and in a special way made important positive discrimination for the upliftment of the Dalits and the Tribals. We have at length discussed the manifold contribution of Dr. Ambedkar in denouncing untouchability and also examined his contribution with regard to their emancipation.

Over the years, the ruling caste and class also engaged itself in various welfare measures for the upliftment of the Dalits and the downtrodden. The State enacted legislative measures to protect the Dalits from atrocities and to ensure their development. Some of these provisions are as follows:

- The Constitution (First Amendment) Act 1951, enjoining upon the State to make special provisions for the advancement of weaker sections;[16]
- The Protection of Civil Rights (Anti-Untouchability) Act 1955;
- The Bonded Labour (Abolition) Act, 1976;
- The Scheduled Castes and the Scheduled Tribes (Prevention of Atrocities) Act, 1989 [For the full text, refer to Appendix 1];
- The National Commission for Scheduled Castes and the Scheduled Tribes 1990;
- Employment of Manual Scavengers and Construction of Dry Latrines (Prohibition) Act, 1993.

These are some of the Acts passed and commissions constituted by the central government. Besides these, Acts like land reform and abolition of money lending etc., also were supposed to be directed towards the benefits of the Dalits. Following the steps of the central government, the states too constituted different commissions and enacted welfare programmes. For example, the state of Tamil Nadu enacted the Tamil Nadu Acquisition of Land for Harijan Welfare Scheme Act 1978. The Bihar government came out with the Bihar Reservation of Vacancies in Posts and Services (for SC, ST and OBC) Act 1991.

Irrespective of all these constitutional provisions, the socio-economic conditions of the Dalits deteriorated further. This is because the Dalits were not only discriminated against but they were also deprived of basic necessities of life. This forced them to depend upon the dominant castes who in turn exploited them to the maximum. Since the dominant castes were the ones who had to ensure that justice is carried out, there was no possibility of Dalits ever obtaining justice that the Constitution has legalised. Moreover, even in the international forums it is the upper caste bureaucrats and officials who represented the country and hence they never exposed the caste discrimination the Dalits were subjected too.

In the international arena, the issue of caste discrimination was raised as a point for discussion very late. In 1969, India ratified the Convention on the Elimination of all forms of Racial Discrimination (CERD) 1965, in 1969. But none of the Indian delegates ever brought before the UN body the caste discrimination or consider caste discrimination as another form of racial discrimination. Only in 1996 the CERD Committee made its first explicit reference to various forms of caste discriminations, untouchability, and Scheduled Castes etc. This is the view expressed by the Committee, "The Committee states that the term 'descent' mentioned in Article 1 of the Convention does not solely refer to race. The Committee affirms that the situation of the Scheduled Castes and Scheduled Tribes fall within the scope of the Convention on the elimination of All Forms of Racial Discrimination".[17] This was also a bold step in the direction of recognising caste and racial discrimination against the Dalits and the Tribals as similar to racial discrimination practiced elsewhere.

The UN body having spelt out in clear and categorical terms that the deplorable condition of the Dalits and the Tribals falls within the purview of racial discrimination, called upon the Indian ruling caste-class to enact special provisions to eliminate caste discrimination. "Special measures be taken by authorities to prevent acts of discrimination towards Scheduled Castes and Scheduled Tribes and in cases where such acts have been committed, to conduct through investigations, to punish those responsible and provide just and adequate reparation to the victims".[18] But since the perpetrators of atrocities on the Dalits and the Tribals were themselves the upper caste and they were also the ruling class, there was no point in demanding from them that the guilty should be punished. With regard to caste discrimination, the accused and the judge both were the upper castes. This ruled out any possibility of punishment to those who discriminated against the Dalits and the Tribals.

While the dominant castes and the ruling caste continued to turn a blind eye to the atrocities heaped upon the Dalits, the UN bodies kept on demanding various action measures. For example they demanded, "A continuing campaign be undertaken to educate the Indian population on human rights, in line with India's Constitution and universal human rights instruments including CERD and aimed at eliminating the institutionalised thinking of the high caste and the low caste (read exploited caste) mentality".[19] The measure proposed by the UN bodies was in the right direction. But these bodies were not aware of the fact that in the heinous and skewed caste stratification of India, it is not the human rights of the individual that is accepted but the caste rights are upheld as the fundamental rights.

From the responses that the committee was receiving it realised that it is not the dearth of constitutional provisions or legal measures that has resulted in the dehumanised state of the Dalits and the Tribals in India but the lack of political will which is the real reason. The Committee argued in clear terms, "It is noted that although constitutional provisions and legal tests exist to abolish untouchability and to protect the members of the Scheduled Castes and Tribes, and although social and educational policies have been adopted to improve the situation of members of scheduled castes and tribes and to protect them from abuses, widespread discrimination against them and the relative impunity of those who abuse them point to the limited effort of these measures. The Committee is particularly concerned at reports that people belonging to the Scheduled Castes and Scheduled Tribes are often prevented from using public wells or from entering cafes or restaurants and that their children are sometimes separated from other children in school, in violation of Article of 5 (f) of the Convention".[20]

Going further one can also identify similar performance by the Government of India. The International Convention on Civil and Political Rights (ICCPR) was ratified by the ruling dispensation of India only in 1973. But the Committee itself took another 20 years to expose the Indian Government's lack of political will in implementing these rights. The Committee noted in its report [1997], "Despite measures taken by the government, members of the Scheduled Castes and Scheduled Tribes, as well as the so-called backward classes and ethnic and national minorities continue to endure severe social discrimination and to suffer disproportionately from many violations of their rights under the Covenant, *inter alia*, inter-caste violence, bonded labour and discrimination of all kinds. It regrets that the de facto perpetuation of the caste system entrenches social differences and contributes to these violations. The Committee also recommended that further measures be adopted, including education programmes at national and state levels to combat all forms of discrimination against these vulnerable groups".[21]

One of the instruments employed by the United Nations was to appoint a Special Rapporteur to investigate into an issue that calls for international attention. During 1996 and 1997, the UN Special Rapporteur on Racism and Racial Discrimination enquired with the Indian Government about the situation of 'untouchables' in the country, requesting the relevant information to be sent to his office. The Special Rapporteur's report exposes the real intent of ruling dispensation of the country. "The report recalls that communications concerning the situation of untouchables in India were sent to the government in December 1996 and August 1997. In its reply, the government rejected allegations that it tolerated untouchability, provided the Special Rapporteur with a list of the measures taken to curb discrimination between castes and maintained that a practice that is so old can not be eliminated soon. The Special Rapporteur noted the discrepancy between the facts alleged and the government's reply and stated that a visit to India would permit him to evaluate the situation in cooperation with the government and the communities concerned".[22]

It is significant to note that the Indian Government till date has not permitted the Special Rapporteur to visit India. Hence, the Committee reported that, "The Committee is concerned with the continuing discrimination, including violence, suffered by women of the Dalit community, despite the passage of the Scheduled Castes and the Scheduled Tribes (Prevention of Atrocities) Act of 1989". The government of India often employs some social anthropologists to demonstrate that caste is different from race.

The Subcommission on Promotion and Protection of Human Rights met on 9th August 2001 discussed Discrimination on the Basis of Work and Descent. The Subcommission Expert R.K.W Goonesekere stated in his report, "Discrimination based on work or descent was based on long history and had serious consequences for individuals belonging to various groups and communities. These were placed at the lower end of a hierarchical order". In his report he noted about India, "India had taken steps, to improve the plight of the Dalits, including through affirmative action programmes first undertaken more than 50 years ago. Yet these efforts had very little effect, and she had been shaken by some of the details of discrimination against Dalits she had come across".[23]

Against this realistic perception of the situation, Ambassador Savitri Kundai of India disputed some of the findings in the working paper. She argued that the working paper overlooked recent constitutional amendments and it failed to take note of the progress that India had made with the castes in question, including one of the far reaching affirmative action programmes in the world. The Ambassador following the line of argument presented by the Indian ruling class in similar international arena repeatedly highlighted the great benefits that have accrued to the Dalits due to affirmative action. Further, the Ambassador also vehemently defended the fact that atrocities on the Dalits are on the decrease.[24]

As stated above while many intellectuals, activists and organisations and other human rights activists tried to raise the issue in national as well as in the international forums, the ruling dispensation tried to throttle all their attempts. At the preparatory meeting for the World Conference Against Racism, held in Tehran in February 2001, the Indian government reiterated its stand once again. It stated that 'introducing caste into the ambit of the WCAR at Durban would amount to diluting the issue of racial discrimination'. Moreover, the Indian official delegation unraveled the agenda of the ruling dispensation. It stated in unequivocal terms that 'the problem of caste is internal and therefore out of the purview of the UN'.

This attitude and the behaviour of the Indian ruling class are not unprecedented. It has always taken a highly parochial stand on issues when its interests are at stake. That is the reason why it would go all out to project its so called traditional stance that apartheid is the serious issue affecting the world and all efforts should be directed to put an end to it. By speaking so, the ruling dispensation of India is projecting an image that it is interested in global issues and also that it has set its own house in order.

Soli Sorabjee, the Auditor General of India once again with the upper caste mindset upheld the view that ' no country is immune from the virus of racism whose roots lie in the hearts and the minds of the people'. This is to project that one is broadminded and is against any form of discrimination. But in the usual shrewdness he went on to decry the attempt to raise the caste issue in the world conference. "There are some misconceived attempts by some NGOs to equate racism with caste-based discrimination which is based on birth and occupation and has nothing to do with the race of a person'.[25]

It is a historical accident that within the western framework racism did not include casteism. And hence, caste discrimination was not considered equal to racial discrimination. Similarly since the issues of indigenous people are a global phenomenon, they found reception among the UN bodies and other agents. But since caste and caste discrimination was an Indian phenomenon or at the most the South-Asian phenomenon, it never found favour in the international bodies. But the heart of the matter is that if a category does not fit neatly into the definition of internationally dominant communities or countries it does not mean that discrimination is absent in another country or in other forms. Since racism is defined from the western paradigm, casteism is 'eliminated' from their purview, irrespective of the fact that a more appalling and dreadful form of discrimination is practiced in the caste-ridden society.

Caste-Race Debate

At this juncture it is expedient to look at some of the ways in which caste has been interpreted in relation to race. The term caste has been defined in a number of different ways. As a noun it is used to refer to an abstract principle based on which certain behaviours are carried out in society. The noun form also is used to denote a particular kind of social group. As an adjective the term caste is employed to signify the quality of the principles of behaviour or the character of the social group. Going into the root of the matter one notices the following evolution of the term. "The Portuguese seafarers who traded mainly on the west coast of India in the 16th and 17th centuries described groups they called *castas* (from which derive the English and French words caste), meaning 'species' or 'breeds' of animals or plants and 'tribes', 'races', 'clans', or 'lineages' among men".[26] Since the reality of caste was defined by the westerners the understanding of this phenomenon also took an alien form. The Indian dominant caste also used this understanding to argue in all the forums that racism does not exist in India.

Even a sociological understanding of the term *jati* brings out some of the salient features of the interface between caste and race. "One of the commonest words for genus in most Indian languages, *jati*, is derived from an Indo-European verbal root meaning 'genesis', 'origin', or 'birth'. It is applied to any species of living things including gods and humans. Among humans, *jati* can designate a distinct sex, a race, a caste, or a tribe, a population, the followers of an occupation or a religion, or a nation".[27] Thus in sociological understanding often race and caste are inter-changeably used. This type of understanding also takes into account the descent-based occupation by the members of a particular caste.

Here, a brief note on race will not be out of place. Classically, the differences among the races in a species have been identified by their morphology, that is, their observable physical structure. In the sociological understanding, race is a biological concept. Races are recognised by a combination of geographic, ecological and morphological factors and, increasingly, in the last third of the twentieth century, by analysis of the distribution of gene frequencies for numbers of essentially non-morphological, biochemical components. As long as one focused on the morphological traits alone, it was sometimes not difficult to convince oneself that races were distinctly differentiated, one from another. But the moment one moved away from explaining race within biological arena, other considerations of race came to the fore demanding a serious comprehension.

The term race is a sociological concept like any other word to explain the social grouping of a society. Though the term race sounds a neutral reality, interaction between two different races exposes the racial discrimination inherent in this interaction. There are also the notion of racial purity, superior and inferior races, race and mental differences, race and culture. Racially discriminatory practices make certain assumptions about race, some overt, some tacit. These include the assumptions that races are pure and distinct entities; all members of a race look alike and think alike, which assumption, in turn is based upon the idea that how one behaves depends entirely or mainly on one's genes; some races are better than others. But the scientific study of human population has provided no evidence to validate any one of these assumptions. Culture, language and outlook are not inseparably bound up with particular morphological or genetic racial features.[28]

In extension it can be stated that caste is also a concept used by a particular segment of human population to understand social groupings as race is used to understand social stratification in another socio-cultural milieu. Though race and caste are two different concepts utilised in two different social settings, both of them are employed to explain social groupings of human race. Further, if one ventures to enter into the ideology of discrimination and the principles that provide the basis for discriminatory behaviour, one would encounter social seclusion and segregation operative in both the cases. Above all, both in racial and caste discrimination not just social grouping is at stake but political domination, cultural deprivation and economic exploitation are at the foundation. Thus, a serious and deeper comprehension of racial and caste discrimination would lead to the understanding that caste and race are two different concepts to refer to similar social discriminatory principles and practices.

The Amnesty International in its report 2001, "Racism and the Administration of Justice" argues, "Racism is an attack on the very notion of universal human rights. It systematically denies certain people their full human rights just because of their colour, race, ethnicity, descent or national origin. It is an assault on a fundamental principle underlying the Universal Declaration of Human Rights (UDHR) – that human rights are everyone's birthright and apply to all without distinction. It undermines all human rights, be they civil, political, economic, social or cultural".[29] The report goes on to lament the fact that inspite of very many national and international tools for the eradication of racism, racial discrimination persists in different forms today.

Caste- Race and Social Scientists

It is also interesting to note how some of the armchair social scientists have responded to the entire debate on caste and race in the run up to World Conference Against Racism. Prof. Andre Beteille of Delhi University argued that "Interested parties within and outside the UN would like to bring caste discrimination in general and the practice of untouchability in particular within the purview of racial discrimination. The practice of untouchability is indeed reprehensible and must be condemned by one and all; but that does not mean that we must begin to regard it as a form of racial discrimination. The Scheduled Castes of India taken together are no more a race than are the Brahmins taken together. Every social group cannot be regarded as race simply because we want to protect it against prejudice and discrimination. ... We cannot throw out the concept of race by the front door when it is misused for asserting social superiority and bring it again through the back door to misuse it in the cause of the oppressed. The metaphor of race is a dangerous weapon whether it is used for asserting white supremacy or making demands on the basis of disadvantaged groups".[30]

Beteille represents the typical Indian colonial-upper caste mindset. It is colonial because it is ethnocentric in its totality. An ethnocentric mindset always regards the attempts by the other communities as not adhering to the 'proper way of proceeding while arguing ones case'. Beteille has done precisely this when he jumbles with the words saying that 'you throw it by the front door and bring it through the backdoor'.[31] Further the comments of Beteille also exhibit a dominant caste mindset. This is clear from the statement 'the practice of untouchability is reprehensible and must be condemned by one and all". This is how a typical upper caste mindset works. They project themselves as person above caste feelings and practices. But in private practice caste discrimination. This is obvious from the fact that the intellectuals like Beteille would not be ready even for the sake of discussion to place caste discrimination at the same plain with racial discrimination. While these social scientists immediately react to issues raised by the Dalit intellectuals and activists, they will not react to atrocities committed on the Dalits and downtrodden or to the anti-people policies enacted by the ruling elite.

In sharp contrast to mainline social scientists there are other intellectuals who have exposed the monstrous nature of caste discrimination. Kalpana Kannabiran highlights 'In the Draft Declaration on Gender and Racism drafted in February 2001, the National Federation of Dalit Women (NFDW) resolved to fight the specific oppression of women from marginalised groups, whose situation as Dalit/Indigenous/Minority is only compounded by their being women. Apart from the fact of social exclusion at various levels, the NFDW asserted that "descent based discrimination based on caste results in the violent appropriation of and sexual control over Dalit women by men of the dominant castes, evident in the systemic rape of Dalit women and the perpetuation of forced prostitution in the name of religion through the *devadasi* system".[32]

At this stage it is also imperative to keep in focus the understanding of caste maintained by some of the international bodies and countries. As stated above since racial discrimination was the most visible form of discrimination and since it is prevalent in many countries the international bodies and human right groups waged a struggle against racism and apartheid. But it took ages for the international bodies to recognise the fact that caste discrimination is equal to or even more horrendous than racial discrimination. While some of the westerners perceive the dehumanising effect of caste discrimination, some others fail to perceive this reality.

WCAR, Caste Discrimination and Indian Government

The stand taken by the Indian Government on the whole issue of whether caste discrimination should be taken to WCAR for discussion or that caste discrimination should form one of the agendas of the WCAR was deplorable. The ruling dispensation was of the view that caste is not an issue to be deliberated upon in the UN conferences. It even raised this phobia that if UN bodies discuss caste issue during the WCAR, then these bodies are infringing upon the sovereignty of the country. The Indian Government further argued, that the World Conference was to deliberate upon racial discrimination and the UN should not redirect its attention from discussing a 'burning international issue'. Much more hilarious was the fact that the political establishment of the country also saw 'undesirable and foreign hands' which are trying to dilute the focus of present conference by insisting on including all forms of discrimination. Above all, the ruling caste and class was spreading this myth that the Indian State has produced enough legal mechanisms and provisions to tackle caste discrimination.

To succeed in its attempts, the government had appointed a National Committee to look into the question of including caste discrimination on the agenda of World Conference Against Racism. The task of this Committee was to evolve consensus on the official government position at the UN conference. But in reality, the ruling elite by appointing this committee succeeded in attaining two goals with one stroke. By appointing a committee of this nature, they have projected an image that the Indian government is serious about the issue of discrimination. Secondly, by appointing a high level committee of this nature, the government had ensured the presence of a strong contingence in the UN Conference to throttle every attempt made by the Dalit intellectuals and activists.

It is significant that the 28 member Committee was once again a slap on the face of the Dalit and downtrodden communities. This is because, this Committee had more people from dominant castes who are usually against the Dalits. Hence, Dalit intellectuals, activists, human rights activists and concerned citizens expressed their distrust in the credibility of this Committee. In a memorandum handed over to the representatives of the United Nations, these people stated that they do not have confidence in the so-called National Committee set up by the Prime Minister Atal Bihari Vajpayee for the Durban Conference. They argued that the Indian government was trying to stop such a discussion at Durban in a naked display of the prejudiced casteist policy of the ruling political parties and classes. They also feared that the committee would only articulate the point of view of the religious and social groups who have subjugated the Dalits through the millennia [For the entire text refer to Appendix 2].[33]

At this juncture it is expedient to examine the manner in which other countries have responded to the issue of caste discrimination. Teesta Setalvad in her analysis exposes the fact that "In stark contrast to the Indian governmental position was the Nepal government's candour on the same issue, confronted as it is with recent assertions of Nepali Dalits who account for not less than 15 percent of the total population. The government of the only Hindu Kingdom in the world openly admitted that caste is the source of acute discrimination and segregation within Nepal. This, it held, was a serious issue that falls under the theme of the forthcoming conference and should, therefore, form part of the official deliberations at the WCAR at Durban".[34]

The Dalits of Nepal were better placed than their Indian counterparts, when it came to representing their cause at the domestic and in international arena. Under the forum National Dalit NGO Preparatory Committee for WCAR, Nepal, the Dalit activists, intellectuals and human rights activists took a bold step. For instance they demanded, "Making the case for ending caste-based discrimination, an admission of the truth, reconciliation through affirmative action and the formation of a UN Dalit Commission for South Asia".[35] The Government of Nepal while did not make any major move to include caste discrimination as one of the agendas of WCAR, it atleast did not block the Dalit activists from participating in the conference and raising the issue.

The Indian Government stood exposed on another ground too. Instead of being magnanimous and accepting before the world community that the discrimination of the Dalits is going on unabated even after all the legal measures enacted by the Independent India, the Government delegation deemed it essential to critique those who spearheaded the Dalit cause. Mr. Omar Abdullah, Minister of State for External Affairs who led the Indian delegation in his address at the WCAR stated "In the run up to the World Conference, there has been propaganda, highly exaggerated and misleading, often based on anecdotal evidence, regarding caste-based discrimination in India. We in India have faced this evil squarely" [See Appendix 3 for entire text of the speech by Omar Abdullah]. Mr. Abdulla instead of being applauded for his statement was decried by many delegates. The Indian dailies are full of incidents of atrocities committed on the Dalits every day. Does Mr. Abdullah read newspapers?[36]

The negative stand taken by the Indian government was irrespective of the fact that the UN General Secretary Kofi Annan urged the leaders to guide national dialogue on racism. He stated, 'With your power as leaders, you can move the machinery of government to put in place the constitutional, legislative and administrative guarantees that protect against discrimination. From your position, you can tackle the problems that fuel intolerance, such as employment... The path ahead must be one of dialogue: inclusive and constructive, with give and take, respect and mutual understanding. But more than any agreement on a document reached here in Durban, it is real progress in people's day-to-day lives that will be the ultimate test of whether this Conference succeeds.'[37] This seemed to be only a wishful thinking since the Indian state did not even allow a discussion on the issue during the conference.

Mary Robinson, the UN High Commissioner for Human Rights went one step further and called for greater generosity. She said "Three things I would ask for in the week ahead from all parties and especially from delegates:

- the first is generosity of spirit. It is no small issue we are dealing with in Durban: it is no time to be small-minded.
- secondly, I call for flexibility and a willingness to meet the views of the others. Progress can only be made on that basis and the urgency of devising new strategies to combat racism and discrimination requires it.
- finally, I would appeal for a sense of vision. I remain convinced that this can be a defining moment for the international community that we have the capacity at the start of this century to work for a better and fairer world.[38]

Thabo Mbeki, the President of South Africa addressing the Delegates of the World Conference, stated 'We have gathered as we have, because we are united in our resolve to ensure that every human being leads a life of dignity. We meet here because we are determined to ensure that nobody anywhere should be subjected to the insult and offence of being despised by another or others because of his or her race, colour, nationality or origin. Together we are committed to the realisation of the objective that every human being should enjoy human rights as equals with other human beings, with every right and possibility to determine both their future and the destiny of their countries. To these masses, human solidarity is not a foreign concept. To them, this world conference must convey the message that the peoples of the world are inspired by a new internationalism that says that we are determined to unite in action to repair the gross human damage that was caused in the past. It must inspire them with the knowledge that as government, as non-governmental organisations, as countries and as peoples, were are ready now, to dedicate our minds, our skills and our resources to the creation of a new world free of racism, racial discrimination, xenophobia and related intolerances.[39]

All these pleas made by the UN authorities and leaders of other countries fell on deaf years with regard to Indian political establishment. The ruling class of India not only tried to stifle the efforts of the Dalit activists, intellectuals and human rights activists of India and abroad from raising the issue at the international forum but also tried to discredit those who tried to do so. Significantly, the ruling class in Nepal allowed their citizens to raise the issue at the WCAR. It is reported that in the Tehran Conference Nepal officially admitted that caste is a concern in South Asia but India was able to pressurize Nepal to withdraw this stand.[40] With regard to India, since the upper castes and upper classes can survive and thrive only by depriving and discriminating against the Dalits they are not ready to accept the fact that caste discrimination is inherent in the Indian social order and this needs to be squarely looked. The deep-rooted caste bias has minimized even the limited space provided by democratic polity.

WCAR and The National Human Rights Commission

The National Human Rights Commission's (NHRC) clear and categorical stand that the inclusion of Dalit discrimination as one of the agenda of the WCAR gave unprecedented support to the Dalit struggle. This is contrary to the Government's stand as discussed above which continued to project that the caste discrimination is an internal issue. And the government also was engaged in the debate 'caste is race' or 'caste is not race'. The bold stand of the National Human Rights Commission was lauded by the Commissioner for United Nations Human Rights Commission (UNHRC), who declared that, "I congratulate the principled stand taken by the NHRC, which stood up to help the Dalits and extended moral support".[41] Ms. Robinson also took note of the manner in which the Dalit activists and human rights activists highlighted the plight of the Dalits and other discriminated masses due to which the issue was brought before the international community.

In contrast to the stand taken by the Government of India, the NHRC took issue-based approach. Justice K. Ramasamy, Member NHRC who represented the NHRC drew attention of all who were present at Durban to the historical roots of discrimination as well as the assertion to do away with discrimination. "There has never been a UN Conference where there has been such a strong quest for the recognition of historical injustices"; and asserted that: "In different parts of the world, people are hurting because of problems of inequality or injustice and are pressing their case at this Conference." Indeed, no part of the world is exempt from such pain. India is no exception [For the full text of the speech see Appendix 4].

Justice Ramasamy went on to highlight the issue of caste discrimination in India and the measures that need to be taken to eliminate discrimination. "The National Human Rights Commission of India, for which I have the honour of speaking at this Conference, has therefore considered it its duty to listen attentively to those in our country who have been the victims of historical injustices, and who are hurting because of discrimination and inequality. I refer in particular to those who, under our Constitution, comprise the Scheduled Castes and Scheduled Tribes - the Dalits and Adivasis of India - with the protection of whose human rights our Commission is itself deeply involved. It was to hear their voices, and to benefit from an exchange of views with them, and with eminent jurists, academics and human rights activists, that our Commission organized two major consultations in August 2001, in Bangalore and Delhi respectively, as steps preparatory to the formulation of the views of our Commission for this Conference. The Commission has naturally also taken note of the discussions leading to the drafting of the document that has been submitted by the Preparatory Committee to this Conference, and in particular of the individual liberty guaranteed by the Constitution or embodied in the International Covenants".[42]

The National Human Rights Commission did not just make an eloquent speech at Durban and then stay content. It had also organized National Seminar-cum-Public Consultation at Bangalore and New Delhi on 3rd and 11th August 2001 respectively just before the commencement of Durban Conference.[43] The NHRC had invited academicians, intellectuals, human rights activists and Dalit activists for these seminars and based on the deliberations it formed its own opinion about caste discrimination. Maintaining its stand that caste discrimination is historical injustice it also supported the move to present caste discrimination as one of the agendas in the World Conference Against Racism. This stand of the NHRC is all the more significant because the National Commission for Scheduled Castes and Scheduled Tribes did not deem it necessary to issue a statement on the entire debate or the issue at hand.

WCAR, Caste Discrimination and Dalit Activists

There were many efforts by individual Dalit and human rights activists as well as Dalit and human rights organisations and forums to make the caste discrimination visible in the international arena. Here it is expedient to review the campaign undertaken by the National Campaign on Dalit Human Rights or what came to be popularly known as NCDHR.[44] Historically speaking, the NCDHR was launched in December 1998 by concerned human rights activists who worked among Dalits and were studying the effectiveness of the implementation of Scheduled Caste and Scheduled Tribe (Prevention of Atrocities) Act, 1989 in different states of India.

Though the National Campaign on Dalit Human Rights began as a forum that tried to examine the effective functioning of the Prevention of Atrocities Act 1955, in course of time it became a platform, which provided scope and space for Dalit and human rights activists and intellectuals to seriously take the issue of Dalit discrimination to the international arena. But there is another important aspect to the NCDHR. That is, it was led by the Dalit human rights activists and intellectuals with the support and solidarity from movements and organisations committed to women, labour and human rights, as well as academicians, intellectuals and other peoples organisations and institutions throughout the country who work to protect and promote the human rights of Dalits. Thus, this Campaign became a broad platform for Dalit, downtrodden and other exploited masses of India.

Here instead of going into the details it is appropriate to highlight the programmes conducted by the National Campaign on Dalit Human Rights.

1. A memorandum on the social condition of the Dalits was presented to Shri. K.R. Narayan, the honourable President of India in December 1998.
2. In April 1999, the NCDHR Published the Black Paper: Broken Promises and Dalits Betrayed, which documents overall situation affecting Dalit rights all over India. Through this publication, the campaign group demanded a white paper from the ruling class of India.

3. The National Dalit Women's Conference was held on 8th December 1999 in New Delhi. Over 300 women delegates from all over India participated in the conference and they worked out Dalit Women's Charter of Gender Rights and Demands.
4. The Campaign undertook a massive nationwide signature campaign and gave a memorandum to Shri. Atal Bihari Vajpayee, the honourable Prime Minister on 9th December 1999 with 25,00,000 signatures, denouncing the discrimination the Dalits are subjected to in an independent country and also called for elimination of these discrimination.
5. The NCDHR organized National Public Hearing in May 2000, where independent jury heard 54 cases of Dalit atrocities from 14 Indian states, in the presence of members of National Human Rights Commission and National Commission on Scheduled Castes and Scheduled Tribes.
6. The Campaign also held Global Conference Against Racism and Caste Based Discrimination, Occupation and Descent Based Discrimination Against Dalits 1st – 4th March 2001 in New Delhi. The participants included delegates from Srilanka, Nepal, Bangladesh, Pakistan, USA, UK, Netherlands, Germany, Denmark, Canada and from other countries and delegates from all over India.
7. On 3rd July 2001, the NCDHR organized the global protest day to object to Indian Government's act of blocking the inclusion of caste discrimination in the agenda of WCAR.
8. The Campaign also organized Pre-Durban National Conference – cum – Training 13th – 15th August 2001 in Hyderabad to prepare the delegates going to Durban so as to make the caste discrimination visible in the international arena.
9. The NCDHR organized and mobilized over 200 Dalit activists, intellectuals and human rights activists to participate in the WCAR and pressed for the inclusion of caste discrimination in the agenda of WCAR.[45]

Over and above, the National Campaign on Dalit Human Rights undertook the following activities: Anti-Untouchability Weeks; Rallies, Marches and Public Meetings; Exhibitions and Cultural Programmes; Fact-Finding Investigations; Meeting with Dalit Politicians and Members of Parliament; Press Meets and Interviews; Legal Aid and Awareness Camps; Awareness Seminars & Workshops on Human Rights; Posters, Handbills and Pamphlet campaigns; Dalit Scholars, Writers and Cultural Persons meets etc. Thus innumerable activities were carried at the local, state and national levels.

These raised the awareness of the Dalit masses and the non-Dalits and made them to examine the caste system. At the international level, the NCDHR carried out the campaign at three fronts: Formation and activities of International Dalit Solidarity Networks; Programmes undertaken by the International Human Rights activists; and finally, advocacy and lobbying efforts at the UN level and in different countries.[46] Just before the World Conference Against Racism, the Government of India announced a National Committee for Durban Conference to represent its viewpoints in the WCAR. The National Campaign for Dalit Human Rights sent a memorandum to the United Nations expressing its no confidence in the Prime Minister Atal Behari Vajpayee's National Committee. They also reiterated the demand of the Dalits that Durban Conference on Racial Discrimination should discuss Casteism [For the full text of the memorandum see Appendix 5].[47]

The NCDHR has further carried out the campaign even after the WCAR held in Durban in 2001. As stated above, though the issue of caste discrimination was not included as one of the issues of racial discrimination in the WCAR, the Campaign was successful in the sense of providing visibility to the discrimination suffered by the Dalits. The representatives of the NCDHR were also present in the UN CERD 61 Session Geneva, Switzerland, 10 August 2002 and presented the matter. Thus, the four-year campaign in the final analysis provided the necessary scope and space for the Dalit intellectuals and activists to represent their cause at the WCAR.

Dalit Discourse at Durban

The representatives of the global community who were present for the NGO forum could identify four major burning issues that caught the imagination of everyone in Durban and the entire human body. These were: the Palestinian Struggle for Statehood; the struggle of the Dalit for emancipation and liberation from the clutches of caste system; the issue of 'Landlessness is Racial discrimination' in Africa; the struggle for Self-determination of the Indigenous Peoples. Significantly, the last three issues have many aspects in common and thus there was an instinctive support and solidarity towards each other.

A careful reading of the processes that took place in Durban conference unravels the fact that the discourse about discrimination of the Dalits has moved from the internal arena to the international forum. Both in the NGO Forum as well as in the Inter-Governmental Conference, discrimination of the Dalits found an echo. Any serious analyst would discern the inclusion of caste discrimination in the WCAR NGO Forum Declaration as a historical success of the Dalit movement in contemporary history. There are critics who would immediately argue that there is not even a mention of caste in the WCAR Declaration. They would also point out that even the earlier inclusion of descent and occupation based discrimination has been deleted. The argument is accepted that if caste discrimination were included, there would have been lots of space for putting pressure on the Indian Government to enact what it ratified under the United Nations treatise. Though this did not come through, all is not lost. The WCAR NGO Forum Declaration also provides scope for Dalit discourse.[48]

Here below we present those Articles that deal with caste discrimination both in the Declaration and in the Programme of Action.[49]

A. The WCAR NGO Forum Declaration

84. Work and descent based discrimination, including caste discrimination and untouchability, being a historically entrenched, false ideological construct sanctioned by religion and culture, which

is hereditary in nature and affects over 300 million people in the Asia Pacific and African regions at the personal, social and structural levels, irrespective of their religious affiliation.

85. The practice of untouchability, rooted in the caste system, stigmatises 260 million Dalits in South Asia as 'polluted' or 'impure', thereby denying them entry into places of religious worship, participation in religious festivals, assigning them menial and degrading work including cleaning toilets, skinning and disposal of dead animals, digging graves and sweeping, and the forced prostitution of Dalit women and girls through the traditional system of temple prostitution (Devadasi).

86. The system of 'Hidden apartheid' based on caste practices of distinction, exclusion and restrictions denies Dalits' enjoyment of their economic, social, political, cultural and religious rights, exposing them to all forms of violence and manifests itself in the segregation of housing settlements and cemeteries, segregation in tea stalls ('two-cup' system), denial of access to common drinking water, restaurants, places of worship, restrictions on marriage and other insidious measures all of which inhibit their development as equals.

87. Caste discrimination and 'untouchability' practised against generations of Dalits for centuries together amounts to systemic 'generational and cultural Daliticide', which is the mass-scale destruction of their individual and collective identity, dignity and self-respect for generations through cultural methods and practices.

88. Any action or even any sign of an attempt to act by Dalits either individually or collectively to assert their rights is met with extreme measures of violence such as burning or destruction of their homes, property and crops, social boycott, rape or gang rape of Dalit women and murder by dominant caste individuals or groups, police or the bureaucracy, and that in such instances the State often acts with impunity and in connivance with these perpetrators.

89. Work and descent based discrimination against the Buraku people of Japan has existed for over 400 years and continues to be experienced today by over 3 million people in relation to marriage, employment and education, with new forms of discrimination emerging such as discriminatory propaganda and incitement to discrimination against them, especially on the Internet.

90. The vulnerability of the victims of work and descent based discrimination, including caste discrimination and untouchability, is aggravated by legal systems and law enforcement machinery that fail to protect them and hence are responsible for the continued perpetuation of discrimination, and by States that are themselves often the law-breakers.

B. The WCAR NGO Forum Programme of Action

267. Enact suitable legislation to recognise and eradicate discrimination based on work and descent, including caste discrimination and untouchability against Dalits, Buraku people and other affected communities, in those countries where such legislation does not exist; and in countries where legislation banning such discrimination already exists, take immediate steps to create transparent and effective monitoring mechanisms including the establishment of time-bound programmes to ensure effective implementation of such legislation, even where the perpetrators are States or State agents.

268. Declare work and descent based discrimination, including caste discrimination and untouchability, as Crimes against Humanity and enact and enforce legislation to guarantee the right to life and security, particularly the women and children of these communities, to criminalise violence, atrocities and incitement to discrimination and violence committed against these communities, and to effectively and speedily prosecute offenders at all levels.

269. Enforce speedy and effective legal and programmatic measures to abolish the traditional practice of the Devadasi system and to rehabilitate the Dalit women and improve the quality of their lives by giving them access to arable lands, proper housing, gainful employment and education.

270. Undertake a survey of the situation of the Buraku people in Japan to ascertain the nature and extent of the discrimination they continue to face despite the enactment of temporary 'Special Measures' by the Government of Japan, and take all necessary

legal, administrative and other measures to eradicate such discrimination.

271. Ensure that these communities, who have contributed to the nation-building process through their massive but unrecognised and silent labour, are protected by law from exploitation of their labour, including the implementation of laws that provide for a living wage and prohibit child labour, bonded labour and manual scavenging. Also implement laws relating to land reform that would guarantee access to and control of land for these communities, and ensure that these lands are officially registered in the name of women of these communities.

272. Create and strengthen transparent policies and systems of affirmative action, irrespective of religious affiliation, that enhance the access of these communities, especially their women, to higher government posts, including scientific institutions, and to posts in the government administration, the judiciary, law enforcement agencies and the private sector, including multinational corporations.

273. Allocate adequate funds to guarantee the enjoyment of their rights to livelihood, land, education, housing, potable water, sanitation, health and employment opportunities, with special emphasis on their women, and establish effective monitoring mechanisms to ensure full and proper utilisation of available funds.

274. Undertake mass-scale public awareness raising and educational initiatives, with the active support of NGOs and other segments of civil society, in order to promote positive changes in attitudes towards and within communities discriminated against on the basis of work and descent based discrimination, for which the necessary budget allocation shall be earmarked by the State.

275. Introduce measures of reparation for the centuries-old wrong doings committed against these communities through legislation and appropriate machineries for the purpose of restitution, monetary compensation, rehabilitation and for ensuring guarantees of non-repetition.

276. The United Nations to ensure the implementation by the States of all relevant recommendations and resolutions of the UN human rights treaty monitoring bodies and of the UN Sub-

Commission on the Promotion of Human Rights, and immediately appoint a UN Special Rapporteur to study the question of work and descent based discrimination, including caste discrimination and untouchability, against these communities in different parts of the world.

277. NGOs to lobby to ensure that the relevant Governments are made accountable to Parliament and to the UN Committee on the Elimination of Racial Discrimination for their implementation of policies and programmes aimed at eradicating work and descent based discrimination, including caste discrimination and untouchability, by constitutionally mandating their Governments to submit and openly discuss the annual reports of National Human Rights Institutions.

The NGO Forum, which preceded the WCAR in an unprecedented manner, took note of the caste discrimination and the deprivation of the Dalits. Along with the Declaration, the NGO Forum's Programme of Action demanded that various governments enact suitable legislation to recognise and eradicate discrimination based on work and descent, including caste discrimination and untouchability.

The Programme of Action further identified caste discrimination a crime against humanity and called for time bound action for the removal of atrocities. It went on to demand redistribution of land, legal provisions to protect the rights of the Dalits and other discriminated communities. A determined demand was also raised by the NGOs that sufficient financial provisions should be made for the upliftment of the Dalits in a time bound manner. With these, the NGO forum also called for international enforcements like the appointment of a Special Rapporteur to examine the complaints about various forms of discrimination and human rights violation. A fresh demand was made by the Special Rapporteur in1996 but this proposal was also turned down by the Indian Government.

The WCAR NGO Forum Declaration has clearly and categorically stated that caste discrimination is one of the most horrendous forms of discrimination based on work and descent and hence all the agencies should concentrate their efforts to eradicate caste. The NGO Forum Declaration and Programme of Action of the World Conference Against Racism, devoted 8 articles [Articles 84-90] in the Declaration and 11 articles [267-277] in the Programme of Action exclusively on caste, discrimination suffered by the Dalits etc. Thus it is for the first time, the term Dalit has come to the international arena of discourse. More submissive term like 'weaker sections' or administrative term like 'Scheduled Caste' or abusive term like '*harijan*' did not find inclusion in the discourse.

Going further, the Declaration categorised the centuries old caste discrimination as "hidden apartheid". Caste discrimination and 'untouchability' practised against generations of Dalits for centuries together amounts to systemic 'cultural Dalitocide', which is the mass-scale destruction of their individual and collective identity, self-respect and self-determination for generations through oppressive cultural methods and practices. The social fact that is emphasised here is that while racial discrimination that existed in other parts of the globe reduced the victims of apartheid into a state of inferior beings, the caste discrimination engaged in 'generational bondage' of the Dalits.

The Declaration and the Programme of Action finalised by the Inter-Governmental Conference eloquently speaks about racial discrimination and other forms of intolerances but fails once again to deal with caste discrimination. "We declare for the purpose of the present Declaration and Programme of Action, the victims of racism, racial discrimination, xenophobia and related intolerance are individuals or groups of individuals who are or have been negatively affected by, subjected to, or targets of these scourges.... The World Conference Against Racism urges States in their national efforts, and in cooperation with other States, regional and international organisations and financial institutions, to promote the use of public and private investment in consultation with the affected communities in order to eradicate poverty, particularly in those areas in which victims of racism, racial discrimination, xenophobia and related intolerance predominantly live. The WCAR also urges States to take all necessary and appropriate measures to end enslavement and contemporary forms of slavery-like practices, to initiate constructive dialogue among States and implement measures with a view to correcting the problems and the damage resulting therefrom".[50]

In contrast to the stand of the Inter-Governmental Conference, the Programme of Action suggested by the NGO Forum has provided concrete measures to annihilate caste discrimination. The delegates of the NGO forum have demanded that from the governments of the member countries to enact suitable legislation to recognise and eradicate discrimination based on work and descent, including caste discrimination and untouchability against Dalits, Buraku people and other affected communities, in those countries where such legislation does not exist; and in countries where legislation banning such discrimination already exists, take immediate steps to create transparent and effective monitoring mechanisms including the establishment of time-bound programmes to ensure effective implementation of such legislation, even where the perpetrators are States or State agents.[51]

This is a major achievement for the Dalit activists, human rights activists and all those who had perceived the validity and the legitimacy of this struggle and made efforts to continue this campaign. There was enormous criticism in some circles that the attempt to take the Dalit issue to the United Nations is unwarranted. Even the most 'enlightened' Indians were weary of this move. Moreover there was pessimism in some quarters that the Dalits activists would gain nothing by 'internationalising the issue'. Inspite of all these rumblings and ramblings, the concerted efforts to make visible the caste discrimination at the international level had its impact on the world body. Above all it is the victory of the common masses from the Dalits and the downtrodden communities who have entered into protracted struggle for continuing their lives and for ensuring and maintaining human rights at all cost.

Conclusion

As stated above the World Conference Against Racism held at Durban in 2001, was the third of its kind against racism. It is in this conference the caste discrimination in general and the exclusion, subordination and exploitation that the Dalits were subjected to in particular was made visible in the international arena for the first time. At that level of discourse this was a new beginning, which would have its historical consequence.

The Dalit activists and organizations, human rights activists and NGO's were well aware of the power equations at the UN bodies and conferences. These representatives of the Dalit cause were also conscious of the fact that they would be able to break grounds at the NGO conference and in the inter-governmental conference, political and trade interest would take dominance. Hence, they left no stone unturned in their efforts to provide visibility to the caste discrimination in the NGO forum. They were also conscious of the fact that raising the issue of caste discrimination at the Durban conference will not eliminate caste oppression. But they wanted to use a global forum to seek solidarity to annihilate untouchability and other forms of human rights violation.

The Dalit leadership was acutely aware of the fact that the Indian Government will deploy all the power and the resources at its disposal to deny any discussion on the caste issue. Above all these individuals and organizations were aware of the fact that the Indian Government will engage in arms-twisting exercise if any NGO attempts to bring up the issue at the World Conference. But this did not deterr them from agitating that their agenda that caste discrimination is horrendous than the racial discrimination and this should be included in the WCAR. They have been trying to unite the Dalits and human rights activists under one broad forum to wage a long drawn-out struggle at all levels. Here Dr. Ambedkar's vision provides scope for a broad-based struggle for Dalit Human Rights. He had declared, " If you wish that you should be the master of political power you have to organise yourselves for this. Then only you will be able to engage yourselves in the struggle for human rights in the political arena that will emerge in the future".

One can identify few factors that lie deep-rooted in the Indian social psyche and structure, which prevented any representation of the issues related to the Dalits, Tribals and the downtrodden in national and international arena. Given the socio-political structure of the country, all those who represented India in the international arena invariably came from the dominant castes who themselves never suffered any stigma in terms of caste or were victims of caste oppression. Hence, it is foolhardy to expect them to rake up the issue in the forums of United Nations. But much more crucial than these personal background of the government representatives is the fact that these representatives were the spokesperson of the official stand with regard to caste discrimination. Even if they themselves were not casteist in principle and behaviour, in their official capacity they have to toe the line of the establishment.

This scenario against the dominated and subjugated Dalits was changed in their favour for the first time in the international deliberations, by the efforts of the Dalit intellectuals, activists, human rights organisations. While starting from the local to the national level Dalit forums like the National Campaign on Dalit Human Rights mobilized and organized Dalits and their compatriots, they also for the first time in a concrete manner worked towards international Dalit solidarity. It is these collective efforts, which ultimately enabled the United Nation's Committee on the Elimination of Racial Discrimination to draft General Recommendation of Caste based discrimination.[52] This is a historic decision, which would go a long way in maintaining the pressure on the Indian government to take into account the lives and the struggles of 160 million population.

This victory though partial would contribute in continuing the struggle to force the Indian ruling class that the exclusion, deprivation, exploitation and discrimination suffered by the Dalits are due to untouchability and the caste system. To pretend that untouchability has been abolished by law and that it is not practiced in India or to claim that caste system is of the past is to play the same old tune. Instead it is demanded of the dominant caste rulers to look into the degrading social reality and take appropriate and time-bound steps, which in turn would contribute in nation building. These efforts also posed a challenge to the perception of the international community that racism is only one form of discrimination and that other shades of discrimination also need to be equally taken into consideration.

It appears appropriate to conclude this section with the words of Harish Bansode[53] a Dalit poet from Maharashtra

We have begun a new life
We have found our new temples
Regained our lost faith
All are equal here

References

1. The First and the Second World Conferences were termed as World Conference to Combat Racism and Racial Discrimination. But the Third World Conference was termed as World Conference Against Racism, Racial Discrimination, Xenophobia and Related Intolerances. Thus, the deliberations in this conference was not limited to racism alone but every other forms of discrimination was brought under the purview of international human rights activists, government representatives, representatives of United Nations and the global community.
2. Shiv Vishwanathan. Durban and Dalit Discourse. 'Economic and political Weekly' 36 (33): August 18-24, 2001: 3123-3127. This article was written in response to my book 'Casteism is more Horrendous than Racism: Dalits and Durban Discourse'. Indian Social Institute: New Delhi, 2001.
3. World Conference Against Racism, United Nations Department of Public Information. May 2001, p. 3.
4. *Ibid.*
5. The UNRISD was established in 1963 to promote research on the most pressing social issues of development. For more details about UNRISD email to liu@unrisd.org and consult worldwide Web Site at http://www.unrisd.org
6. UNRISD Conference on Racism and Public Policy. Durban, 3 September 2001.
7. *Ibid.*
8. World Conference Against Racism, United Nations Department of Public Information. May 2001, p. 4.
9. *Ibid.*
10. Background Material for National Seminar on Racism. The National Human Rights Commission: New Delhi. Vol. 1 and 2. August 2001. Vol. 1, p. 7.
11. Durban 2001: United Against Racism. Newsletter of the World Conference Against Racism Secretariat. Issue 3, April 2001, p. 4.
12. *Ibid.*, p. 8.
13. The United Nations Declaration on the Elimination of All Forms of

Racial Discrimination, 1963. Human Rights: A Compilation of International Instruments, Vol. 1, United Nations; New York, 1994, p. 61.

14. I have highlighted only some of the provisions, which are directly related to the lives of the Dalits. There are many more such provisions and instruments worked out at the international level for the protection of the rights of the marginalised and vulnerable communities. Refer to, Human Rights: A Compilation of International Instruments. United Nations, New York, 1988. Also see, D. Bhaskara Rao (ed). International Encylopedia of Human Rights: International Instruments of Human Rights. Part I & II. Discovery Publishing House: New Delhi, 2001.
15. The final document of the World Conference Against Racism was made available after a long time. Due to some differences the document was to be finalised after ensuring consensus and it was communicated to all. With the attack on the World Trade Centre, the finalisation of the document was delayed further. For the final document refer to Declaration and Programme of Action. World Conference Against Racism, Racial Discrimination, Xenophobia and Related Intolerance. United Nations: New York. March 2002.
16. Article 15 of the Constitution prohibits discrimination on grounds of religion, race, caste, sex or place of birth. By introducing First Amendment in 1951, the State introduced another clause, "Nothing in this article or in clause (2) of Article 29 shall prevent the State from making any special provision for the advancement of any socially and educationally backward classes of citizens or for the Scheduled Castes and the Scheduled Tribes.
17. United Nations Committee on Elimination of all forms of Racial Discrimination; CERD /C/304/Add 13, September 17, 1996.
18. *Ibid.*
19. *Ibid.*
20. *Ibid.*
21. The UN Committee on Civil and Political Rights, Consideration of the Government of India Report to the Human Rights Committee; CCPR/C/79/Add 81, August 4, 1997.
22. The UN Special Rapporteur on Racism and Racial Discrimination.
23. United Nations Press Release. 9th August, Geneva 2001. p. 4.
24. *Ibid.*
25. The Times of India, New Delhi, March 4, 2001.
26. Marriott and Inden. 1985: 348. Quoted in Declan Quigley: The

Interpretation of Caste, Clarendon Press, Oxford, 1993, p. 4.

27. *Ibid.*, p. 5.
28. Adam Kuper and Jessica Kuper 1985. Race: The Social Science Encyclopedia, Routledge: London, 1985.
29. Amnesty International Report, New Delhi, 2001.
30. Andre Beteille. Race and Caste. The Hindu, New Delhi, March 10, 2001.
31. Interestingly this is what armchair social scientists like Beteille have done for a long time. Mr. L.G. Havanur responding to Beteille's statement "Treating caste as a form of race is politically mischievous; what is worse, it is scientifically, nonsensical" argues that Indian Government and Andre Beteille have taken recourse obviously to selective anthropological and ethnographic meaning, in forming their subjective opinions. They are also oblivious to the contents of charter, declarations, conventions, reports of the UN bodies basic legal documents for member states to pass statutes and law for their countries.
32. Kalpana Kannabiran. Caste, the academy and Dalit women. *The Hindu*, New Delhi, 20.6.2001.
33. Dalit Protest at UN Office, Express No Confidence in PM's National Committee. National Campaign For Dalit Human Rights. Delhi Office. Press Statement Issued on 3rd July 2001.
34. Teesta Setalvad. Hidden Apartheid. *Communalism Combat*, Mumbai. April 2001, p 8.
35. Document issued by National Dalit NGO Preparatory Committee for WCAR, Nepal.
36. Prakash Louis. Globalising Caste or Natinalising Hypocrisy? Subalterns, New Delhi, October-December 2001.
37. United Nations Information Centre. New York. September 2001.
38. Mary Robinson. Focus on Fundamental Aims, New Strategies Needed to Fight Racism, UN High Commissioner for Human Rights Tells Conference. United Nations Information Centre, Geneva: September 2001.
39. Thabo Mbeki. 21st Century to Restore Human Dignity to all. Inaugural address of the President of South Africa. The Independent: Durban. September 1st, 2001.
40. National Campaign on Dalit Human Rights: WCAR Secretariat. Secundrabad: Andhra Pradesh, p 2.
41. NCHR Support for Dalits praised. The Hindu New Delhi, 6/9/2001.

42. Justice K. Ramaswamy, Abstract of Statement of the National Human Rights Commission of India.
43. For more details refer Background Material for National Seminar on Racism. The National Human Rights Commission, New Delhi, Vol. 1 and 2. August 2001.
44. Most of the material related to the activities of National Campaign on Dalit Human Rights could be found in the kit provided by the Campaign group in the Global Conference Against Racism 1st – 4th March 2001 in New Delhi and Pre-Durban National Conference – cum – Training 13th – 15th August 2001 in Hyderabad.
45. *Ibid.*
46. *Ibid.*
47. Memorandum to the United Naitons. The National Campaign for Dalit Human Rights. New Delhi. 3rd July 2001.
48. Prakash Louis. Regaining Our Lost Faith. Seminar, 508, December 2001, pp. 25-29.
49. Declaration and the Programme of Action of the WCAR NGO Forum, Durban, 03, September 2001.
50. Declaration and the Programme of Action of the World Conference Against Racism, Racial Discrimination, Xenophobia and Related Forms of Intolerance. 31 August-7 September 2001, Durban, South Africa. United Nations Information Centre, New Delhi. Articles 1 of Declaration and Articles 1& 2 of Programme of Action.
51. Ibid.
52. Press Statement. At the UN CERD 61 Session, Geneva, Switzerland, 10 August 2002
53. Steven M. Parish. Hierarchy and its Discontents: Culture and Politics of Consciousness in Caste Society. University Pennsylvania Press: Philadelphia, 1996, p. 82.

5

Post Durban Dalit Discourse

Contemporary Dalit discourse fundamentally focuses on the barbarity and the cruelty that the Dalits were subjected to for centuries, which also matters to them in everyday existence.[1] Any historical reading of the Dalit struggles abounds with the penetrating insights that the Dalits suffered all manners and modes of discrimination, deprivation and dehumanization. But it is of seminal significance that the individual and collective, social and historical experience of domination and servitude, which the Dalits suffered, provide the urge for Dalit movements and contextualise them. Going further, it also needs to be stated here that inspite of the atrocities the ability and the resolve of the Dalits to carry on their struggle is on the ascent. It is this social context, which provides the direction and determination to the Dalit movements and Dalit discourse.

In the run up to the Durban Conference, any careful observer of Indian social reality would have recognised, the leadership of the campaign to take the caste discrimination to UN conference was vested with the Dalits to a great extent. This is not to deny that others who had provided leadership all these years were relegated to the background or that their presence was not substantial. On the contrary, the argument is that for the first time, historical and social discrimination of the Dalits found expression and impact through the words and deeds of the Dalit women and men at the international forum. Also, it needs to be stated that the success of the campaign was in incorporating Dalit and non-Dalit leadership and organizing national and international solidarity, which has given impetus for furthering the discourse on the Dalit struggles and movements.

Contemporary Dalit Discourse

One of the central issues in the present Dalit discourse is whether the Dalit community should engage itself in fighting for upholding the provisions of reservation or formulate a broader movement to demand due share of the Dalits in the natural resources, labour rights to the Dalits, along with social dignity and self-determination. Most often, the struggle for the continuation of reservation is carried out by the economically and socially mobile segment of the Dalit population. The common Dalit masses who have not directly benefited from the reservation policy continue their basic struggle for *roti, kapada aur makan,* (food, shelter and clothing). Some of the Dalits who benefited out of the reservation policy to become socially mobile provide leadership in the Dalit assertion. But even this contribution has limited impact on the entire community.

Ownership of land becomes a crucial issue in a country like India where agriculture is the mainstay of the rural masses. The legitimate claim by the Dalis for share in land is always countered by the upper castes, by citing the 'historical role' of the Dalits as agricultural labourers. In extension it is argued that the Dalits were not landholders at any point of time. Later to substantiate their position, the following argument is often presented, 'lack of sense of private property among Dalits' were circulated arguing that the Dalits sold out the land, which they got under the land reform policies, and 'squandered the money'. It was also argued that the Dalits do not have the habit of saving for future since they are happy go lucky people. But various research studies present contrary facts. According to a study on people's perception of land reforms in Uttar Pradesh the small plot of land given under the land reforms had to be sold since it was in the midst of land owned by Gujjars. The dominant caste harassed the Dalits so much that the Dalits were forced to sell the land and continue as agricultural labourers.[2]

Land reform laws have been enforced for the last 50 years in the country and election manifestos, Independence Day promises or *Gandhi Jayanti* speeches were marked with the stress on providing land to the landless. But an examination of 50 years of implementation of land reforms reveals an appalling picture. Out of 78 lakh acres that were declared surplus and earmarked for distribution only 66 lakh acres, that is, only 83.68 per cent of the land has been taken possession by the administration. Going further, one also notices that out of the 78 lakh acres declared surplus and to be distributed among the landless, only 52 lakh acres, that is, 65.85 per cent of the land taken possession have been distributed. The total amount of land distributed among the Dalits is only 28 lakhs, that is only 35.60 per cent.[3] This empirical data disproves the tall claims made by the ruling establishment, that the Dalits are the beneficiaries of land reform policies.

To make the matters worse, the ruling establishment has already announced its priorities for changes in the land legislation policies that would make the situation more difficult for the Dalits. The National Agricultural Policy states that 'Private sector participation will be promoted through contract farming and land leasing arrangements to allow accelerated technology transfer, capital inflow and assured markets for crop production, especially of oil seeds, cotton and horticultural crops' The Policy document goes on to say, 'the legislative and regulatory framework will be appropriately amended and strengthened to achieve these objectives'.[4] Once private sector enters into agriculture too, land will not be available to the Dalits. The private sector would go for technology driven agriculture and thus the Dalits would loose even the possibilities of earning their living by selling their labour.

The anti-people, anti-Dalit orientation of the National Agricultural Policy has been criticized by Dalit intellectuals. Anand Teltumbde argues that "The impetus to export agriculture in the reforms is bringing in corporate and contract system in the agriculture. The government has already identified the Land Ceiling Act as the main obstacle in the process, which would be suitably changed. Directionally, the emergent corporate farms will gobble up smallholdings of the marginal to middle farmers and push them into the herd of job seeking millions. Corporatisation of agriculture always leads to de-peasantisation and simultaneously reduction in labour absorption... This emergent scenario is certainly going to aggravate the unemployment problem further rather than solving it".[5]

The continued attempt by the lower castes to be not only cultivators but also owner-cultivators was resisted with all might and power by the dominant castes. By maintaining the lower castes as agricultural labourers, the landed upper caste gentry not only ensured a continued flow of farm labourers but also this process guaranteed to themselves and enhanced their scheme of bondage and slavery of the Dalits. Historical studies amply demonstrate this social fact that in regions like Bihar where there was a close interface between feudalism and caste hierarchy, agricultural labourers in effect were bonded laboures and they in turn were predominantly from the Dalit communities. Gyan Prakash in his study about the Bhuiyans[6] of Bihar argues that 'The bondage unleased on the poor of the south Bihar and Chota Nagpur enabled the nineteenth-century expansion of an agricultural production that, far from introducing major improvements in the technical basis of agriculture, relief on the intensification of labour exploitation. Paddy cultivation, in a context marked by the growth of estates and the accumulation of tenant holdings by rich peasants and petty landlords, increased the need for labour and made labour control more critical. This was because of sharp fluctuations in labour demand, characteristic of paddy cultivation, became more acute when landlords enlarged their estates and rich peasants accumulated more lands than they could cultivate with family labour. In these circumstances, landlords and rich peasants acquired labour control by expanding the bonded labour system'.[7]

In this regard the Dalit intellectuals are called upon to examine the place and role of Naxalite movement to draw lessons from it. Naxalite movement, which began in a non-descript village named Naxalbari of West Bengal, has continued to operate for more than three decades. The revolt of the poor peasants, labourers and tea garden workers was initiated against the tyranny of the local landlords, police and anti-social elements. Most of the cadres, sympathizers and leaders of this struggle came from the Dalit, Tribal and backward caste communities. Marxist-Leninist and Maoist thought provided the basis of the struggle. But primarily it is the oppressive local conditions, which gave the impetus for protest and revolt. One of the reasons for the Naxalite movement to spread to other parts of the country, which continues even now, is that it addresses the issues of the toiling masses who are all invariably from the lower castes. For the last three decades the movement has been engaged in the struggle for minimum wages, redistribution of land and resources, social dignity of the lower castes in several regions of the country.[8]

Untouchability is one of the most horrendous forms of exploitation that humanity has ever witnessed. Every Dalit shudders and suffers under this dehumanizing form of social interaction. There are also indications that untouchability did not take this tyrannical form as long as it was practiced only by the upper castes. But when the lower castes began to practice untouchability towards each other, untouchability became to the present rigid; inhuman form.[9] In this context, the social conditions and social forces that contributed in the enforcement of strict and inflexible practice of untouchability among the Dalits in particular and between the Dalits and non-Dalits in general needs to be probed more.

"On 4th November 2001 at Ramlila grounds over 1 million Dalits are going to embrace Buddhism".[10] This was a proclamation made by the *Dhamma Chakra* group under the leadership of Ram Raj I.R.S [With his own conversion to Buddhism on that day he is known as Udit Raj]. It is another matter if 1 million participants could be accommodated in that ground. But even these kinds of announcements are indicative of the social processes that are churning within the Dalit community. The Dalit intellectuals have to seriously and systematically examine the process of conversion as well as its outcome. Conversion in general possesses two fundamental threats to the existing religious realities. On the one hand, conversion makes a strong proposal that its boundaries are permeable and vulnerable for external forces. On the other hand, it also registers the social fact that what was held as unshakable and unalterable beliefs and practices stand shattered. For the Dalit intellectuals conversion cannot be moving from one religion to another religion. It can also provide a paradigm for social change.

Dalit Children and Child Labour seem to go hand in hand. Even the government documents acknowledge the fact that most parents of the working children belong to Scheduled Castes Scheduled Tribes and other weaker sections of the society.[11] Dalit children seem to suffer from multiple discrimination due to their age, economic deprivation, low caste status, cultural and educational isolation. Like in other issues, in the discussion about child labour too, the administration lists out programmes under which the parents of children withdrawn from work and children themselves could be covered. These programmes and schemes are IRDP, EAS, JRY, DWCRA, DPEP, ICDS, National Literacy Campaigns, School Health Projects (SHP), TRYSEM, Indira Awas Yojna, Prime Minister's Rozgar Yojna, Mid-day Meal Schemes.

Here it needs to be stated that the government machinery fails to raise question if these schemes have been carried out for last few decades, why there has been no tangible change in the lives of the child labourers in general and the lives of the Dalit child labourers who are supposed to be the special beneficiaries of these schemes. Almost all of the Acts, schemes and policies worked to eradicate child labour in India have been generic in nature and not Dalit children specific.[12] The Dalit movements too have not really focused on the Dalit children and much less on Dalit girl child. The multiple discrimination and exploitation these children undergo deprives them any prospects for a better future. Thus, they are lost to the community. The Dalit leadership in collaboration with civil society and human rights activists should seriously look into mechanisms to eradicate child labour and provide a better future for their children. This once again cannot be done unless the social order itself is not altered in their favour.

One of the overarching strength of the Dalit community is that the Dalit women enjoyed considerable freedom both spatially and temporally, which does not mean that they shared equality with their men in all respects. Still comparatively free existence of Dalit women is evident as we move down in the caste order. Absence of dowry system and the consequent dowry deaths is a main indicator in this regard. But as the Dalits get educated, urbanised and economically mobile they fall into the trap of non-Dalit practices like dowry, restrictions on women's movements etc. But interestingly, one can hear feeble but saner voices which demand that the dominant castes better learn from the Dalits about the principles and practices of providing freedom to their women.[13] Dalits themselves are called upon to ensure that the Dalit women do not become victims of patriarchy of Hindu social order within the Dalit community.

The Dalit discourse should also see the continuum that exists with regard to Dalit assertion. This continuum could be presented as follows: Atrocities —— Agony —— Anger— Aggression. While the non-Dalits see only or mostly, the anger and the aggression of Dalit assertion, the Dalits see all the four aspects in a continuum. A clear case of Dalit anger and assertion was witnessed in Mumbai on July 11th, 1997[14]. The vandalization of the statue of Bhimrao Ambedkar in Ramabai Ambedkar Nagar in Mumbai sparked off violent protests and revolts by the Dalits. This led to police firing in which about 11 people were killed. This is not the first instance of desecration of a statue in Maharastra. It is stated that in the last 5 years about 508 such incidents have been reported[15]. But the social fact that needs to be paid attention is that this incident like previous incidents had led to revolt, where the nature of the agitation was severe and violent than the earlier ones. This response spilled over to other states and in Gujarat where the Bharatiya Dalit Panthers gave a call for a bandh in Gujarat. The Dalits are also aware of the social fact that it is their anger, which has given them the prowess to withstand heinous crimes committed against them.

In an era of globalisation, Dalits whose lives and struggles were limited to local space are finding scope for international solidarity. In the recent past many international Dalit solidarity forums have come into existence. Some of their operations could be seen immediately before and during the Durban conference -World Conference Against Racism- held in the year 2001.[16] However, the question remains unanswered, 'Will this solidarity and the benefits that accrue out of this broader alliance get limited to a small minority of Dalit elites, intellectuals, social scientists and social activists? Or would it provide space for the common masses to engage in an interface with all forms of attempts for liberation of all the exploited masses?'

The Dalit discourse should also seriously and comprehensively take note of the polarisation that is taking place in the arena of Dalit movements and Dalit struggles. Polarisation can be witnessed in the realm of leadership. A prominent question is that -should the leadership of Dalit movements remain at the hands of the non-Dalits or should it be solely in the hands of the Dalits. Should a sociological understanding of the Dalit movements become inclusive and be confined to the purview of the Dalit intellectuals or since the Dalit movements themselves are the logical outcome of caste interaction should it not be open-ended.

Moreover, there are points of convergence and difference among the Dalits. There is no shying away from the fact that there is no differences and that the non-Dalits are making a mountain of a mole. At regular intervals, these divisions also come to the fore and lead to conflict and crisis. Few would argue that due to reservation and the consequent social mobility some from the Dalit community have climbed up the ladder and are not in any way paying back to the community, which has supported their cause. Another argument is that some of those who benefited from reservation and have moved to middle class have become blind to the plight of their community. Some would go the extent of calling them 'Brahminical Dalits' and the rest 'Dalits among the Dalits'.[17] This further aggravates the distance between these two groups. Instead of perceiving this phenomenon as a malaise or unfortunate outgrowth of reservation policy, it would augur well for the Dalit community to view this as part of social phenomenon and see what needs to be done to bridge the gap.

In the same vein, in most of the discourse about Dalit movements for liberation, a fact that is stressed constantly is that there is no unity among the Dalits. At this stage it is not sociologically tenable to place a counter argument that there is no unity among members of other castes.[18] But the most important issue is to examine the root cause of the division among the Dalit leadership. Interestingly, even the social scientists and activists from the non-Dalit communities fail to examine the reasons behind these difference. Further, while they focus upon the nature and content of polarisation among the Dalit leadership, they fail to pay attention to the forces that continue to work against their unity.

Gail Omvedt provides some sociological insights in this regard. She states, 'Politically many forces worked to absorb Dalit protest. The Tilakite tradition in Nagpur provided the patronage links to Hindu nationalism, most importantly through B.S. Moonje,[19] a Hindu Mahasabha leader, and Hedgewar, the founder of Rashtriya Swayamsevak Sangh (RSS). Gavai who had been involved in many Dalit conferences during the 1920, eventually supported a Hindu Mahasabha proposal for compromise during the 1932 clash between Ambedkar and Gandhi. He joined the Hindu Mahasabha in 1933 and harshly criticised Ambedkar's call for conversion in 1935. Thaware another Dalit leader, who was involved with Gavai in the Depressed Classes Association, also joined the Hindu Mahasabha in 1941 and became a member of its executive. Khandekar who was part of Depressed Classes Association in 1930, opposed conversion move initiated by Ambedkar and finally joined Congress in 1942.[20] This countervailing force from the non-Dalit communities needs to be examined systematically not only to counter their argument but also to ensure that space is provided for a broader Dalit struggle.

Dalit intellectuals need to go into the root causes behind the emergence of Dalit movements. Also, they should examine the reasons behind their limited presence and impact at the pan-Indian level. The eruption of Dalit Panthers in early 1970s was an unprecedented Dalit assertion.[21] This appeared to be a sparkle, which was hoped to set the discriminatory forest aflame. According to Anand Teltumbde, 'There could be varied explanations for the paradigm shift in Dalit politics marked by the Dalit Panthers. Remarkably, they spoke the language of defiance and militancy, which created waves. These waves had shaken the foundations of the established order in the country and in essence demonstrated what the wrath of the wretched could be. It provided a valuable insight that was pathetically missing in the Dalit politics. Going by their manifesto, Dalit Panthers had broken many new grounds in terms of radicalising the political space for the Dalit movement. They imparted the proletarian-radical class identity to Dalits and linked their struggles to the struggles of all oppressed people over the globe.[22] Though this was a radical move, in the ultimate analysis it was done without much substance and thus it died out.

Dalit assertion is being expressed through popularizing symbols of Dalit heroes, leaders and reformers. The Bahujan Samaj Party (BSP) has created a wealth of symbols , which can be seen in the naming of new districts in Uttar Pradesh and naming them after such personalities as Shahuji Maharaj, Mahamaya, Ravidas et.al. This was one of the most notable actions during the six-month regime of Mayawati in Uttar Pradesh in 1997. By engaging in this exercise of creating new districts and naming them on the heroes and famous personalities from the Dalit communities, the BSP appropriates to itself the exclusive role of symbolically ameliorating the social positioning of the Dalits in the state. The symbolic language becomes a source of solace for those who have seldom found a place at the threshold of the social history of India. The Bundelkhand region, marked by greater inequality due to the larger land holdings of the upper castes with a demographic balance in favour of the Dalits, has become a battle ground between two sets of symbols and language: the one connected with Laxmi Bai which is still in the one set of literature and the other with Jhalkhari Bai which is still in the process of construction through the resurrection of the living memories.

The efforts of the BSP towards the glorification and mythicisation of Jhalkari Bai in a reconstructed framework can also be perceived as the politicisation of an existing memory. It aims at the mobilisation of the bearers of this memory to subserve the political ends of the party. To accomplish this objective three models of articulation have been implemented. A) oral: the political ends are communicated in the form of an oral transmission, a mode popular in the region and practised from very early times; b) Print and Visual: Pamphlets, dramas and other kinds of literature sketching out their identity is circulated amongst them. The statue of Jhalkari Bai in Jhansi built under the BSP patronage during the regime of

Mayawati, much larger size and represents her face and features as similar to those of the Rani; c) ritual: Ritualism is observed in the organisation of festivals and functions around the personality of Jhalkari Bai, such as commemoration has been a repeated instance in the past.

It is noteworthy that Jhalkari Bai was brought back in to public memory by an upper caste literary figure, Brindavan Lal Verma, but contemporary constructions of the myth are presented in the form of a reaction against the earlier representations. These representations have now become victorious and have a great presence in the memory of the people, but have been tailored to the demands of the political interest. In order to ensure the permanence of the memory of Jhalkari Bai many alluring features have been added to her personality. Authority depends upon legitimacy and legitimacy, in turn, depends on mass support. This support is elicited through the reconstruction and invocation of the past. Repetitive thrust strengthen memory and for this both old and modern mediums are being used.[23]

Dalit discourse and Dalit movements provide scope for forging a broad alliance between all the exploited masses, that is, the Dalits, the Tribals, women, the most backward castes and the minorities. It is this broad alliance, which will enhance the liberative power of the struggling masses. But the possibility of this broader alliance has been a contentious question subjected to variety of interpretations. This is not because of any inherent obstacles to the broader alliance formation between these communities. Anyone who wants to work in this direction should comprehend both the similarities and differences that exist between these communities. These similarities and differences are social in nature. But an underlying and unifying factor is that all these communities are the exploited masses of this country and society.[24] The dominant castes at times make it appear that the Dalits and the Tribals form part of the Hindu fold and the minority Muslims are the 'enemy other' who need to be done away with for the well-being and progress of the country. Efforts like these have contributed in the recent Gujarat Pogrom.[25] On the other hand, the recent experiment in Kerala where the Dalits and the fisherfolk showed solidarity with the Tribals who have been fighting for land rights. It is this united struggle, which resulted in success.

It is not outlandish to argue that the Dalit discourse set in by the Dalit intellectuals will have to immediately and irrevocably address these burning issues. Dalit discourse needs to begin from the lives and the struggles of the Dalit masses. But its credibility can be examined only in the background of its contribution to the liberation and emancipation of all the exploited and subjugated masses of this country. In extension, it would also network and align with many other struggles and revolts against exclusion, deprivation and discrimination of individuals and community. Would the Dalit intellectuals, leaders and activists become the countervailing force to the oppressive forces among the dominant castes is the million-dollar question today.

Pre-Durban Initiatives

In the recent times providing visibility to the Dalit issues at the international arena has found greater success than ever. Another fact, which needs to be equally underlined is that Dalit issue attained visibility worldwide not just by the efforts of any individual or group of individuals but due to the struggle carried out by many individuals, groups, organisations, forums at the local, national and international level. At the international level the formation of International Dalit Solidarity Network provided the impetus for internationalizing the issue. At this juncture it is expedient to briefly review the pre-Durban Initiatives so as to place the discourse at the right perspective. The ensuing discussion would feature some of the oganisations[26] that played a catalyst role in making the Dalit issue visible at the international arena as well as the efforts made by them.

The Federation of Ambedkarites and Buddhist Council is one of the earliest Dalit oganisations based in United Kingdom. From 1970 this Council began to highlight the plights of the Dalits in India. In the beginning the independent organsiations concentrated more on religious and cultural activities like constructing Guru Ravi Dass centers or celebrating the birthday of Dr. Ambedkar etc. But once they federated themselves under the Council, they began to engage in issues affecting the Dalit communities in India.

The Ambedkar Mission of Canada based in Toronto was founded in mid-1970s by Mr. Darshan Chaudhary, an immigrant from Punjab. The Ambedkar Mission attempted to bring together the Dalits settled in Canada. This is a human rights organisation, which in collaboration with other human rights organisations and Buddhist organisations tried to highlight the human rights violations of Dalits in India. They also organize events like annual birthday celebrations of Dr. B.R. Ambedkar and contribute Ambedkar's literature to the University of Toronto, other than organizing seminars on Dalit issues.[27]

In 1978, the Dalits in United States formed an organization called Vision, with the prime objective to fight for human rights of the Dalits. Members of Vision protested in front of the United Nation's headquarters in New York City when then Prime Minister Morarji Desai addressed the U.N. General Assembly. In 1982, Vision organized a protest against the Prime Minister Mrs. Indira Gandhi against her government's failure to protect the Dalits from the atrocities they were subjected to by the dominant castes.

An academic event of telling impact was a seminar organized on the theme, "Economic Reforms and Dalits in India" by Oxford University in England on 8th November 1996. Anand Teltumbde noted during the seminar, "The Dalits in India being the poorest of the poor, have been hit the hardest by new economic polity. There are social disabilities, largely reinforced by, and sustained on, economic deprivation, and are bound to become sharpened with these policies". He suggested that, "As pre-requisites to reform, there could be radical land reform, infrastructural projects, universalisation of primary education, a primary health care system and reinforcement of positive discrimination in favour of Dalits. The policy of positive discrimination in favour of Dalits will have to be reinforced much more vigorously in all sectors of economy than ever before."[28] Organising a seminar in Oxford University should be seen as a major move in the direction of finding an extended ideological space for Dalit cause at the international level.

The Dalit International Organisation organized the "First World Convention on A New Vision Towards a Casteless Society" on October 10-11, 1998 at Kuala Lumpur, Malaysia. It is interesting to take note of the reasons behind holding this international Convention in Malaysia. Dalits have been living in Malaysia over hundred years. They were brought as plantation workers by the British. But for decades they considered themselves to be Tamilians brought from India as plantation workers and lived in that way. But for the last two decades, there have been awareness among them and thus they organized the First World Convention in the attempt to build a casteless society. This increase in social consciousness among the Dalits was due to the rising political consciousness among them. Dalits like Mr. M.G. Pandithan were part of Malaysian Indian Congress, a party of the Indians. But the dominant caste Indians did not tolerate the assertion of the Dalits and Mr. M.G. Pandithan was thrown out of Malaysian Indian Congress Party on December 24, 1988. This gave a crude shock to the Dalit community. Finally, Mr. Pandithan formed "Indian Progressive Front". It is this mobilization and organization of the Dalits, which led to the holding of the First World Convention on the theme 'A New Vision Towards a Casteless Society'. It is also significant to note that Mr. Kanshi Ram the leader of Bahujan Samaj Party delivered the keynote address in this convention.[29]

Dalit Organizations in United Kingdom played a major role in highlighting the plight of the Dalits in India. Voice Of Dalit International or VODI was one such forum that highlighted the cause of the Dalits. VODI[30] was founded in 1999 to internalize the discriminatory practices of caste, which is similar to that of apartheid and affect approximately 250 million people who live within the Indian subcontinent and an estimated 1 million living abroad including 2 million in the UK. Further, VOD International champions the rights of all individuals to equality and freedom through integrated and effective programmes [31]

It is important to note here that even before the Dalit activists and intellectuals went to Durban to represent their case, Dalits in United Kingdom had already organized a two-day International Conference on Dalit Human rights. This conference was jointly organised by Voice of Dalit International (VODI) and the Dalit Solidarity Network, UK, at Shri Guru Ravidass Community Centre,

London during 16-17 September 2000.[32] The conference was unique in the sense that Representatives from all denominations of Dalit community of United Kingdom like the Shri Guru Ravidass, Bhagwan Valmiki, Amedkarite and Buddhists and Christians not only attended and participated in the conference but also generously donated money and other resources for the conference. The conference was well attended by the Dalits living in India and abroad. The overall objective of the Conference was to draw the attention of the international community towards the oppressive aspects of the caste system and atrocities in India against the Dalits under the system, which is similar to apartheid and slavery, and to plan for Dalit Human Rights and Development in the New Millennium with the participation of Overseas Dalit Organisations.

The following were some of the recommendations made by the London Conference: "Economic and educational development of the Dalits must be given priority in our approach to help the Dalit brethren in India... Despite all legal measures, untouchability is parctised in different forms in India and hence our prime task should be to fight against untouchability and to abolish the caste system, which promotes untouchability... at the international level, an in depth "Dalit Research/Information Center" be established in the North to communicate and feed regular information to Governments, civil society organizations and other advocacy groups in the North...Create network organisations all over the world, and ensure that the voice of Dalits is heard at the highest levels nationally and internationally.... UN agencies such as WHO, UNDP, UNICEF and UNIFEM should focus on the Human Rights implications of violence against Dalit women and develop programmes like legal training, to safeguard the rights of the Dalit women"[33] [For London Declaration see Appendix 6].

We made passing reference in the previous chapter to National Campaign for Dalit Human Rights or NCDHR as the campaign which got noticed both at the domestic front and at international level. In this chapter we would examine at length the contribution made by NCDHR to internationalize Dalit cause. "The National Campaign for Dalit Human Rights was born in 1998 out of the initiatives of concerned human rights activists in India working among the Dalits. Thought we had just completed the 50th year of our independence, the prevalence of "untouchability" continued unabated in many parts of the country in spite of our Constitutional and international commitment to the contrary. In conjunction with the 50th Anniversary of the Universal Declaration of Human Rights, we called for an urgent national campaign highlighting Dalit Human Rights and upholding that 'Dalit Rights are Human Rights'. National Campaign for Dalit Human Rights is a platform launched and led by Dalit Human Rights activists, both women and men, with support and solidarity from movements and organisations committed to women, labour and human rights as well as other people's organisations and institutions throughout the country. Academicians and intellectuals who work to protect and promote human rights are also part of the forum'.[34]

The overall objectives[35] of the NCDHR were to

- Create awareness and support Dalit Human Rights by highlighting the issues of Dalit Human Rights in civil society;
- Strengthen the unity and solidarity of Dalits and Dalit movements across the nation and the world;
- Prepare Status Reports or Black Papers on Dalits covering the areas of Livelihood, Education, Land & Labour, Gender Equity for Dalit Women, Life & Security, and Reservation and Employment;
- Pressurise Central and State Governments and state and national level statutory bodies to give top priority to Dalit Rights;
- Pressurise statutory bodies of the UN and other international organisations to give top priority to Dalit issues;
- Highlight the culture and contribution of Dalit Communities to society.[36]

The Charter of Dalit Human Rights as propounded by NCDHR once again spells out the demands of the campaign forum. "We demand that a global effort be made to abolish untouchability in all its manifestations and its practice be considered a heinous crime against humanity and be punished in the severest form possible... We demand that the State should not only effectively ensure the prevention of atrocities on Dalits by the civil society but also guarantee the right of reservation to Dalits and all other most backward castes in all private enterprises and companies which enjoy one or more forms of subsidy from the Government ... We demand that the UN will respond seriously to violations of Dalit rights through the appointment of a special Rapporteur or Working Group on the practice of untouchability in Asia and include 'caste discrimination' in Article I of the Convention on the Elimination of Racial Discrimination"[37].

So, it is discernible to a careful reader of the campaigns undertaken by the Dalit organisations that how they began to put pressure not only on Indian government but also on the international bodies to do away with untouchability.

Post-Durban Initiatives

The Bhopal Conference

Following the World Conference Against Racism in August-September 2001 in Durban 'The Bhopal Conference' with the theme, "Charting A New Course For Dalits For The 21st Century" was held at Bhopal, Madhya Pradesh, India 12th – 13th January 2002. As the invitation letter from the Chief Minister of Madhya Pradesh indicated, this National Conference was organized by the Government of Madhya Pradesh,[38] with the aim of framing 'Dalit Agenda for the 21st Century'.[39] Since the ruling political party, the Congress organised the conference it raised many questions.

The objective of the Bhopal Conference reads as follows: "Even after 54 years of Independence, our models of development have done little to change the fate of the teeming millions of Dalits (Scheduled Castes and Scheduled Tribes) of the country. The Indian State, apart from practicing distributive democracy of its own resources and institutions, should also consider persuading the society to reconcile to the notion of sharing its assets and institutions which the SC/STs, whom history has treated in an extremely unfair manner. The Bhopal Conference is aimed at providing an open forum for a free and frank debate on Dalit questions before the nation".[40] Leaving out the confusion and the criticism that overshadowed the Bhopal Conference, one can identify similar resolves as envisaged by the earlier conferences and declarations.

The Bhopal Declaration stated

"We, intellectuals and activists assembled at the Bhopal Conference, 12-13 January 2002, to deliberate the issues concerning the welfare of and justice to the 250 million and, Declaring our belief in Babasaheb Dr. B.R. Ambedkar's ideal of Social Democracy and his prophecy that, "A democratic form of Government presupposes a democratic form of society. The formal framework of democracy is of no value and would indeed be a misfit if there was no social democracy", Mindful of the fact that even after 54 years of Independence, the Dalit community is denied of its basic human rights and is also at the receiving end of the most brutal and oppressive forms of discrimination and exclusion, Reaffirming that concerted action by society as a whole - especially coordination among the political leadership, officials and grassroots activists - is necessary for the over-all development of the most oppressed of India."[41]

The Bhopal Conference made the following demands:

"Bring down the ceiling limit of private land ownership, and from the declared surplus land, government revenue lands and temple lands, distribute within five years a minimum of five acres of cultivable land to each Dalit household with registration in the name of Dalit women. Provide the initially required accessories and capital to make their livelihood sustainable and secure.

Enact legislation and enforce it stringently to enable Dalits have an equitable share in the appropriation and use of the rural and urban common property resources.

Enact legislation and enforce the right of Dalit agricultural labourers to living wages, to gender parity in wages, to job security, to better working conditions and welfare measures, and ensure punitive measures against offenders.

Enforce with stringent measures the Bonded Labour System (Abolition) Act, 1976 and abolish forthwith child labour to ensure freedom with dignity for all the Dalits, and accordingly make suitable amendments in the appropriate legislations.

Implement compulsory, free and high quality education for all Dalits immediately, make allocation of funds proportionate to the number and level of the illiterates, ensure compensation to those families which forfeit their income from child-labour, increase the number and amount of scholarships, and provide better infrastructural facilities in Sc and ST schools and offer market-oriented vocational and technical education.

Implement effectively in letter and spirit the SC and ST (Prevention of Atrocities) Act, 1989 & Rules 1995. Provide arms licenses to the SCs & STs for self-defence purposes, make the setting up of Dalit self-defence groups from village onwards mandatory, and specially train Dalit women to handle weapons in self-defence against the perpetrators of crimes and atrocities.

Make reservation mandatory in the private and corporate sector in the same proportion as in the public sector and government institutions and develop the capacities and skills of Dalits to help them cope up with the demands of these different sectors"[42] [For more details on this see Appendix 7].

VOD International Dalit Conference

It is remarkable to note that as a follow up of the International Conference on Dalit Human rights, Voice Of Dalit International [VODI] organized another International Dalit Conference in the Indian Social Institute, New Delhi, India during 19-20th Feburary2003. The conference was specially organized on the issue of "Dalit and International Developmental Aid".[43] In this context the conference was aimed at providing an overview of the foreign aid contributed to Indian development sector and the role played by 'International non governmental development aid agencies' (NGAA) and bilateral and multilateral agencies in this area. The conference also examined the role played by Indian non-governmental organisations (NGOs) in the poverty alleviation programme.

It was also highlighted in the conference that by the end of 1997, the volume of foreign contributions to NGO sector had reached nearly $568 million (Rs. 26,000 million), a growth rate of 643%

over the last decade. Further it was revealed that this money was cornered by the NGOs run by the dominant castes. Hence the conference recommended the following steps to be taken to rectify the situation: "An in-depth study be carried out on the place of caste in the approach of NGAAs in India and other south Asian countries to ascertain to what degree caste is a factor in formulating NGAA programme and to make recommendations to the Dalit Solidarity Network and its member bodies, to partner organisations and where appropriate to Government agencies... The declaration of the conference read "We recommend that an in-depth Dalit Research Information Centre be established, either in south Asia or more probably the North, to communicate regular information to Governments, civil society organisations and other advocacy groups, primarily in the North... We suggest that all relevant organisations and agencies ensure adequate representation of Dalits at senior levels. We urge that adequate support and funds should be allocated in developing leadership skills, capacity and professionalism among the Dalit youth in the hope that they may be in a position to fill posts at a senior level in the future.[44]

MHOW Declaration – Bharatiya Janata Party's Dalit Agenda

While Congress Party facilitated the Bhopal Conference, the ruling *Bharatiya Janata Party* (BJP) did not want to lag behind. Under the theme, "Towards Integral Development of the Scheduled Castes" the Bharatiya Janata Party's Madhya Pradesh State unit had organized a conference in May 2003 in Mhow.[45] The choice of the location is very revealing. Mhow is the birthplace of Dr. Bhimrao Ambedkar.[46] With elections round the corner for the State legislature in Madhya Pradesh, this move is seen as an attempt to ensure Dalit vote bank for the BJP.

The Declaration of the Conference begins stating that the Constitution has provided political independence to the Scheduled Castes, but economic equality and social unity needs to be ensured further. It further states that the present Congress Government under the Chief Minister is known for making false promises. Making reference to the Bhopal Conference, the document also states that the Bhopal Declaration is the handiwork of the Chief Minister and his stooges. Against this backdrop if one examines the atrocities committed on the Dalits in general and Dalit women in particular, Madhya Pradesh is leading in atrocities on Dalits. In this regard, the document further promises that the Bharatiya Janata Party would ensure to the Scheduled Castes social dignity, economic development and participation in political power.[47]

The Mhow Declaration concludes with a set of recommendations. "Effective schemes to promote local self-employment among the Scheduled Castes are to be initiated. To ensure that no Dalit should goes to sleep with empty stomach, schemes need to be worked out. Among the Scheduled Caste agricultural labourers those who are landless should be provided with five acres of land. This land should be without any dispute of ownership. To develop the land allotted, Rs. 1,000.00 per acre should be provided so that the beneficiaries can begin the cultivation. In this age of competition, with the provisions made in the Constitution through reservation, the Dalits should be prepared to face competition".[48] A cursory glance at this declaration would suggest that like many other declarations it also indicate the compulsions of political parties engaged in this exercise. But a careful examination of these declarations would unravel the fact that there is some common trend in all of them. However, these recommendations if converted into action plans, have scope for change.

International Dalit Conference, Vancouver

An International Dalit Conference was organized in Vancouver from 15th to 16th May 2003. This conference was organized by the Association for International Dalit Conference, Canada. The objectives of the Conference as stated by the organizers were, "The International Dalit Conference 2003 is a sincere attempt by the Dalit Diaspora to present the world a true picture of the status of Dalits in India and world over and debate, discuss and deliberate their future vision for the 21st century and issue a Vancouver Declaration so as to create an opinion all over the world and in India in support of the global movement of Dalits. There is also a strong need to change the strategies of Dalit struggle for self-respect, empowerment, justice and peace".[49]

It is significant to note that the Vancouver Conference Declaration draws its inspiration from Dr. Ambedkar. "WE, THE DALITS, from all over the globe having assembled at the International Dalit Conference, to deliberate the issues concerning the 250 million Dalits (Scheduled Castes and Scheduled Tribes) of India and their future in the 21st century,

INSPIRED by that great thinker and philosopher of the oppressed. Babasaheb Dr. B. R. Ambedkar,

REDEDICATE ourselves to his mission to bring about a democratic and peaceful transformation of India whereby all its citizens, irrespective of their gender, caste, creed, language and region, will enjoy the fruits of equality and justice,

WHEREAS the world has entered the third millennium and is progressing towards accomplishing the goals of Liberty, Equality and Fraternity, and whereas India has failed to eradicate untouchability and caste and descent-based discrimination and is yet to achieve basic fundamental human rights,

CALL UPON the Dalits of the world to unite in their activism in the true spirit of interfaith and multiculturalism, and resolve to work tirelessly for the upliftment of the community."[50]

The Vancouver Declaration goes on to demand, "The rightful and proportionate share of Dalits and tribals in India's national institutions, wealth and capital must be recognized. Economic exclusion hitherto practiced in the name of caste must be done away with. The community should have equitable access to means of production and economic empowerment...The United Nations and its affiliates, and non-governmental agencies concerned with human rights, social and economic development, must recognise that the Dalits are a special group and create separate Dalit divisions managed by the Dalits themselves. Their programmes and projects should have special Dalit components as well as special focus in their reports. The World Bank and other International Financial Institutions should attach conditional special component clause and must ensure the rightful share of the Dalits in the funds they lend to India for socio-economic and sustainable development. Sustained efforts must be made at the United Nations to expedite the process of formally equating caste-based discrimination with Racial discrimination".[51] [For more details on the Vancouver Declaration, refer to Appendix 8].

These conferences are representative in nature of many of the efforts made by the Dalit individuals and organisations and human rights activists at the post-Durban period. From the above presentation, it becomes clear that serious attempts were made both at the national and international arena to keep the Dalit discourse alive. It is not argued that the Dalit activists have won the battle. But that the struggle goes on and it is taking definite direction.

Dalit Intellectuals

The place and role of Dalit activists, intellectuals and leaders becomes all the more crucial since the Dalit struggle should go on unabated for the emancipation of all the Dalits. Further, they also need to examine the strategies adopted by the dominant castes who are waiting at the wings to suppress and repress any attempt by the Dalits and the downtrodden to raise their head against exclusion, deprivation and discrimination. One of the most central and crucial question in this regard is, 'How do the Dalit intellectuals comprehend the methods and the means used by the dominant castes to throttle any attempt to stage a protest against the existing social order and for restructuring the social order on an equal footing?' The dominant castes use time-tested weapons like repression, cooption and distortion to discredit or disable Dalit movements. The dominant castes also engage in calumny and defamation to immobilize the struggle. It is here the Dalit intellectuals, activists, NGOs etc., are called upon to continue to engage in the emancipatory struggle of the Dalits.

Antonio Gramsci's contribution to the debate on leadership and intellectuals rightly fits here. He considers intellectuals as persons who are creators and distributors of culture. While discussing about leadership, Gramsci identifies two types of intellectuals. 1) Organic intellectuals and 2) Traditional intellectuals. The former is one who works consciously for his own social class, convinced that it has a historical "right" at a given moment. Further, he states that they are formed in the process of the formation of new historical classes. Gramsci defines the later as those who carried out their intellectual activities in traditional intellectual institutions like the Church, trade unions and the academy."[52]

R. Eyerman and A. Jamison taking clue from Gramsci classified two categories of intellectuals, that is, movement intellectuals and establishment intellectuals. According to them, 'Movement intellectuals are those who carry out their tasks within a social movement, and establishment intellectuals are those who are formed within established social institutional contexts'.[53] Eyerman and Jamison go on to argue, "All intellectuals emerge in particular contexts: no one is born an intellectual. Rather, those both commonly and in more scholarly accounts referred to as intellectuals are formed in the process of social interaction, through the carrying out of intellectual activities in particular social contexts. One such especially significant context is that opened up by a social movement".

Movements' literature in general devoted some pages for the discussion of leadership. But with regard to Dalit movements, since the Dalits themselves were at the receiving end not only of the skewed and unequal caste order but also of the prejudiced notions in social sciences, the emergence of Dalit intellectuals with an identity of their own did not figure in the purview of the mainline social sciences. Some social scientists have done comparatively better analysis of the place and role of leadership within the Dalit movements. Yet, they also seem to perceive the Dalit leadership from typically academic exercise, where the Dalit worldview does not seem to figure substantially. For example, Sudha Pai in her well-reached work on the ascendance of Bahujan Samaj Party,[54] has tried to combine both a sympathetic as well as critical approach. But while the objective of the study was to examine the agenda of BSP based on its emergence and establishment, the study seems to take into account only the manifest dimensions of its achievements and fail to take note of the latent dimensions with regard to Dalit mobilization and organization. The book also considers the fact that the evaluation of BSP should be done at a wider context. But then one of the elements of the wider context identified by the author is colonial legacy during which no anti-caste or social reform movement took place in Uttar Pradesh. The author identifies this as one of the major handicap faced by the Dalit parties. Once again to argue based on one event, that is, the Shergarhi incident that the BSP is not a social movement interested in transformation but is an opportunistic political party is reductionist in character, ignoring the social importance the BSP has for the Dalit assertion.[55]

While discussing Dalit intellectual activism, Gopal Guru argues that 'Increased intellectual activism has marked Dalit-Bahujan cultural life at both the national and the regional levels in recent years. An interesting feature of this development is that the growth is well outside the formal education sites that are supposed to be the normal locations for such a flourish'.[56]

Gopal Guru identifies five trends in Dalit intellectual activism.

(1) State Sponsored Dalit Intellectual Activism. In this type of activism the initiative to organise the intellectual meets are taken by the state and hence it also decides their agenda. The themes are hence diluted so that they remain purely empirical and merely supply the context to design welfare policies for Dalits. These efforts, hence, ultimately turn out to be prescriptive in nature. The participants only suggest some policy initiatives or corrective measures. State-sponsored Dalit intellectualism thus transforms the Dalit intellectuals from critical reflexive thinkers to 'official intellectuals' often working overtime to offer legitimacy to state. This state sponsored intellectual activism also induces a fierce competition among the thinkers themselves as they vie to become "official intellectuals". Obviously, the sites for such intellectual activism are the centres of power, particularly the state and national capitals, places that house the planning commissions or the secretariats that lure the official intellectuals. Dalit scholars and bureaucrats both lead these efforts. The bureaucrats like to be called scholars, and in fact, expect an intellectual status equal or even superior to the Dalit academic elite in formal educational institutions.

(2) Dalit-Bahujan Intellectuals. This category represents bureaucrats whose intellectual initiatives are organised well outside the state system. These are based on the moral, material and intellectual resources raised through contribution of the Dalit-Bahujan bureaucrats themselves who want the members of their segment to make some sacrifice for the sake of the community. Thus, these efforts also have a communitarian angle.

(3) Bureaucrat-Turned-Intellectuals. This group of intellectuals organise intellectual activism with the blessing, influence and political support of the Dalit-Bahujan political parties. In this case, Dalit intellectual activism receives political support rather indirectly for the obvious reason that the Dalit bureaucrats do not wish to provoke any governmental actions. In fact, some of them are likely to be harassed by other Dalit-Bahujan leaders (say, of the ruling party or coalition) who would not like any Dalit opponent or rival to gain any intellectual respectability form such meetings. Thus, the support is tactical and contingent.

(4) Political Party Intellectuals. Certain political parties also try to organise Dalit intellectual activities directly. These efforts are basically confined to the State of Maharashtra and are initiated by the Republican Party of India led by Prakash Ambedkar. The conclave called '*Vidvata Sabha*' is held regularly since 1997.

(5) NGO Based Dalit Intellectuals. Certain Dalit NGOs, particularly in southern India, also organise such intellectual activities. This NGO based Dalit intellectual activism has emerged on the background of the failure of formal educational institutions led by Dalits or supported by the central or state governments to fulfill these functions. The formal academic sphere has failed to create an institutional form of Dalit intellectualism. In fact, universities unfortunately suffer from the worst kind of intellectual fragmentation of the 'Dalit think-tank' in the country.[57]

Gopal Guru goes on to state that first four are institutionalised intellectual efforts since they operate within a particular framework of understanding of Dalit issues. These are also institutionalised efforts because they do not engage in genuine interrogation within about the contribution of the Dalit intellectuals and activists for the liberation and emancipation of the Dalit masses.

Going further, one need to reiterate the social fact that the Dalit intellectuals, activists and the common masses have to learn lessons from history about the leadership for their emancipation. Some of the success stories need to be examined so as to delineate the social process at work and identify the forces that are anti-Dalit and recognize those who perceive Dalit rights to be human rights and search for alliances. According to Eleanor Zelliot, the essential factors in the processes by which the Mahar movement grew were:

1. A leadership released from traditional service and followers with some economic freedom;
2. Grievances understood and felt by both the "elite" members of the caste and the masses;
3. Some form of legitimization of the new non-traditional Mahar ambition both within the caste and among members of the elite in the larger society;
4. A group of "brokers" — men who could serve as links between the caste and the institutions of power in society, or who knew how to use modern channels of change;
5. Channels for communication, both within the group and from the group to the public;
6. Some form of protection for protesters when the overstepping of traditional boundaries brought retaliation.

Without any of these factors, the Mahar movement would have taken a different path, or would have narrowed its aims, or would have remained a minor protest.[58]

Let us briefly examine the perspectives of Mahatma Jotiba Phule and Dr. Ambedkar about leadership from the marginalised communities. With the data available to him Phule dreamt of a *masiha* who would liberate the depressed classes. "If and when the children of the *Shurdras* and the *Ati Shudras* including the Bhils and Kolis, whom the Brahmans have condemned as low castes, untouchables and subhuman beings, take to acquiring true knowledge, in course of time they would attain it and then it might happen that a great man would spring up from amongst them, would shower flowers on our tombs and declare victory and joy in our names".[59]

Dr. Ambedkar was immensely aware of the contributions made by his predecessors for Dalit liberation and emancipation. Writing about Phule he stated, "The greatest *Shudra* of Modern India who made the lower classes of Hindus conscience of their slavery to the higher classes and who preached the gospel that for Indian social democracy was more vital than independence from foreign rule".[60]

While Dr, Ambedkar envisaged a written Constitution for the maintenance of social democracy in India and attempted to maintain its political structure, for him the causes of the depressed classes was the foremost in mind. "So far as I am concerned, the untouchables' interest will take precedence over the interests of the country. I am not going to support a tyrannizing majority simply because it happens to speak in the name of the country. I am not going to support a party because it happens to speak in the name of the country. I shall not do that. Let everybody here and everywhere understand that this is my position. As between the country and myself, the country will have precedence; as between the country and the depressed classes, the depressed classes will have precedence-the country will have no precedence."[61]

It is in the fitness of things to state here that the Dalits have been carrying out anti-caste struggle in general and anti-untouchability movements in particular for centuries. With the run up to the World Conference Against Racism, social activists, political leaders, representatives of the voluntary sector were engaged in ensuring the fact that the caste and descent based discrimination is brought to center stage not only in the national forums but at the international plane too. The central focus of the demand of the Dalit activists and intellectuals was that caste discrimination has been and continues to be institutional in nature. They are part of the descent and occupation based oppression, subjugation, exclusion, separation and social ostracism. Though casteism may not fall under the category of racism *per se*, caste discrimination is similar to if not more horrendous than racial discrimination. From the perspective of human rights, caste discrimination is violation of fundamental human rights of over 160 million Indians. As stated above this violation of basic human rights of the Dalits are rooted and grounded on hate, intolerance, discrimination, prejudice, enmity and abhorrence.

Against this backdrop, Dalits have been waging a relentless war making every effort to annihilate caste and liberate themselves from the dehumanizing social order. To carry on this struggle, they have also been trying to build Dalit organizations at the local level. The formation of *Dalit Sangharsh Samitis* or the Dalit Struggle Forums is the outcome of these long-standing efforts. At the national level a forum like the National Campaign for Dalit Human Rights (NCDHR) carried out campaigns against caste discrimination. In its Final Declaration at the end of the Global Conference Against Racism and Caste based Discrimination held from 1-4th March 2001, New Delhi it demanded the following: ' We affirm that caste is the basis for the segregation and oppression of peoples in terms of their descent and occupation and this is a form of apartheid and a distinct form of racism that equally victimises irrespective of religion. We assert that untouchability is a crime against humanity. We demand that caste-based discrimination be included in the agenda of the World Conference Against Racism'.[62]

At the international arena, the International Dalit Solidarity Network has provided ideological, infrastructural and financial support to carry on the campaign further. The International Dalit Solidarity Network and the Dalits of India in a joint declaration have clearly and categorically stated, 'We acknowledge that discrimination based on work (occupation) and descent (untouchability arising out of caste discrimination) has historically been a feature of societies in different regions of the world and has affected a significant proportion overall (240 million) of the world's population and we declare that such discrimination is prohibited by international human rights law'.[63] Thus in the last few years consistent efforts have been made to raise the caste discrimination in league with racial discrimination.

The Campaign on Trail

As repeatedly stated earlier, the Dalit struggle for liberation and emancipation has in no way reached its logical conclusion. It forges ahead with renewed vigour and vitality inspite of all odds against it. One of the major advancement is the successful campaign in terms of providing visibility to Dalit discrimination at the international level, which is profiled in the present and previous chapters. Expectedly, the struggle continues in a multi-dimensional, multi-faceted manner.

The follow up of the Durban conference was the review of including 'descent and occupation based discrimination' under the purview of racial discrimination. The following communication from NGO Liaison Officer of the High Commissioner for Human Rights once again brought the racial discrimination issue for review: "Dear NGO representatives, General Assembly Resolution A/56/266, of 27 March 2002, entitled: "Comprehensive implementation and follow-up to the World Conference against Racism, Racial Discrimination, Xenophobia and Related Intolerance" requests the High Commissioner for Human Rights to report annually to the General Assembly on progress made in the implementation of the provisions of the Durban Declaration and Programme of Action. In this context, the Office would like to invite all NGOs with ECOSOC status, as well as organisations which were accredited specifically to the World Conference against Racism, Racial Discrimination, Xenophobia and Related Intolerance, to forward their contributions to the Anti-Discrimination Unit by 21 June 2002."[64]

In a Press Statement issued by the National Campaign for Dalit Human Rights Delegation, the following progress made in the attempt to include caste discrimination in the agenda of racial discrimination could be discerned:

At the UN CERD 61 Session, Geneva, Switzerland, 10 August 2002 a Historic Decision was adopted by UN Committee on the Elimination of Racial Discrimination (UN CERD) to draft General Recommendation of Caste based discrimination. Mr. Rajesh Prasad, a representative of the Permanent Mission of India to the UN, stated that the "thematic discussion has been transformed into a debate of the situation allegedly (pertaining) to a particular country". He said that the abhorrent practice of untouchability had been specifically abolished by the Constitution and manual scavenging was outlawed. "There are special schemes for the economic welfare of the Scheduled Castes and Scheduled Tribes." He acknowledged that there is often deficiency in implementation and that laws have to be better enforced. He said the tools to bring about change are in place and are available within the Indian democratic polity itself and do not have to be sought elsewhere. He also contested the interpretation of the CERD committee to cover Caste based discrimination as the Convention (ICERD) refers to 'racial descent'.

Members of UN CERD felt otherwise. "This is a historic opportunity. We must have the courage to take this opportunity. Within CERD there is an unanimity to take the issue of Caste", declared Mr. Sicilianos, a member of the UN CERD during the debate on second and final day of the Thematic Discussion on the Ground of Descent. His speech reflected the general mood of the other members of the CERD after they have heard the NGOs and movements made their presentation on the previous day, 8 August 2002, which formed the first day of discussion on the ground of descent. Prof. Patrick Thornberry, coordinator of the Thematic discussion, while echoing the previous remarks, noted that the Interpretation from India was not convincing and that they were not progressively interpreting the clauses in the International Convention on Racial Discrimination (ICERD). He also said a General Recommendation will aim to encourage the states to identify issues that need to be addressed and does not and will not target any one country but will continuously engage with the States and work with them to encourage further action on the issue of caste based discrimination and further action on the implementation of the policies and the Acts already in existence to reduce the caste based discrimination.

Another CERD member De Gouttes, explained that there are other clauses, articles, charter bodies and other instruments to cover the other forms of discrimination. He said that this is specifically provided for those discriminated on the ground of descent, which has social origin, wherein one is born into an identity that cannot be changed and there is an absence of social mobility. These characteristics and many other indicators are present in the caste system. He said that it is primarily a national problem – it starts and ends with national responsibility. In many countries there are laws and texts but the problem is implementation. The Chairperson of the CERD, Lon Diaconu said the General Recommendations will attempt to identify specific areas which the Governments can follow and we expect that it will contribute to the resolution of the emerging human problems. On 8 August, the whole of afternoon session was set apart for non- governmental organisations mostly from Africa and the Asian continents who have come to make presentations on the discrimination based on descent. In all there were 23 presentations registered with the secretariat.

There were Joint Statement from 26 NGOs[65] and these NGOs exposed the current and changing patterns of the discrimination based on caste system in the country and condemned the in-human practice of Caste system, which affected millions around the world. In fact many constitutional provisions and laws that have been promulgated are still unattended too. The NGOs recommended the CERD to name Caste-based discrimination as the primary form of descent-based form of discrimination and should effectively bring the Dalits under the purview of the committee. It is indeed a historic decision taken by the CERD to pass a General Recommendation on the Caste Based Discrimination. This implies that Caste based discrimination will be directly addressed with clear guidelines of monitoring by the states within their respective countries as well as reporting to the CERD in its deliberations. The important spin-off is that caste based discrimination will be addressed by the many UN bodies on its own identity and within the parameters of the discrimination being experienced by the Dalits and similar communities across the world. It will mean that every Charter body or relevant international Conventions like CRC (Convention of Child Rights), CEDAW (Convention of Elimination of Discrimination Against Women), ICCPR (International Convention for Civil and Political Rights), ICSECR (International Convention on Social, Economic and Cultural Rights).

Already a beginning was made through the statements by the members of the United Nation's Sub-Commission for Protection and Promotion of Human Rights who had participated in the UN CERD Thematic discussion on the 8 August. They said that while agreeing to the progress in countries like India on setting the standards in Constitution and laws for the protection and promotion of the Scheduled Castes and Tribes, they disagree with the position taken by India that caste based discrimination does not fall under descent based discrimination. Prof. Hampson said that the discrimination felt by the Dalits – humiliation, distinction and exclusion violates the basic right to equality irrespective of race, colour, gender, religion and descent mentioned in all the human rights charters. The members of the Sub-commission are seriously considering the extension to the Study on Discrimination related to Work and Descent. The previous study done by Mr. Goonesekere, and presented at the last years Sub-commission directly confirmed the practice of discrimination based on Caste in India and other South Asian countries and indicted the government of India in failing to implement existing legislation in favour of the Dalits whose rights are violated. NCDHR delegates feel that the flood gates are now in the process of being flung open for addressing the caste based discrimination at the United Nations in its various bodies for deliberation and consideration. They feel this will pressurise the government in India to take the issue of enforcement more seriously. The real work continues to be in the thousands of villages.

NCDHR will continue network with the many Dalit movements, activists, academics and organisations to expose the decrying gap between the Acts and their implementation, as well as the constitutional provisions and their enforcement. It will work towards to building a positive mind-set in the civil society to the rights and concerns of the Dalit women, children and men and communities. It aims to bring the many MPs and MLAs and floor leaders of the political parties in India to take seriously the agenda of protection and promotion of Dalit human rights and its enforcement in the county. NCDHR will also simultaneously network with the many communities around the globe particularly in Asia and Africa which are discriminated on the issue of caste based discrimination to collectively address this issue at the United nations and related multi-lateral organisations.[66]

Finally, it needs to be stated that all the efforts to continue with the discourse of Dalit struggle as well as to initiate concrete actions are painstakingly and progressively making strides. Some of the fundamental issues the Dalit liberation struggles have to squarely answer at this juncture is, "Is our liberation and emancipation only 'freedom from' or 'freedom to' or is it both?" Moreover, where does the leadership lie and what form of leadership does Dalit movement need today? It is expedient to conclude this chapter with the prophetic words of Dr. Ambedkar. 'Blessed are those who experience this fact that we have to liberate those people among whom we are born. Blessed are those who offer everything for the elimination of slavery. Blessed are those who without taking into account pain and please, dignity and indignity, problems and crisis, cyclone and earthquake continue to struggle till then when the untouchables do not attain their human rights and dignity'.[67]

References

1. Prakash Louis. Casteism is more Horrendous than Racism; Durban and Dalit discourse. Indian Social Institute, New Delhi 2001. Also see Shiv Vishwanathan, The Race for Caste: Prolegomena to the Durban Conference, Economic and Political Weekly, July 7, 2001, pp. 2512-2516 and Shiv Vishwanathan, Durban and Dalit Discourse. Economic and Political Weekly, August 18, 2001, pp. 3123-3127.
2. People's Perception of Land Reform Policies and Practices: A Comparative Study of Eastern, Western and Central Regions of Uttar Pradesh. Indian Social Institute: New Delhi, June 2001.
3. B.B. Mohanty. Land Distribution among the Scheduled Castes and Tribes. Economic and Political Weekly. Bombay. October 6, 2001, p 3863.
4. The National Agricultural Policy. Department of Agriculture and Cooperation. Ministry of Agriculture. Government of India, July 2000. Refer for other recent National Policies to Prakash Louis. Policy Documents of the Government of India. Indian Social Institute: New Delhi. 2003.
5. Anand Teltumbde. Impact of New Economic Reforms on Dalits in India. Unpublished paper presented in the Seminar on 'Economic Reforms and Dalits in India' organised by the University of Oxford, on November 8, 1996.
6. Buiyans are considered to be at the lowest rung of the caste order

not only in terms of the upper castes but among the Dalits too.

7. Gyan Prakash. Bonded Histories: Genealogies of Labor Servitude in Colonial India. Cambridge University Press, Cambridge, 1990, p. 169.
8. For a study of this orientation, see, Prakash Louis, People Power: The Naxalite Movement in Central Bihar. Wordsmiths: New Delhi, 2002. Workshops and consultations are being organized in different parts of the country to understand the points of convergence and difference between the Dalit movement and Naxalite movement.
9. Kancha Ilaiah. God as Political Philosopher: Buddha's Challenge to Brahminism. Samya: Calcutta, 2000, p. 32.
10. Refer to National Dailies of 4th and 5th November 2001.
11. Towards Eliminating Child Labour. V.V. Giri National Labour Institute, Noida: India. September 1995, p. 12.
12. For more on this debate refer Prakash Louis. Caste, Child, Labour and Exploitation: Civil Society and Dalit Children. A paper presented in the National Seminar on 'Building Better Tomorrow for the Dalit Children' organized by Bachpan Bachao Andolan at Indian Social Institute, New Delhi June 2003.
13. Manisha. *Avarna se kuch seeken savarna*. Rashtriya Sahara: (New Delhi). 18.12.2000, p. 6.
14. J.V. Deshpande. Behind Dalit Anger. Economic and Political Weekly, Bombay. August 16-23 1997. pp. 2090-91.
15. A.K.Jha. Dalit Ascendancy. The Times of India, New Delhi, 26.7.97, p. 8.
16. Prakash Louis. Casteism is more Horrendous than Racism; Durban and Dalit discourse. Indian Social Institute, New Delhi 2001.
17. These discussions are held at the meetings, workshops, and consultations, which mostly end up in accusation and counter-accusation.
18. There are proverbs in many parts of India indicating the powerful divisions in particular castes whether they are lower or higher. In north Indian villages there is a proverb doing the rounds "*theen kanujya aur thera vichar*" which means ' where there are 3 members from the Kanuj caste, there will be 13 opinions'. This is a clear indication of the division that is prevalent in any caste group.
19. It is of seminal significance to underscore this socio-historical fact that it was B.S. Moonje, a Maharashtrian Brahmin who was sent to Italy and Germany to understand the tenets of fascism so that the Hindu social order could be built on similar foundations. This clearly

indicates the internal and external links of the Hindutva forces whose only aim was to continue to maintain the hegemony and monopoly of the Brahminical social order. For more details refer to Marzia Casolari, Hindutva Foreign Tie-up in the 1930s" Archival Evidence. In Economic and Political Weekly, January 22, 2000, p 218. , and Prakash Louis, The Emerging Hindutva Force: The Ascent of the Hindu Nationalism, Indian Social Institute, 2000.

20. Gail Omvedt. Dalits and the Democratic Revolution: Dr. Ambedkar and the Dalit Movement in Colonial India. Sage Publications, New Delhi, 1994, p. 111.
21. Lata Murugkar. Dalit Panther Movement in Maharastra. Popular Prakashan: Bombay, 1991.
22. Anand Teltumbde. Ambedkar for the Post-Ambedkar Dalit Movement. Sugawa Prakashan: Pune 1997, p. 16.
23. Badrinarayan. Documenting Dissent: Contesting Fables, Contested Memories and Dalit Political Discourse. Indian Institute of Advanced Study, Shimla, 2001, pp. 149-150.
24. While in the last two decades, efforts have been made to explore the possibilities of forming a broad alliance between the weaker sections, the genocide that took place in Gujarat, impressed upon the immediacy of forming this alliance.
25. The Gujarat Pogrom. A Compilation of Various Reports. Indian Social Institute: New Delhi, 2002.
26. I am describing here only the International organisations and major forums or campaigns. For a discussion on Indian organisations refer to R.K. Kshirsagar. Dalit movement in India and its leaders. New Delhi: M.D. Publications Pvt Ltd, 1994.
27. Laxmi N. Berwa. Asian Dalit Solidarity. ISPCK: Delhi, 2000, pp. 136.
28. Anand Teltumbde, in P.G. Jogdand (ed), New Economic Policy and Dalits. Rawat Publications: Jaipur. 2000, pp. 91-138.
29. Refer to a booklet compiled by M. Gopinath and Pramod Kureel. 'Rulers alone can create casteless society. A message from Dadasaheb Kanshi Ram to the victimized castes. 1998.
30. Interestingly, VOD International was supported by Dalit Solidarity Network (DSN) a UK based forum. The DSN is composed of human rights motivated individuals, groups and leading NGOs like Amnesty International, Anti-Slavery International and Minority Rights Groups.
31. Dalits in the New Millennium. Report of the Proceedings of

International Conference on Dalit Human Rights. VOD International: London. 2000. Back cover page.

32. *Ibid.*
33. Ibid., pp. 19-24.
34. Sketches of the Campaign. National Campaign for Dalit Human Rights. Secundrabad. Unpublished paper.
35. *Ibid.*
36. From the objectives of the NCDHR, it is clear that it was not constituted to represent the Dalit issue in the World Conference Against Racism though pressurizing the UN and other international organisations was one of the objectives.
37. National Campaign Manifesto: 1998. Dalit Human Rights – 10th December 1998- 15th August 1999. Secundrabad, India.
38. There has been lot of criticism about the Bhopal Conference. The main one was that it was an attempt by the State Congress Government to ensure its vote bank among the Dalits and the Tribals, and to succeed in this, the State Government co-opted some Dalit intellectuals to draft the Bhopal Declaration.
39. Invitation sent by Mr. Digvijay Singh. Chief Minister of Madhya Pradesh, dated 18.12.2001.
40. The Bhopal Document. Charting A New Course For Dalits For The 21st Century. Madhya Pradesh Government: Bhopal. 2001.
41. Declaration of the Bhopal Conference date. Bhopal: Madhya Pradesh. 12-13 January 2002.
42. *Ibid.*
43. David Haslam. Dalits and International Development Aid. A Dalit Solidarity Network Paper. Dalit Solidarity Network: London. February 2003. [An unpublished document]
44. *Ibid.*
45. Mhow Declaration. Towards Integral Development of the Scheduled Castes. Scheduled Caste Forum of Bharatiya Janata Party, Madhya Pradesh. May 2003. Translated from Hindi by the author.
46. The document of the Mhow Declaration begins with the vision of Dr. Ambedkar. The document does not stop with that and goes on to speak about the contributions made by Gandhi, Sant Ravidas, Sant Kabir, Mahatma Jyotiba Phule and Pandit Deendayal Upadhyay.
47. *Ibid.*
48. *Ibid.*
49. The Vancouver Vision on Diversity. The Association for International

Dalit Conference. Canada, 2003, pp. 2 & 7.

50. Vancouver Declaration Adopted Unanimously by The International Dalit Conference Vancouver, Canada, May 16-18, 2003.
51. *Ibid.*
52. Antonio Gramsci. Selection from the Prison Note Books. The Noonday Pess: New York. 1971, pp. 43-44 & 203-205.
53. R. Eyerman and A. Jamison. Social Movements: A Cognitive Approach. Polity Press, Cambridge, 1991, p. 101.
54. Sudha Pai. "Dalit Assertion and the Unfinished Democratic Revolution: The Bahujan Samaj Party in Uttar Pradesh. Sage Publications: New Delhi. 2002.
55. *Ibid.*
56. Gopal Guru and V.Geetha. Dalit Intellectual Activism: Recent Trends. Vikas Adhyayan Kendra Publication, New Delhi, p. 1.
57. Ibid. The National Campaign for Dalit Human Rights, which from 1998 has been campaigning for Dalit human rights, could be classified as a Dalit NGO-led campaign.
58. Eleanor Zelliot. From Untouchables to Dalit: Essays on Ambedkar Movement. Manohar, Delhi, 1992, p. 34.
59. Jotiba Phule, Sarvajanik Satya Dharma Pustika, Marathi, as quoted in J.R. Kamble, Rise and Awakening of Depressed Classes in India. National Publishing House, Delhi, 1979, p. 56.
60. Dr. B.R. Ambedkar. Writings and Speeches, Vol. 7, p. i.
61. Bombay Legislative Council Debates, Vol, XXIII, pp. 708-721.
62. Final Declaration. The National Campaign for Dalit Human Rights, Global Conference. I am grateful to the Campaign Committee for giving me the material prepared for the campaign ,which have extensively used this material for the preparation of this book.
63. Draft Declaration. International Dalit Solidarity Network and the Dalits of India.
64. NGO Liaison Officer. UNOG-OHCHR, Geneva.
65. Names of the 26 NGOs who made the joint statement. International Dalit Solidarity Network), National Campaign on Dalit Human Rights, India, National Federation of Dalit Women, Sakshi-Dalit Human Rights Watch – Andhra Pradesh, Centre for Dalit Human Rights, Rajasthan, AP Jogini Vyvastha Vyathireka Porata Sanghatan, Lutheran World Federation-Geneva, International Movement Against discrimination and Racism – Japan, Buraku Liberation League, Nepalese Dalit NGO Federation, Human Development

Organisation - Sri Lanka, National Dalit Commission (Nepal), RADDHO (Senegal), AFRAD- Somali Association, Timidria – Niger, Centre Minority Rights Development (Kenya).

66. Press Statement issued by the National Campaign for Dalit Human rights Delegation. 10 August 2002.
67. Dr. Ambedkar's Writings and Speeches *(Hindi).* Education Department, Government of Maharashtra, 1987, Vol. 10.

6

Dalit Assertion and Emancipation

Dalit assertion and Dalit struggle for emancipation have come to stay. Seclusion, deprivation, exploitation and discrimination of the Dalits are historical as well as everyday phenomenon. In the same manner, Dalit protest, revolt and movements are also historical and contemporary processes. Right through the book it has been argued that atrocities and discrimination suffered by the Dalits and their assertion for liberation are two sides of the same coin. It is these two interlinked processes, which has provided a new identity to the Dalits. But these processes have followed one of the most relevant discursive paths as well as action programmes. This emerging identity in its turn has strengthened its resolve to fight every forms of discrimination and also determine the path for liberation.

If one delves deep into the social basis of Dalit discrimination, it would become clear the antagonism that exists between the Dalits and the non-Dalits. The heart of the matter is that the lower castes are considered to be the antithesis of the upper caste. The very presence of the Dalits and the downtrodden invariably challenges the claim that Indian society and nation are founded on high principles. The talk of India being an ancient civilization is countered by the skewed and oppressive caste system. Moreover, the Dalits today more than ever are challenging the very foundation on which the Indian society and polity are erected. As they are becoming acutely aware of the cumulative effective of social segregation, economic deprivation, political discrimination and cultural subordination, they are in a mission of overthrowing the very society and polity, which promises citizenhood for them.

The continued awareness building processes that were going on among the Dalits and the downtrodden have driven home this message, that poverty, illiteracy, ignorance and alcoholism etc., are only the symptoms of much greater malice that is affecting the entire Indian society. The fundamental issues are denial of access to resources, of participation in political processes, exclusion from social milieu and subjugation to an ideology of servitude and bondage. This is not limited to individual level and the entire Dalit community is reduced to this subjugated and dominated state of affairs. Hence, the Dalits are denying this social order as 'given' and are making every attempt to restructure the social order. Going further, they are demanding equal share in every resource, centers of power and struggle for equal dignity and right as human beings and as citizens of the country.

There is also another significant awareness that is gaining prominence among the Dalits, that is, the Dalits are becoming conscious of the fact that they are the real producers, creators, and upholders of all that is social, political, economic, cultural and religious. But they are also aware of the debilitating fact that they are denied of any share from the products of their labour and imagination. Hence, they are defying all that is available as 'social', 'religious', 'traditional' and 'national'. This force and power has led them to raise questions about the very legitimacy and validity of all the powers being concentrated in the hands of the dominant castes and classes. This has sent a danger signal to the dominant castes and has sounded death bell to the caste system. Hence, the Dalits are subjected to ruthless and brutal atrocities and repression.

If one even gleans through the Annual Reports of the Commission for the Scheduled Castes and Scheduled Tribes, the volumes of atrocities unleashed on the Dalits become amply clear. Significantly, the number of atrocities committed on the Dalits, would make one realize that the number of crimes committed under the categories defined under 'Prevention of Atrocities Act' is the highest. This goes to establish the fact that even when legal provisions are in place for the protection of the rights of the weaker sections, the ground reality is very different. Consequently, the Dalits and the downtrodden are loosing faith in the legal and constitutional provisions on the one hand, and on the other, their frustration is converted into aggression.

Factors Behind Dalit Movements

It is also expedient at this juncture to briefly recount some of the factors that were responsible for the rise of Dalit revolts, protests and movements in India. The Bhakti movements created a philosophical base for social equality and set in motion a new trend towards social and spiritual equality. Secondly, recruitment to martial services not only provided gainful economic employment but also functioned as moral booster. Thirdly, Dalit reform movements while advocating belief in casteless society, prohibition of idol worship, meat eating, liquor etc., also laid more emphasis on mobilization and organization of the downtrodden. Modern education opened up avenues for social mobility. Mahatma Jotiba Phule established Satya Shodhak Samaj in 1873 at Pune for the social and religious uplift of the untouchables and other backward communities.[1] Dalits as argued above, resorted to religious conversions as a means to liberate themselves from the clutches of inhuman caste system. Affirmative action or reservation policy provided scope and space for educated Dalits to become socially mobile and also provide leadership for the community. Finally, emergence of Dalit organisations, Dalit NGOs, Dalit intellectual class and Dalit political parties have enhanced the ability for political mobilization.

A careful examination of Dalit struggles would also unravel some of the inanimate factors behind Dalit movements. Land reform measures generated hope for owning land. The Dalits were and are aware of the fact that they cannot purchase land since owning land has become unaffordable by them. But they are hopeful that within the land reform policy enactment they would have some access to land from the common property resources, which till recently was the prerogative of the dominant caste landed gentry. Urbanisation and industrialization provided employment outside the caste-ridden village system and in return enhanced the scope for social mobility.[2] It is not proposed here that migration to urban centers have altogether altered the life situation of the Dalits.[3] But most of those who moved out of the rural areas have escaped from physical torture and mental agony they were subjected to every day in the villages.

One of the most vital and decisive factors in the reinterpretation of Dalit identity by the Dalits themselves was politicization of the Dalits. Politicization means' 'the orientation of people to political perspectives and political actions'. The first attempt to politicize the Dalits was done when the British government abandoned the practice of recruiting the Dalits into army. Dr. Ambedkar in 1941 convinced the government to recruit the Mahars into military. In the second place one sees the emergence of caste associations, which try to highlight the plight of the Dalits. Finally the founding of organizations like the Independent Party, the Depressed Classes League and the Scheduled Caste Federation also contributed in the politicization of the Dalits.

Most of the struggles and movements in India have been divided in terms of pre and post-independent era. But once again this division does not explain the true development of the Dalit struggle and the factors that generated these movements. It is expedient to divide them in terms of pre-Ambedkar and post-Ambedkar era.

1. Pre-Ambedkar era: the efforts of this period were mostly reformative in nature, often less co-ordinated and even isolated. Demands were more in the nature of reservation in educational institutions, temple entries etc, internal and external reforms etc.
2. Post-Ambedkar era: the struggles of this phase were mostly transformative, challenging the very ethos of the stratified society. Also the response of the Dalits was ubiquitous, that is, universal and overwhelming. Moreover, the dominant caste took cognizance of the movements.[5]

One question continues to be raised in the discourse on Dalit liberation is: What does Dalit liberation or emancipation or revolution really mean? Gail Omvedt presents a historical note to this question. "Ambedkar had argued, in one of his tracts, *Mukti Kon Pathe*? (What Path to Liberation?), that a necessary condition was the overthrow of "Hindu" religious-ideological hegemony. He had tended to see economic and social oppression as separate structures, taking up 'cultural' (religious, ideological) change as the way to challenge Hinduism, socialism as the way to overcome economic exploitation. But always Dr. Ambedkar, and all the militant Dalit activists of India, had seen the necessity of combined struggle, dealing with both social and economic issues. At times it seemed as if a mechanical stress on economic solutions was met with an equally mechanical insistence on cultural-religious ones; indeed the most militant organisations of the new movement, the Dalit Panthers, split on this issues in 1974-75 with one faction associated with 'Buddhism' and the other 'Marxism'. Yet this was a temporary break; nearly all came to agree on the need for combining 'class-caste struggle'.[6]

Dalit Women and Dalit Movements

Significantly, while the caste and class question came to occupy centre stage in the Dalit movement, the question of direct participation of Dalit women took time to be engaged in the central discourse of Dalit struggles. There are some questions, which continue to remain unanswered with regard to Dalit women. These are as following; What did Dalit women gain from Dalit movement? Have Dalit women gained equal status with men cadres and leaders in Dalit movements? The Hindu society is not only hierarchical but it is also inherently patriarchal. Hence, women in Hindu society are denied access to property and resources. They are also deprived of equal power and authority but invested with greater responsibility and accountability. Since Hinduisation of Dalits has been going on successfully, have the Dalit women also been brought under the purview of patriarchy? What is the place and role of Dalit women in their family, Dalit communities and finally in Dalit movements?

It is a fact that from 18th century onwards some attempts were made to liberate the Dalit women from the clutches of double oppression. In 1852 schools were opened for the education of Dalit women. In 1930 small-scale industries were started for the Dalit women. Hostels were opened for the Women's Conference for Dalit women in 1935 and from then on education was opened up for the women in a big way. Dr. Ambedkar too focused on some of the important aspects of reform among Dalit women. 1. He stressed the fact that education of girls should be equal to that of the boys; 2. He also opposed early marriage of girls since it stalls their education and mobility; 3. He insisted on the need to take the consent of the girls before marriage. He had also said that the true index of development of any society is the development of women. During his life time itself, women took part in temple entry, protest marches etc., and were also got imprisoned. Encouraged by this Dr. Ambedkar organized Mahila Parishad or Women's Conference in 1942 in Nagpur. Women's Conferences were also organized in Nasik in 1942, in Kanpur in 1944, and in Bombay 1945. It is from these concerted efforts that leaders among Dalit women emerged.[7]

But one should not loose sight of some salient features of Dalit women in general and Dalit women's participation in struggles in particular. 1. Within the Dalit movements, women's specific issues are neglected. 2. Emergence of women's leadership has not been encouraged. 3. There is a fear to allow the emergence of an independent women's movement within Dalit movement, due to the fear that this would weaken the movement.

Response of Dominant Castes

It is logical that one refers to the response of the dominant castes towards the emerging Dalit leadership and Dalit movement. One can broadly identify the following responses: 1) Initiate welfare measures like reservation in educational institutions, jobs, electoral arena. These welfare measures are supposed to placate the anger of the Dalits towards establishment. Some would even go to the extent of organizing inter-dining and inter-caste marriage. 2. To maintain status quo, the dominant castes would introduce reform movements. While the reform movements are supposed to draw the Dalits into 'mainline' social order, the leadership continues to remain with the dominant castes. *Swaadhyay* movement, which was operative in Gujarat, could be cited as an example of this reality.[8] 3. Co-opt potential leaders and thus destroy movements. 4. Boycott Dalit leaders and movements and ultimately Dalit communities. 5. The dominant castes could also engage in maligning the names of the leaders and the movements. 6. Finally, terrorise the Dalits and commit atrocities and engage in repressive measures. Interestingly, the state also conducts its affairs in a similar manner towards Dalits and Dalit movements.

Broader Alliance of the Exploited

As stated in the foregoing pages, Dalit discrimination was provided visibility at the international arena during the World Conference Against Racism held in Durban in 2001. This is a major achievement for the Dalit activists, human rights activists and all those who had perceived the validity and the legitimacy of this struggle. Above all it is the victory of the common masses from the Dalits and the downtrodden communities, since their cause has found echo in the international human rights forum.

Efforts of this nature over the years, has also demanded a joint search for building broad alliance between all the discriminated and exploited masses in India. At various times attempts were made to unite the Dalits and the tribals or the Dalit and the Muslims or search for common platforms for Dalit and women's movements or search for shared aims and actions between the radical left movements or the Naxalite movements and the Dalit movements.

For instance, in early 1960s there was alliance formed between the *Jataos*[9] and the Muslims in Uttar Pradesh. R. Kamble stated, "In my fact finding tour of important districts in Uttar Pradesh especially Aligarh, Moradabad and Lucknow during 1962 elections, I came across a militant attitude in the *Jatao* community. Their political awakening was unprecedented. Strangely enough the Muslims and *Chamars* have grouped themselves together and their slogan is "*Jatao Muslim bhai-bhai, Hindu Kaum kahan se ayi*", [meaning 'The Jataos and the Muslims are in alliance and there is no scope for the Hindus']. This is a new phenomenon in Indian politics. Sri B.P. Morya a Jatao was elected to the Lok Sabha on a general seat defeating a rival caste Hindu Congress candidate. Many prominent Muslims have joined Republican Party, which is a leading party in India representing these classes."[10]

Finally to unravel the emerging Dalit consciousness and Dalit movements in India it is imperative that the social contradictions of the wider caste society as well as the contradictions within the Dalit communities should be viewed. The Dalits have not been the forerunners but have been the flag bearers of most of the social movements that have unfolded in various parts of India. Whether it is the trade union movements, left movements or even the radical left movements, it is the Dalits and the downtrodden of this country who have born the brunt of all these movements. The countless repressions and the massacres that have taken place in many parts of the country bear ample testimony to this sociological fact. Interestingly, the leadership of most of these movements is still in the hands of the dominant castes.[11] The reason for this is not just lack of education or lack of ability to mobilize and organize the labouring masses or lack of economic resources. But the reasons for this social reality should be searched in the very Indian social order, which is anti-Dalit. Learning from this social and historical fact, the Dalits are making ceaseless attempts to forge a unified Dalit struggle. The Dalits are also moving further than their own conventional realm to search for space to build broader alliance with other exploited masses of this country.

Taken together, whether it is in the social or in the political realm the Dalits of India have amply demonstrated that they will not take things lying any more. Further, they have also demonstrated their resolve that they are no more vote bank of the upper castes but are equal partners in power equations. Though the Dalits of India have not initiated and mobilized a pan-Indian Dalit movement *per se,* yet they have begun to assert their constitutional rights in unparalleled terms through political participation both in the electoral processes and also in ruling position. Going further, they have also asserted their demand for a major share in the political power. They have also stated their resolve not to remain the cadres or flag bearers of the upper castes but determine their emancipation on their own terms. In this context it is not farfetched to state that Dalit assertion for liberation and emancipation has come to stay in the caste ridden Indian society.

In this regard the prophetic words of Jagjivan Ram has a pointer for the Dalit assertion. He had declared, "The Liberation struggle of the Scheduled Castes has begun. There are many hurdles and impediments on the way. The fight is unequal. But struggle we must without any respite and without a pause. We must liberate ourselves for in our liberation lies the emancipation of mankind."[12]

Dr. Ambedkar was also well aware of the crucial fact that the problems confronting the depressed classes are more fundamental than a social issue, which could be done away with social reforms, "It is wrong to say that the problem of the untouchables is a social problem. For, it is quite unlike the problem of dowry, widow remarriage, age of consent, etc., which are illustrations of what are called social problems. Essentially, it is the problem of quite a different nature... the problem of the untouchables is fundamentally a political problem... of minority versus majority groups."[13]

There are many questions that need to be raised with regard to Dalit atrocities and Dalit assertion. Social exclusion, deprivation and discrimination of the Dalits have led to conservative solidarity[14] among the Dalits. The question that needs to be raised today is how does this conservative solidarity be transformed into radical solidarity? Many of the Dalit organisations, NGOs, political formations are busy in welfare and developmental activities among the Dalits. Since the Dalits are and have been economically deprived and dispossessed, developmental activities need to be undertaken in a big way with them. While carrying out developmental measures, how does political socialization of the Dalit masses be undertaken in a systematic manner is a serious question today.

There have been many attempts to build a pan-Indian Dalit movement. These efforts need to be carried out in the most premeditated method. In the process, Dalit activists and intellectuals also need to pay attention to the subtle and informal protests that go on unabated. The principal question is how does the everyday forms of resistance[15] contribute in the revolts, protests and movements? It is a well acknowledged fact that reservation has been one of the instruments for social mobility. There have been some rumblings from the dominant castes to do away with reservation or to dilute it by promising to offer reservation to the 'poor among the dominant castes'. While continuing the pressure to provide reservation till that time when the Dalits themselves would oppose reservation policy, how does the Dalit leadership initiate struggle and wage movements for access over resources, control over land and labour?

Finally, the discrimination that the Dalits are subjected to is much more horrendous than racial discrimination. This has had cumulative impact on the Dalits and has deprived them of the right to be human. But in the same time, the agony and the anguish of the Dalits have given rise to protests and assertions. Over the years, they have come to realize that they have to assert themselves for their human and constitutional rights and also the right to live a human life. This resolve alone has the potential to liberate them from the clutches of social exclusion, economic deprivation, cultural subjugation and political powerlessness. Thus, the political sociology of the Dalits while highlighting the atrocities heaped on the Dalits also unravels the assertion that is gathering up unabated among this discriminated community. This paradigm shift in the Dalit struggles and movements have provided the potent and force for a unified struggle of all the exploited masses. The need of the hour today is to forge this integrated struggle of the exploited masses for the restructuring of the entire Indian social order.

References

1. Rosalind O'Hanlon. Caste, Conflict and Ideology: Mahatma Jyotirao Phule and low Caste protest in nineteenth-century western India. Cambridge University Press, 1985.
2. R.K. Kshirsagar. Dalit movement in India and its leaders. M.D. Publications Pvt Ltd: New Delhi. 1994.
3. Margaret Antony and G. Maheshwaran. Social Segregation and Slums: The Plight of the Dalits in the Slums of Delhi. Indian Social Institute: New Delhi, 2001.
4. For more on this theme, refer, Anand Teltumbde. Ambedkar in And For The Post-Ambedkar Dalit Movement. Sugawa Prakashan: Pune, 1997.
5. Gail Omvedt. Dalits and Democratic Revolution. Dr. Ambedkar and the Dalit Movement in Colonial India. Sage Publications: New Delhi, 1994, p 338.
6. Sandeep Pendse. Dalit Movements At Cross Roads. Vikas Adhyayn Kendra: Mumbai, 1994.

7. What has the Dalit Movement Offered to Women? Urmila Power in Pendse: Dalit Movements At Cross Roads. *Vikas Adhyayan Kendra, Bombay,* 1994.
8. Ghanshyam Shah. The BJP and the Backward Castes in Gujarat. In Praful Bidwai (ed) Religion, Religiosity and Communalism. Manohar Publications: New Delhi, 1996.
9. Jataos are one of the sub-castes among Dalit community in Uttar Prdesh. They are also called 'Charmars' or Ravidasis'.
10. R. Kamble, Rise and Awakening of Depressed Classes in India. National Publishing House, Delhi, 1979, p 101.
11. Gulab Jha. Caste and the Communist Movement. Common Wealth Publishers: New Delhi. 1990. In this study about the Communist Party of Madhubani district of Bihar State, which is a stronghold of Communist Party of India, Gulab Jha argues that the upper caste in Madhubani constituted about 18.1% but occupied 57.8% of leadership roles and have produced only 25.7% of martyrs during the struggle. The Scheduled Castes on the other hand comprised 12.8% of population held only 26.6% of leadership position but had the highest share of the martyrs, about 34.3%. This goes to state that even in left parties the Scheduled Castes continue to be flag bearers and not leaders.
12. Jagjivan Ram. Caste Challenges in India. Vision Books: New Delhi, 1980. Ibid. p 6.
13. Dr.B.R. Ambedkar, What Congress and Gandhi have done to Untouchables, Bombay, 1946, p 190.
14. Conservative solidarity in political sociology means a sense of being deprived, excluded and discriminated. Radical solidarity taking this exploitative and oppressive milieu engages in assertion and self-determination.
15. James C. Scott. Weapons of the Weak: Everyday Form of Peasant Resistance in Southeast Asia. Frank Cass: London. 1986.

APPENDIX 1

The Scheduled Castes and the Scheduled Tribes (Prevention of Atrocities) Act, 1989

Objective: This Act is enacted to prevent the commission of offences of atrocities against the members of the Scheduled Castes and the Scheduled Tribes and to provide special courts for the trial of such offences and for the relief and rehabilitation of the victims of such offences.

Atrocities: atrocity means an offence punishable under section 3 of the act.

1. Forces a member of the Scheduled Castes and the Scheduled Tribes to drink or eat any inedible or obnoxious substance.
2. Acts with intent to cause injury, insult or annoyance to any member of a Scheduled Caste and the Scheduled Tribe the by dumping excreta, waste matter, carcasses or any other obnoxious substance in his premises or neighbourhood.
3. Forcibly removes clothes from the persons of a member of a Scheduled Caste and the Scheduled Tribe or parade him naked or with painted face or body or commits act which is derogatory to human dignity.
4. Wrongfully occupies or cultivates any land owned by, or allotted to or notified by any competent authority to be allotted to a member of a Scheduled Caste and the Scheduled Tribe or gets the land to him transferred.
5. Wrongfully dispossesses a member of a Scheduled Caste and the Scheduled Tribe from his land or premises or interferes with the enjoyment of his rights over any land, premises or water.

6. Compels or entices a member of the Scheduled Caste and the Scheduled Tribe to do "beggar" or other similar forms of forced or bonded labour other than any compulsory service for public purposes imposed by Government.
7. Forces or intimidates a member of a Scheduled Caste and the Scheduled Tribe not to vote or to vote to a particular candidate or to vote in a manner other than that provided by law.
8. Institutes false, malicious or vexatious suit or criminal or other legal proceedings against a member of a Scheduled Caste and the Scheduled Tribe.
9. Gives any false or frivolous information to any public servant and thereby causes such public servant to use his lawful power to the injury or annoyance of a member of a Scheduled Caste and the Scheduled Tribe.
10. Intentionally insults or intimidates with intent to humiliate a member of a Scheduled Caste and the Scheduled Tribe in any place within public view.
11. Assaults or uses force to any woman belonging to a Scheduled Caste and the Scheduled Tribe with intent to dishonour or outrage her modesty.
12. Being in a position to dominate the will of a woman belonging to a Scheduled Caste and the Scheduled Tribe and uses the position to explain her sexually to which she would not have otherwise agreed.
13. Corrupts or fouls the water of any spring, reservoir or any other source ordinarily used by members of the Scheduled Caste and the Scheduled Tribe so as to render it less fit for the purpose for which it is ordinarily used.
14. Denies a member of a Scheduled Caste and the Scheduled Tribe any customary right of passage to a place of public resort to obstructs such member so as to prevent him from using or having access to a place of public resort to which other members of public or any section thereof have a right to use to access to.

15. Forces or causes a member of a Scheduled Caste and the Scheduled Tribe to leave his house, village or other places of residence.

For all these offences a person shall be punishable with imprisonment for a term which shall not be less than six months but which may extend to five years and with fine.

APPENDIX 2

National Campaign on Dalit Human Rights

Delhi Office: 38/2996 Beadon Pura, Karol Bagh, New Delhi 11005
Phone: 585 4967, 581 7738 Email: mimroth@indiatimes.com

MEMORANDUM TO THE UNITED NATIONS, 3rd July 2001

No Confidence in Prime Minister Atal Behari Vajpayee's National Committee for Durban Conference

To the Secretary General and Member States of the United Nations:

Today, 3rd July, is a historic day. This day in 1928 in Mahad, Dr. Baba Sahib Dr Bhimrao Ambedkar led a massive movement to challenge the validity of the restrictions set against the Dalits by the Orthodox Scriptures and the inhuman behaviour of the self styled Upper castes.

On this historic day, the Dalits of India and other Asian, African, Pacific and Caribbean countries express their deep concern over the fact that the Government of India has deliberately injured democratic processes and the sentiments and feelings of the hundreds of millions of Dalits in opposing inclusion of Caste in the agenda of the United Nations World Conference Against Racism, Racial discrimination, Xenophobia and Related Intolerance. The UN conference is to beheld in Durban, South Africa from 31 August 2001.

The position that the government of India has taken in several meetings leading up to the Durban conference, and the propaganda it has unleashed, violates the very superstructure of Equity and Justice of the Indian Constitution and is tantamount to further violence against its own citizens.

The Prime Minister of India has tried to divert global attention by setting up a so-called National Committee under the chairmanship of the Union Minister for External Affairs to facilitate India's participation in the World Conference to be held at Durban, South Africa from 31 August to 7 September. A look at the membership of this committee clearly shows the upper caste bias of this committee.

The Dalits of India have no confidence in the Prime Minister's National Committee. We fear this committee will only articulate the point of view of the religious and social groups who have subjugated the Dalits through the millennia.

The record of these groups is tainted with the blood of millions of innocent people, the tears of women who have been raped, and the cries of others who have been robbed of basic human dignity. In doing so, these groups have violated all canons of civilisational norms which are today enshrined in the Charter of the United Nations and its other special resolutions on Human Rights.

The historic injury to an entire people is sufficient and adequate mandate for an immediate international discussion on discrimination based on descent and occupation-based Caste, a discrimination that has been ratified and even sanctified for more than three thousand years, is justified by dominant groups even to this day, and continues to be practiced with barbaric savagery in many countries of South Asia, including Nepal, Bangladesh, Pakistan, Sri Lanka, and of course, in India, apart from other parts of the world.

The United Nations Sub Committee has already appointed an Expert Member, Advocate Goonashekharan, of Sri Lanka, to conduct an in-depth study of the issue. We urge him to review the Draft Declaration and include the following clauses proposed by the International Dalit Solidarity Network and the Dalits of India:

"For insertion under Para 20 of the Draft Declaration:

We acknowledge that discrimination based on work (occupation) and descent (untouchability arising out of caste discrimination) has historically been a feature of societies in different regions of the world and has affected a significant proportion overall (240 million) of the world's population and we declare that such discrimination is prohibited by international human rights law. (UN Sub Commission on Human Rights Resolution 2000/4)

For insertion in the Draft Program of Action as Chapter X bis, Para 53 bis titled Discrimination on the basis of work and descent (Caste):

The World Conference affirms that discrimination on the basis of work and descent involves a complex and deeply entrenched obstacle to the realization of the civil, cultural, economic, political and social rights of members of the affected communities and that while most closely associated with caste systems in South Asia, this type of discrimination is encountered in other parts of the world as well.

The World Conference therefore:

(i) calls upon the Office of the United Nations Commissioner for Human Rights to undertake an in depth study of the question of discrimination on the basis of work and descent, in co-operation with the Committee for the Elimination of Racial Discrimination.

(ii) encourages Governments concerned to undertake public awareness raising and educational initiatives in order to promote positive changes in attitudes towards and within communities discriminated against on the basis of work and descent."

This is the demand of 240 million affected people of the world. We will not countenance hypocrisy any more, nor will we be satiated by platitudes. We urge the Secretary General and Member States of the United nations to encourage a World discussion on caste-based discrimination to finally exorcise this evil, which has poisoned society for all too long.

The mandate for the Durban Conference is clear and unambiguous. The Durban Conference is meant to discuss Discrimination, Intolerance and xenophobia deriving out of race. We firmly believe this Mandate is sufficient and adequate for an immediate international discussion on discrimination based on Caste — which is defined by descent – a discrimination that has been ratified, even sanctified, for more than three thousand years, is justified by dominant groups even to this day, and continues to be practiced with barbaric savagery in many countries of South Asia, including Nepal, Bangladesh, Pakistan, Sri Lanka, and of course, in India.

To characterise Caste as an internal matter of India and to state that any discussion on it as an intrusion on Indian sovereignty goes counter to historical facts, and militates against evolution of contemporary philosophical, juridical and political norms and principles of equality, enshrined both in the Indian Constitution and in the Statutes and Special Resolutions of the United Nations.

'Caste is Race Plus'. Inflicted by birth, sanctified by religion, glorified by tradition, Caste has had brutal repercussions for a fifth of India's population through the generations. Social scientists have highlighted the conspiracy to subjugate the Dalit Bahujans by attempting to construct the Indian nation on the basis of purity of blood, language and culture. With revivalism, a fascist culture centered on the purity of the Aryan race, superiority of Sanskrit over other languages and brahmanic culture are imposed on the country.

The Indian legal system has consistently recognised and acknowledged the existence in Indian society of discrimination based on caste as a form of racial discrimination. The existence of discrimination on the basis of descent and occupation has been the subject matter of a number of Legislative measures including Constitutional provisions and judicial decisions of the Supreme Court of India and the High Courts of different States. The discrimination based on caste is at least equated with, or dealt at par with discrimination based on race.

The Constitutional provisions not only juxtapose caste with race and sex as prohibited grounds of discrimination but also equate caste discrimination with racial discrimination. Article 15 of the Constitution of India, which outlaws discrimination on grounds of religion, race, caste, sex or place of birth, treats caste at par with race as a prohibited ground of discrimination. Similarly, Article 16 while declaring equality of opportunity in matters of public employment as a fundamental right not only specifies caste as a prohibited ground of discrimination at par with race but also protects and declares the provision for reservation in educational institutions, job opportunities and legislatures (a form of affirmative action). Article 17 while declaring the abolition of untouchability has in effect accepted the existence of caste based discrimination and its effect of untouchability as racial discrimination. Article 23 prohibits forced labour as a form of discrimination. Similarly in Article 29 while declaring the fundamental rights of protection of the interest of minority rights, caste discrimination in admission into educational institutions is prohibited at par with racial discrimination. The provisions relating to reservation of seats for SCs/STs (Castes and Tribes listed in the Schedule appended to the Constitution of India) in the House of People (Lok Sabha) and in the Legislative Assemblies of the State (Article 331 and 332) do recognise the mischief of caste discrimination and attempt to remedy the same, which is a clear proof of the Constitution of India acknowledging caste discrimination as a form of racial discrimination. Article 335, mandating that the claims of SCs/STs to services and posts in connection with the affairs of the Union of India and the States, also reflects the acknowledgement of existençe of caste discrimination as a form of racial discrimination. Article 338, which provides for National Commission for SCs/STs also reflects the said Constitutional acknowledgement. The provisions of Article 341 providing for the specification of the SCs for the purpose of the Constitution clearly show that the castes are not only equated with races but the scheduled castes include race. It is clear therefore, that according to the Indian Constitution the concept of SCs is inclusive of the concept of race. Thus caste-based discrimination is not only a form of racial discrimination but is more than racial discrimination. Article 341 is extracted here below:

"341. Scheduled Castes – (1) The President may with respect to any State or Union territory, and where it is a State after consultation with the Governor thereof, by public notification, specify the castes, races or tribes or parts of or groups within castes, races or tribes which shall for the purposes of this Constitution be deemed to be Scheduled Castes in relation to that State or Union territory, as the case may be.

(2) Parliament may by law include in or exclude from the list of Scheduled Castes specified in a notification issued under clause (1) any caste, race or tribe or part of said a notification issued under the said clause shall be varied by any subsequent notification".

Several Legislative measures relating to SCs/STs clearly prove the existence of caste discrimination even more violent and more dangerous than racial discrimination in Indian society but also shows the ineffectiveness of the governmental measures already taken. The two particular legislations worth pointing out are (a) The Removal of Untouchability Act, 1955 which was improved and renamed subsequently as Protection of Civil Rights Act 1976 prescribing more stringent measures and (b) The SCs/STs (Prevention of Atrocities) Act, 1989.

The catena of judgments relating to the caste based discrimination against SCs and the remedies against the same shows that caste is recognised and acknowledged by the judicial decisions as a prohibited ground of discrimination not only at par with race but also as a form of racial discrimination. The different definitions of caste adopted by the several decisions of the Supreme Court of India show that for the purposes of treating caste as a prohibited ground of discrimination, caste is race in the Indian context (K.C. Vasant Kumar vs. State of Karnataka, 1985 (Supp.)1 SCR 352). In the said decision caste is even identified as a race or unit of race, as per the definition of caste accepted by Justice Venkataramaiah in the said case. The 9-Judge Constitution Bench in the case of Indira Sawhney vs. Union of India (1992 (Supp) 3 SCC 217 at 714 defines caste in the following terms: "a caste is nothing but a social class – a socially homogeneous class. It is also an occupational grouping, with this difference that its membership is hereditary. One is born into it. Its membership is involuntary. Even if one ceases to follow that occupation, still he remains and continues a member of that group". Thus it is evident from the Constitutional, Legislative and judicial history of India that caste discrimination needs to be identified and treated as a form of racial discrimination, in fact a more virulent form of racial discrimination than the ones found in other countries.

For many years UN bodies such as International Convention on Civil and Political Rights (ICCPR), International Convention on Social, Economic And Cultural Rights (ICESCR), Convention Against Elimination of Racial Discrimination (CERD), CEDAW and International Labour Organisation (ILO) had ignored the existence of caste based discrimination in India. This omission had serious negative repercussions on the ability of the UN to address discrimination against Dalits. Dalits could make little use of the space offered by human right bodies to raise the issue of caste-based discrimination. However, the UN human rights bodies have in recent years acknowledged and addressed the existence, prevalence and persistence of caste based discrimination in India and the rest of South Asia.

The UN Committee on the Elimination of Racial Discrimination in its meeting held on August 7 and 8, 1996, considered the question of discrimination against SCs/STs of India and made explicit reference to caste-based discrimination. The Committee held that "the situation of SCs/STs falls within the scope of the International Convention on the Elimination of All Forms of Racial Discrimination". The 52nd UN sub-committee in Geneva in August 2000 unanimously passed a resolution to prepare a working paper on 'Discrimination based on caste'.

The Dalits want the global community to acknowledge and condemn the caste-based discrimination as a distinct form of racism. UN bodies will be failing in their duty to the people of the world if they do not take this matter at the Durban conference and devise drastic steps to eradicate the caste-based discrimination. The failure to include caste in the Durban discussions will erode the credibility of the United Nations and compromise its historical role.

Signed by, among others, the following:

Advocate P L Mimroth, Member, Core Committee, National campaign on Dalit Human Rights
Prof S K Thorat, Jawahar Lal Nehru University
Mrs. Rajni Tilak, President, Centre for Dalit Alternate Media
Mr. Asha Ram Gautam, President, Manvadhikar Samta Seva Society
Dr. Vimal Thorat, Member, National Campaign
Dr. Prakash Louis, Executive Director, Indian Social Institute
S. Lourduswamy, Executive Secretary, CBCI SC and STs Commission
Ms Maja Daruwala, Executive Director, Commonwealth Human Rights Initiative
Dr John Dayal, Secretary General, All India Christian Council
Mr. Narendra Kumar, Director, Pairavi

APPENDIX 3

सत्यमेव जयते

Statement By H.e. Mr. Omar Abdullah, Minister of State for External Affairs, India at the World Conference Against Racism, Racial Discrimination, Xenophobia And Related Intolerance Durban

2 September 2001

Madam President,

On behalf of my delegation and on my own behalf, I felicitate you on your election as Chairman of the World Conference against Racism, Racial Discrimination, Xenophobia and Related Intolerance. We are grateful to the Government and the people of South Africa for their warm hospitality and for the excellent arrangements for the Conference.

It is fitting that the World Conference is taking place in your great country. The solidarity of the international community with

South Africa's struggle against apartheid symbolizes mankind's united quest for equality, dignity and justice. We take this opportunity to salute the valiant peoples of Africa. They braved repression, brutality and indignity and remained in the vanguard of the war against racism and racial discrimination. They have set a glorious example.

I would like to record our deep appreciation for the inspiring Inaugural address by President Mbeki. We hope the Conference would be guided by the forward-looking vision he outlined. The thought provoking statements of Secretary General Kofi Annan and High Commissioner for Human Rights, Mrs. Mary Robinson, should assist us in our work.

Madam President,

The international community takes legitimate pride in its historic triumph against apartheid, the most inhuman and abhorrent manifestation of racism. We must show courage and sagacity also in facing up to the heinous consequences of the racist practices of the colonial era. Slavery and slave trade caused untold misery to countless numbers as did imperialism and colonialism. In saying so we do not mire this Conference in the past. Of course, this World Conference must be focused, constructive and forward-looking. We do not wish that we confine ourselves to recriminations for historic wrongs. To do so will neither be purposeful, nor action-oriented, in combating modern manifestations of racism that cry out for urgent action. But, we must study the past to learn lessons for the future. The demise of imperialism and colonialism have not led to the elimination of attitudes, habits and thought processes ingrained in entire populations over generations. We are united in our belief that our global civilization is enriched by diversity. Yet, we witness exclusivism based on racial hatred; violence as an instrumentality for achieving racial cleansing. Sadly, theories of racial superiority continue to be propagated and practised even though recent biological research has conclusively controverted such beliefs. We continue to witness instances of destruction of constitutional order to promote policies based on racial or ethnic discrimination. If we are to move towards a better future, we must rededicate ourselves to our fight against racism and racial discrimination.

Madam President,

Economic disparities sustain and strengthen racist attitudes. As do political platforms and concepts based on racial hatred and discrimination, which regard foreigners as rivals, competitors and a threat to local prosperity, culture and identity. So also immigration, citizenship and refugee laws with racist overtones. We must remain vigilant also against the vulnerability of modern communication technology. The internet has turned the world into a global village. Yet, this technological beneficence is being used by some to spread racial hatred.

Madam President,

It is here in South Africa, indeed in this very city of Durban, that Mahatma Gandhi launched the Satyagraha movement - struggle based on truth - against the racist regime in South Africa. In 1946, India was the first country to raise its voice against apartheid at the United Nations. We have always regarded racism and racial discrimination as the anti-thesis of everything humanity stands for - equality, justice, peace and progress. It is a negation of the Charter of the United Nations and the Universal Declaration of Human Rights.

In our own national, context, inspired by Mahatma Gandhi and guided by the legacy of Dr. Ambedkar and other social reformers, the government is committed to combating and eliminating discrimination in all its manifestation. Over half a century ago, we built into our Constitution, human rights and fundamental freedoms as justiciable principles. It proscribes discrimination on any ground, including race. Appropriate laws supplement this constitutional provision. The Indian Penal Code prohibits dissemination of ideas that promote disharmony on any ground, including race. The Constitution pioneered affirmative action programmes for the socially disadvantaged. We have put in place an administrative and institutional framework to tackle, within out democratic framework, different forms of discrimination. Our independent judiciary, an ever-vigilant media and an active civil society have strengthened the government's efforts for attaining equality and non-discrimination. Our nationhood is based on values of democracy and rule of law, pluralism, tolerance and diversity. We stand resolved to counter the forces that seek to destroy these values.

At the same time, we are humbled by our awareness that much remains to be done. Action at the level of the Government, however important it may be is not enough unless there is a change in social attitudes and values. Change in social attitudes cannot be achieved simply by legislating. Our society has a tradition and capacity for dialogue and building consensus. But as all democratic societies know only too well, such change can only be brought about through education and persuasion. This cannot be achieved overnight.

Madam President,

To ensure that our participation in this Conference is meaningful, constructive and in consonance with our national policies, Prime Minister Vajpayee constituted a National Committee under the chairmanship of External Affairs Minister, Jaswant Singh. The committee deliberated on the issues relating to this Conference, and, in order to ensure proper preparations through a nationwide discussion, heard presentations by NGOs, academics, professionals, representatives of the civil society and others interested in assisting the Committee. The Committee was heartened by the wide spread approbation of the constitutional and legislative provisions against any form of discrimination and of affirmative action programmes. It noted also the call for more concerted efforts at re-orienting ingrained social attitudes. The Committee recommended that there was need to strengthen the national structures and institutions to ensure effective implementation of the Constitutional and legislative provisions, affirmative action programmes and transform social attitudes within our society.

I affirm the commitment of my Government to act on this recommendation.

Madam President,

In the run up to the world Conference, there has been propaganda, highly exaggerated and misleading, often based on anecdotal evidence, regarding caste-based discrimination in India. We in India have faced this evil squarely. We unequivocally condemn this and, indeed, any other form of discrimination. The issue has remained at the top of our national agenda. I have just spoken of our Constitutional, legislative and administrative framework; of our affirmative action programmes for the uplift of the members of the historically disadvantaged castes. We are proud of the positive difference these measures have made. The institutions of our democratic polity, the progressive removal of poverty and the spread of literacy have empowered and given a voice to millions of the weaker sections of our society. We are determined to continue this national endeavour.

Madam President,

We are firmly of the view that the issue of caste is not an appropriate subject for discussion at this Conference. We are here to ensure that there is no state-sponsored, institutionalised, discrimination against any individual citizen or groups of citizens. We are here to ensure that states do not condone or encourage regressive social attitudes. We are not here to engage in social ' engineering within member states. It is neither legitimate nor feasible nor practical for this World Conference or, for that matter, even the UN to legislate, let alone police, individual behaviour in our societies. The battle has to be fought within our respective societies to change thoughts, processes and attitudes; indeed, the hearts and souls of our peoples. This is the task that we pledge ourselves to remain engaged in.

Madam President,

The World Conference should call for effective recourse and remedies for victims of racism, racial discrimination, xenophobia and related intolerance, based on the principles enunciated in the International Convention on the Elimination of all Forms of Racial Discrimination. Promulgation of stringent national laws, against these phenomena, as necessary; their strict implementation; and the setting up of independent national institutions with powers to address problems connected with endemic racism; are some essential steps in the combat against racism. The Conference should also encourage countries to introduce affirmative action in respect of disadvantaged segments of their populations. Special attention needs to be paid to secure, for women and children, who are victims of such discrimination, their basic human rights and dignity. The power of education must be harnessed to instill the right values in young minds.

The UN agencies concerned should be provided with requisite resources to take, within their respective mandates, all possible action to combat racism and racial discrimination. The Inter Parliamentary Union can play a particularly important role by encouraging reflection in national Parliaments. The Conference should encourage the mass media to promote ideas of tolerance and understanding.

Madam President,

As one of the oldest civilisations of the world, India is fully conscious of its responsibility. We will work closely and tirelessly with your delegation and with all other delegations to ensure that the lofty ideals before this World Conference lead us to seek constructive, productive and lasting solutions to our common concern. Thank you, Madam President.

APPENDIX 4

World Conference Against Racism, Racial Discrimination, Xenophobia and Related Intolerance Durban

31 August - 7 September 2001

Abstract of Statement of the National Human Rights Commission Of India [Read By Dr. Justice K. Ramaswamy, Member]

Abstract of Statement

This World Conference Against Racism, Racial Discrimination, Xenophobia & Related Intolerance holds, in reality, a mirror to the soul of each of us.

Our comments therefore require a degree of introspection and honesty not always associated with the expression of views in such gatherings.

Mrs. Robinson has been right in observing:

"There has never been a UN Conference where there has been such a strong quest for the recognition of historical injustices";

and in asserting:

"In different parts of the world, people are hurting because of problems of inequality or injustice and are pressing their case at this Conference."

Indeed, no part of the world is exempt from such pain. India is no exception.

The National Human Rights Commission of India, for which I have the honour of speaking at this Conference, has therefore considered it its duty to listen attentively to those in our country who have been the victims of historical injustices, and who are hurting because of discrimination and inequality. I refer in particular to those who, under our Constitution, comprise the Scheduled Castes and Scheduled Tribes - the Dalits and Adivasis of India - with the protection of whose human rights our Commission is itself deeply involved. It was to hear their voices, and to benefit from an exchange of views with them, and with eminent jurists, academics and human rights activists, that our Commission organized two major consultations in August 2001, in Bangalore and Delhi respectively, as steps preparatory to the formulation of the views of our Commission for this Conference. The Commission has naturally also taken note of the discussions leading to the drafting of the document that has been submitted by the Preparatory Committee to this Conference, and in particular of the individual guaranteed by the Constitution or embodied in the International Covenants.

In the light of this, the Commission is of the opinion that the exchange of views on human rights matters, whether at the national, regional or international level, can all contribute constructively to the promotion and protection of such rights and that this Conference provides a singular opportunity to the international community to deal openly and courageously with the vexed issues of discrimination and inequality as they exist all over the world, in all of their variety, including the forms of discrimination that persist in India and all other countries. In such a context, it is not so much the nomenclature of the form of discrimination that must engage our attention, but the fact of its persistence that must cause concern. Given this perception, the Commission is of the view that the debate on whether race and caste are co-terminus, or similar forms of discrimination, is not the essence of the matter. The Constitution of India in Article 15 expressly prohibits discrimination on either ground, and that Constitutional guarantee must be rigorously implemented. In this connection, the Commission believes deeply in the value of engaging Governments, non-governmental organizations, national institutions, and all concerned elements of civil society in the process of fighting discrimination, and urges that this process be conducted at all levels in a spirit that is genuinely interested in the furtherance of human rights, and not vitiated by self-righteousness or by political and other extraneous considerations.

In furtherance of its statutory responsibilities, the Commission has, thus accorded the highest priority to ending discrimination against Scheduled Castes and Scheduled Tribes and in seeking to eradicate, in particular, two pernicious practices which largely affect members of these communities: these relate to manual scavenging and bonded labour.

The Commission has also taken up the issue of the rights of persons displaced by mega projects, specifically those affected by construction of large dams, many of whom are tribals.

In the final analysis, the Commission believes that the promotion and protection of the human rights of the weakest sections of society are clearly related to their full and proper empowerment. That is why the Commission has urged the adoption and implementation of policies at the Central and State levels that will open the doors of opportunity to them: free and compulsory primary education upto the age of 14 years, as the Constitution requires; access to proper primary health care; freedom from malnutrition and maternal anemia, and the re-allocation of resources to back such programmes in a manner that has true meaning. In addition, the Commission has continued to receive and redress numerous individual complaints that it has received daily from persons who are included among the Scheduled Castes and Scheduled Tribes; these have alleged acts of discrimination, "untouchability", violence against the human person, atrocities of various kinds, and high-handedness by public servants and others.

Economic upliftment and empowerment of Dalits is the most effective tool to combat casteism. More avenues must be opened for the economic betterment of the disadvantaged.

The Commission is acutely aware that the journey to end discrimination, injustice and inequality will be long and often frustrating. But it is convinced that, in this mission, the Constitution of the Republic has shown the way. Legislative and affirmative action programmes are firmly in place, but unquestionably need to be far better implemented. The Commission is convinced that discrimination on any of the grounds contained in the Constitution of India, and these include race, caste and descent, constitute an unacceptable assault on the dignity and worth of the human person and an egregious violation of human rights. The commission holds the view that the instruments of governance in our country, and the energetic and committed non-governmental sector that exists, can unitedly triumph over the historical injustices that have hurt the weakest sections of our country, particularly Dalits and Scheduled Tribes. This is above all a national responsibility and a moral imperative than can and must be honoured.

APPENDIX 5

National Campaign on Dalit Human Rights

Memorandum

Greetings and solidarity from the National Campaign on Dalit Human Rights!

The National Campaign on Dalit Human Rights was born out of an initiative of concerned Human Rights Activists in India working among the Dalits who were engaged in a study of the effectiveness of the implementation of the SC/ST (Prevention of Atrocities) Act. 1989 in the different States in India. This initiative strongly felt that considering the fact that we are in the 50th Anniversary of the Universal Declaration of Human Rights and we, having just completed our 50th year celebrations of independence, the continued prevalence of "untouchability" in many parts of our country in spite of our Constitutional and International commitment to the contrary, called for an urgent national campaign highlighting Dalit Human Rights and upholding that "Dalit Rights are Human Rights".

We wish to place on record that Dalits in India are the people of Mother Earth, people from a labouring community rooted to the community and no power on this Earth has the power to destroy Dalit Power and Dalit Culture. On this occasion we fondly remember our great leader Dr. B.R.Ambedkar and leaders like Mr. Phule and Mr. E.V.R. Periyar who have made their historical contribution for the abolition of the "heinous crime of untouchability" from the face of this earth. We are only attempting to carry on the great march that they have led decades ago.

We are alarmed by the fact that even after 50 years of survival after independence from colonial powers, every hour 2 Dalits are assaulted, every day 3 Dalit Women are raped, every day 2 Dalits are murdered, every day 2 Dalit houses are burnt down. We are ashamed by the fact that much more than the violations that is perpetrated on the Dalits, the Varnashrama Dharma which is referred to as a "religion" is not only an insult to us but to the whole of humanity. We are shocked that the Dalits are deprived of their basic needs by the dominant caste forces in India along with the State which embodies the dominant caste aspirations. We strongly feel that the denial of basic human needs to the Dalits is a violation of our Human Rights.

We are enraged that Human Rights violations against Dalits take place largely in the context of governance which is the power for allocating resources in India. These violations manifest themselves in the denial of the right to livelihood of communities of people and in the lopsided allocation of resources to people drawn from dominant castes. We are also angered and enraged that their function in the village Panchayat Raj system has only resulted in it being a political and cultural form of oppression of our people wherein we are even denied the right to sit as equals with other dominant caste forces. We are deeply anguished that our people have been denied access to resources like land, water and other means of production and whatever we had possessed have been forcefully taken away from us. We are also outraged that the dominant caste, civil society has established its control over the labour of Dalits through the obnoxious system called "bonded labour". We recognise that the denial of education to Dalits throughout our history of oppression has resulted in the dominant caste society establishing its hegemony over the minds of the Dalits in multiple forms. This has ultimately resulted in the denial of the right to free thinking and the freedom of expression. Out people have been denied their right to practice a religion of their choice and have been discriminated against by the state because of their allegiance to one or other religion. We also strongly recognise that caste and gender discrimination is perpetrated in its worst form on Dalit women.

We therefore demand that the Government of India:

1. formally accept that Dalit Rights are Human Rights;
2. effectively implement in spirit and action the SC/ST

(Prevention of Atrocities) Act and Rules in all States and hand over the responsibility of monitoring the implementation of the Act to the National SC/ST Commission;

3. afford full protection to all Dalits participating in the Panchayat Raj institutions and other democratic institutions of the country's polity;
4. restore to us all the land that have been taken away from us;
5. ensure the right of reservation of Dalits and other most backward classes in all private enterprises and companies which enjoy one or more forms of subsidy from the Central or State Government;
6. consider all Dalits as "Scheduled Castes" within the parameters of our Constitution, irrespective of their particular faith and practice of religion.
7. ensure that the Dalit community in India is provided sufficient financial resources for their true social development, since denial of basic needs of Dalits amounts to denial of their Human Rights.

We further demand that the International Human Rights Community:

1. recognise that "Dalit Rights are Human Rights";
2. undertake a global effort to abolish untouchability in all its manifestation and its practice be considered a heinous crime against humanity punishable in the severest form possible in India in particular and in several other Asian countries;
3. bring within the purview of Human Rights forms of discrimination and violations against Dalits, both by the State and by Civil Society;
4. support the demand for the appointment of a Special Rapporteur or Working Group on the practice of untouchability in Asia and the inclusion of caste discrimination in Article 1 of the UN Convention on the Elimination of Racial Discrimination;

We demand that the United Nations:

1. urgently recognise that "Dalit Rights are Human Rights":
2. urgently appoint a Special Rapporteur or Working Group on

the practice of untouchability in Asia;

3. urgently take steps to include caste discrimination in Article 1 of the Convention on the Elimination of Racial Discrimination.

This memorandum is being addressed to:

1. The President of India
2. The Prime Minister of India
3. The Speaker of the Lok Sabha
4. The Chairman of the Rajya Sabha
5. The Leader of the Opposition in the Lok Sabha
6. The Leaders of the Opposition in the Rajya Sabha
7. The Governors of all the Indian States
8. The Chief Ministers of all the Indian States
9. The Speakers of the Assemblies of all the Indian States
10. The Leaders of the Opposition of all Assemblies.
11. The Secretary General of the UN
12. The Chief Human Rights Commissioner of the UN
13. The Chief of Missions of every Indian Mission abroad

APPENDIX 6

International Conference on Dalit Human Rights

London Declaration

We, the Ambedkarites, Buddhists, Ravidassies, Valmikies, Christians and other Dalits of United Kingdom and around the world gathered here for an International Conference on Dalit Human Rights unanimously declare that:

1. We strongly condemn the continuous Human Rights violations against Dalits in all parts of India and ask Indian Government to take immediate steps to:

(a) Stop all Human Rights violations

(b) Punish guilty to the fullest extent of the law

(c) Give satisfactory reparations to the victims

(d) Implement

 (i) the Scheduled Castes/Scheduled Tribes Prevention of Atrocities Act 1989

 (ii) the Concluding Observations of the Committee on the Elimination of Racial Discrimination on the Country Report on India (CERD/C/304/Add.13, 17th September 1996,

 (iii) the concluding Observations of the Committee on Human Rights (Civil and Political Rights) (CCPR/C/79/ADD.81,4 August 1997), and

 (iv) the Concluding Observations of the Committee on the Rights of the Child.(CRC/C/15/Add.115, 23 Feb. 2000)

(e) State a continuing campaign to educate the Indian population Human Rights in line with the Constitution of India and with Universal Human Rights instruments, aimed at eliminating the institutionalized thinking of the high-caste and low-caste mentality (as per CERD Report, para 31, (CERD/C/304/Add.13,17 Sept, 1996)

(f) Start free and compulsory education for all children up to age of 14 as per article 45 of the Constitution (as recommended in UN document no. (CRC/C/15/ADD 15, 23 Feb, 2000), Para 57, 58 and 59)

(g) Provide economic rehabilitation of all landless Dalit labourers in villages, so that they will be no more dependent on dominant caste landlords for their survival, through vocational training, job opportunity and micro economic projects within 3 years.

(h) Provide 22.5% reservation to Scheduled Castes/Tribes for jobs in private sector as most of the jobs are being created in private sector.

(i) Dissolve the Constitution Review Committee, as it is unconstitutional. The Amendment mechanism should be used in all future need as it has been done in the past.

(j) Provide adequate resources and take all necessary steps to strengthen the capacity and effectiveness of National Commission for Scheduled Castes/Tribes.

2. World Bank and other International Financial Institutions should attach conditionality clause, to their aid and loans to India, for improving the Human Rights of Dalits. This should be monitored by UN body and evaluated on a regular basis.

Irene Beckett
(Chairman, VOD International)
London 17th September 2000

APPENDIX 7

The Bhopal Declaration

The Bhopal Conference: Charting A New Course For Dalits For The 21st Century Held at Bhopal, Madhya Pradesh, India, 12-13 January 2002

WE, intellectuals and activists assembled at the Bhopal Conference, 12-13 January 2002, to deliberate the issues concerning the welfare of and justice to the 250 million and,

Declaring our belief in Babasaheb Dr. B. R. Ambedkar's ideal of Social Democracy and his prophecy that, "A democratic form of Government presupposes a democratic form of society. The formal framework of democracy is of no value and would be judged as misfit if there was no social democracy",

Endorsing the ideals of civil society enshrined in the Constitution of India, particularly its Preamble that declares the Indian State's commitment to Justice, Liberty, Equality and Fraternity,

Recognising that the tenets established by the Universal Declaration of Human Rights and various other charters of the United Nations which our nation has acceded to also emphasise the same principles,

Recalling the struggles that Babasaheb had waged for the emancipation of his people and the historic rights he had won for them,

Mindful of the fact that even after 54 years of Independence, the Dalit community is denied of its basic human rights and is also at the receiving end of the most brutal and oppressive forms of discrimination and exclusion,

Reaffirming that concerted action by society as a whole - especially coordination among the political leadership, officials and grassroots activists - is necessary for the over-all development of the most oppressed of India,

Bearing in mind the responsibility to take forward our struggle at this critical juncture in spite of the fact that most political formations are reluctant to pursue any policy favourable to the Dalits,

Recognising that the social consensus over the Dalit cause - reluctantly agreed upon at the time of Independence - has by and large broken down,

Convinced that informed and democratic discourse at all levels is essential to re-negotiate a new consensus over redeeming the pledges of the founding fathers of the Republic to do justice to Dalits,

Convinced also that the national psyche and public discourse in the country accepts uncritically the rigid hierarchy and discrimination caused by caste and thereby denies that caste is a major source of prejudice and brutal violence,

Persuaded that it is the duty of the civil society in the country - insignificant in its influence though it might be - to unite and to promote Democracy - social, economic and political - Justice and Equality,

Emphasizing that Babasaheb's stress on struggle through democratic and constitutional means is relevant today,

Regretting that the post-Ambedkar Dalit intelligentsia has failed both in carrying forward his emancipatory movement as well as making a dent in the country's intellectual life,

Recognizing the need for Dalits to make common cause with other liberation and human rights movements in and outside the country,

Conscious of the hurdles that caste-Hindu society - and its tentacles in government, media, voluntary sector, etc., - is likely to hurl at any serious movement that challenges the entrenched system of discrimination and exclusion,

Noting that women - especially Dalit women - represent the most oppressed sections of our society, and that they face multiple forms of discrimination, including caste-based, religious and patriarchal ideology and practices,

Welcoming the winds of change the world over that are conducive to Inclusion, Equal Opportunity, Diversity, Democratisation and Civil Society, and against discrimination, stereotype, stigma, exclusion and caste society,

Hoping that this country will no longer remain an exception to the global norm of Progress, Equality. Justice, Peace and Social Harmony, and

We hereby Solemnly proclaim that while we rededicate ourselves to work in unison to achieve basic rights of Dalits, we are convinced that unless the following issues are resolved no amount of activism on our part and pro-active measures from the State can liberate the community from the scourges of untouchability and exploitation,

We therefore demand....

21-Point Action Agenda for the 21st Century

1. Bring down the ceiling limit of private land ownership, and from the declared surplus land, government revenue lands and temple lands, distribute within five years a minimum of five acres of cultivable land to each Dalit household with registration in the name of Dalit women. Provide the initially required accessories and capital to make their livelihood sustainable and secure.

2. Enact legislation and enforce it stringently to enable Dalits have an equitable share in the appropriation and use of the rural and urban common property resources.

3. Enact legislation and enforce the right of Dalit agricultural labourers to living wages, to gender parity in wages, to job security, to better working conditions and welfare measures, and ensure punitive measures against offenders.

4. Appoint Statutory Committees at the national and state level to identify within specified time-frame all the Depressed Class lands occupied by non-Dalits, to assess the quantum of compensation to be paid by non-Dalits for their illegal utilization of lands, to identify the original owners and their nearest kith and kin for restoring these lands back to them, to expedite legal proceedings in courts specially appointed for this purpose against the illegal occupants and to ensure punitive measures against them.

5. Ensure the restoration of the alienated lands to the tribals, restore their rights over forest and forest-produce, provide them

with compensation and rehabilitation measures, extend resources and capacity building measures for gainful utilization of their lands and forests and entitle those Dalits displaced due to construction of dams/developmental projects as shareholders of such enterprises.

6. Democratise the capital so as to ensure proportionate share for SCs and STs. Make budgetary allocation for SCs and STs to enable them enter the market economy with adequate investment resources, and develop their capacities and skills for such market enterprises.

7. Enforce with stringent measures the Bonded Labour System (Abolition) Act, 1976 and abolish forthwith child labour to ensure freedom with dignity for all the Dalits, and accordingly make suitable amendments in the appropriate legislations.

8. Amend Art. 21 of the Constitution of India: Fundamental Rights so as to include the following rights for all citizens, but with special emphasis for SCs and STs, and on the basis of two criteria, namely low economic income and without religious discrimination: the rights to a standard of living adequate for the health and well-being of women and men equally, including food, safe drinking water, clothing, housing, public health and medical care, social security and social services; the right to living wage and the right to own 5 acres of cultivable land or to gainful employment.

9. Implement compulsory, free and high quality education for all Dalits immediately, make allocation of funds proportionate to the number and level of the illiterates, ensure compensation to those families which forfeit their income from child-labour, increase the number and amount of scholarships, and provide better infrastructural facilities in Sc and ST schools and offer market-oriented vocational and technical education.

10. Make the reservation quota applicable in all the public and private educational institutions from primary to technical and professional levels. Every SC/ST child with low income-base must be given quality free-education at State's expense. And every English medium school must implement Diversity in Admissions.

11. Recognize SC and ST women as a distinct category among women, and accordingly make segregated data on Dalit women available in census reports, action taken reports and progress reports,

evolve national and state level perspective plan for mainstreaming SC and ST women in developmental programmes, market enterprises, financial allocation, reservation facilities in education, employment and health facilities, and mandate the National and State Commissions for SC and ST and for Women to study and report specifically the status of SC and ST women in their annual reports.

12. Implement effectively in letter and spirit the SC and ST (Prevention of Atrocities) Act, 1989 & Rules 1995, especially with regard to atrocities against Dalit women, and accordingly prosecute the dominant caste leaders and their minions who stoke the fire of caste clashes and the police officials acting in connivance with them. In cases of atrocities against SC/STs, a system of collective punishment has to be evolved as oppressors enjoy community' support and protection and escape the law.

13. Ensure diversity or SC/STs' due representation in all public institutions of India, whether universities or academic or autonomous or registered bodies. Those institutions, which do not abide by the principle of Affirmative Action, must lose recognition and state funding.

14. All private industry/ corporate houses must accept and implement Diversity immediately.

in workforce

15. Every government and private organization must implement Supplier Diversity from socially disadvantaged businesses and Dealership Diversity in all goods and services.

16. Provide arms licences to the SCs & STs for self-defence purposes, make the setting up of Dalit self-defence groups from village onwards mandatory, and specially train Dalit women to handle weapons in self-defence against the perpetrators of crimes and atrocities.

17. Eliminate the humiliating practice of manual scavenging on an urgent footing through effective rehabilitation, alternative and sustainable employment measures and developmental programmes, and prosecute violators of the Employment of Manual Scavengers and Construction of Dry Latrines (Prohibition) Act, 1993, especially the gross violators Railways, Defence and Urban Local bodies.

18. Make it statutory for Parliament and State Assemblies to debate on the Annual Reports of the National and State level Commissions for SC/ST and Safai Karamcharis within the following year, and ensure that these annual reports and the action-taken reports of the government are made public.

19. Make reservation mandatory in the private and corporate sector in the same proportion as in the public sector and government institutions and develop the capacities and skills of Dalits to help them cope up with the demands of these different sectors.

20. Implement policy of reservation to SCs and STs at all levels of judiciary and defence forces.

21. Bring out a Truth Paper in two years on the status of reservation during the past 25 years and place it before Parliament and State Assemblies for debate, and on a war footing fill immediately all the backlog posts meant for Dalits and that, too, only with Dalit candidates.

APPENDIX 8

Vancouver Declaration

Adopted Unanimously
By
The International Dalit Conference
Vancouver, BC, Canada, May 16-18, 2003

WE, THE DALITS, from all over the globe having assembled at the International Dalit Conference, to deliberate the issues concerning the 250 million Dalits (Scheduled Castes and Scheduled Tribes) of India and their future in the 21st century,

INSPIRED by that great thinker and philosopher of the oppressed. Babasaheb Dr. B. R. Ambedkar,

REDEDICATE ourselves to his mission to bring about a democratic and peaceful transformation of India whereby all its citizens, irrespective of their gender, caste, creed, language and region, will enjoy the fruits of equality and justice,

WHEREAS the world has entered the third millennium and is progressing towards accomplishing the goals of Liberty, Equality and Fraternity, and whereas India has failed to eradicate untouchability and caste and descent-based discrimination and is yet to achieve basic fundamental human rights,

CALL UPON the Dalits of the world to unite in their activism in the true spirit of interfaith and multiculturalism, and resolve to work tirelessly for the upliftment of the community,

AFFIRM that every human being has the inherent right to life and dignity and that Black is Beautiful and Dalit is Dignified,

MINDFUL of the fact that the Dalits and tribals, accounting for a fourth of India's one billion population, continue to be the victims of manifold discriminations and violence,

MINDFUL also that women belonging to these sections are the victims of gender-caste discrimination,

SINCERELY BELIEVE that the caste problem is not the problem of Dalits alone but also of the entire nation and without the Annihilation of Caste and the elimination of other primordial identities, India will not be able to realize its full socio-economic potential and claim its rightful place among the community of nations,

UPHOLD our unwavering belief in the Indian Constitution as well as the unity and integrity of India,

TAKE cognizance of the universal ideals enshrined in several international and national covenants and treaties - from the Universal Declaration of the Human Rights to the Bhopal Declaration - and ENDORSE wholeheartedly the Bhopal Declaration in letter and spint,

AFFIRM our mission to support the struggles of oppressed people worldwide and muster all possible support from anywhere for the advancement of the Dalit cause,

RESOLVE to propagate knowledge of Babasaheb as a philosopher of emancipation to all the oppressed anywhere in the world, and to fulfill the pledge,

RESOLVE also to build our own educational, cultural and other institutions for the advancement of the community, we

REDEDICATE ourselves to institutionalize the process started in the Conference through constant coordination and by setting up a formal institutional structure for better networking among the Resident and Non-Resident Indian Dalit community as well as to make use of international institutions and processes to sensitize the world about the plight of the Dalits and Tribals in India,

WE therefore Demand,

1. The rightful and proportionate share of Dalits and tribals in India's national institutions, wealth and capital must be recognized. Economic exclusion hitherto practised in the name of caste must be done away with. The community should have equitable access to means of production and economic empowerment.

2. Since no development is possible without gender justice, women of these groups must be given priority in all developmental

activities. They must have formal, legally sanctioned rights on par with men.

3. Private Corporations and Multi-National Corporations operating in India must recognize and accept their social responsibilities.

4. The United Nations and its affiliates, and non-governmental agencies concerned with human rights, social and economic development, must recognise that the Dalits are a special group and create separate Dalit divisions managed by the Dalits themselves. Their programmes and projects should have special Dalit components as well as special focus in their reports.

5. Dalit Studies must be included in Indian and international educational and research institutions, especially in North America and Europe, and universities should recognise the need to admit Dalit students on priority.

6. The World Bank and other International Financial Institutions should attach conditional special component clause and must ensure the rightful share of the Dalits in the funds they lend to India for socio-economic and sustainable development.

7. The international governmental and non-governmental development aid agencies should focus on Dalit development and empowerment with initiatives to be inbuilt in their system and adopted in the funding programmes.

8. Sustained efforts must be made at the United Nations to expedite the process of formally equating caste-based discrimination with Racial 9+9discrimination.

9. Untouchability is practised in many countries such as Bangladesh, Nepal, Pakistan and Sri Lanka. No effort must be spared to address the problem by the world community.

10. Reorganize the National and State Commissions for SCs and STs as the SC and ST Vigilance Commissions and the decisions of these Commissions should be binding.

11. All laws, rules and regulations meant for protecting the rights of the Dalits must be included in the Ninth Schedule of the Constitution of India, to prevent unjust and lengthy litigation process which always goes against the community.

Bibliography

Books

- Ambedkar, B. R. Emancipation of the Untouchables. Bombay: Thacker & Co. Ltd., 1972.
- Ambedkar, B. R. Writings and Speeches. Education Department, Government of Maharashtra, 1987, Vol. 1-17 in English and 1-15 in Hindi.
- Badrinarayan. Documenting Dissent, Contesting Fables, Contested Memories and Dalit Political Discourse. Shimla: Indian Institute of Advanced Study, 2001.
- Bhave, Sumitra. Pan on Fire: Eight Dalit Women Tell Their Story. New Delhi: Indian Social Institute, 1988.
- Bhargava, G.S. Human Rights Of Dalits (Societal Violation). New Delhi: Gyan Publishing, 1999.
- Breman, Jan. The Labouring Poor in India: Patterns of Exploitation, Subordination, and Exclusion. New Delhi: Oxford University Press, 2003
- Chalam, K.S. (Ed.) Relevance of Ambedkarism in India Jaipur, Ravat Publications, 1993; 209.
- Charsley, Simon R. and Karanth, G K. (Ed.) - Challenging Untouchability: Dalit Initiative and Experience From Karnataka. New Delhi: Sage Publications, 1998.
- Fuller, J. Christopher. (Ed). Caste Today. Delhi: Oxford University Press, 1996.
- Franco, Fernando; Macwan, Jyotsna and Others. The Silken Swing: The Cultural Universe of Dalit Women. Calcutta: Stree, 2000.

- Franco, Fernando. Pain and Awakening: The Dynamics of Dalit Identity in Bihar, Gujarat and Uttar Pradesh. New Delhi: Indian Social Institute, 2002.
- Ghosh, G. K. G, Shukla. Dalit Women. New Delhi: A.P.H. Publishing Corporation, 1997.
- Ghosh, Ashish. Dalits and Peasants: The Emerging Caste-Class Dynamics. Delhi: Gyan Sagar Publications, 1999.
- Guru, Gopal. Dalit Cultural Movement and Dialectics of Dalit Politics in Maharashtra. Mumbai: Vikas Adhyan Kendra. 1997.
- ———————— and V.Geetha. Dalit Intellectual Activism: Recent Trends. Mumbai: Vikas Adhyan Kendra. n.d
- Ilaiah, Kancha. Why I Am Not A Hindu: A Sudra Critique of Hindutva Philosophy, Culture and Political Economy. Calcutta: Samya, 1996.
- ———————— God as a Political Philosopher: Buddha's Challenge to Brahminism. Calcutta: Samya, 2000.
- Jeffrelot, Christophe. India's Silent Revolution: The Rise of the Low Castes in North Indian Politics. Delhi: Permanent Block, 2003.
- Jodhka, Surinder. Community & Identities: Contemporary Discourses on Culture and Politics in India. New Delhi: Sage Publications, 2001
- Jogdand, P.G. (Ed.). Dalit Women: Issues and Perspectives. New Delhi: Gyan Publishing House, 1995.
- ———————— New Economic Policy and Dalits. New Delhi: Rawat Publications, 2000.
- Joshi, Barbara R. Democracy in search of equality: untouchable politics and Indian social change. Delhi: Hindustan Pub. Corp., 1982.
- ———————— Untouchable: Voice of the Dalit liberation movement. New Delhi: Select Book Service Syndicate, 1986.

- Khosla, Dinesh. Myth and reality of the protection of civil rights law: A case study of untouchability in rural India. Delhi: Hindustan Publishing Corporation, 1987.
- Kshirsagar, R. K. Dalit movement in India and its leaders. New Delhi: M.D. Publications Pvt Ltd, 1994.
- Kotani, H. Caste System Untouchability and the Depressed, Delhi, Manohar, 1997.
- Louis, Prakash. The Emerging Hindutva Force: The Ascent of Hindu Nationalism. New Delhi: Indian Social Institute, 2000.
- ——————— Casteism is more Horrendous than Racism: Durban and Dalit Discourse. New Delhi: Indian Social Institute, 2001.
- ——————— People Power: The Naxalite Movement in Central Bihar. New Delhi: Wordsmiths, 2002.
- Lynch, Owen. Politics of Untouchability: Social Movements and Social Change in a City of India. New York: 1969.
- Mahar, J Michael (Ed.). The Untouchables in Contemporary India. Jaipur: Rawat Publications, 1998.
- Manchanda, Ritu. Women, War and Peace in South Asia: Beyond Victimhood to Agency. New Delhi: Sage Publications, 2001.
- Mathew, Joseph. Ideology, Protest and Social Mobility: Case Study of Mahars & Pulayas. New Delhi: Inter-India Publications, 1986.
- Mendelsohn, Oliver and Vicziany, Marika. The Untouchables: Subordination, Poverty and the State in Modern India. New York: Cambridge University Press, 1998.
- Murugkar; Lata. Dalit Panther Movement in Maharastra. Bombay: Popular Prakashan, 1991.
- O'Hanlon, Rosalind. Caste, Conflict and Ideology: Mahatma Jotirao Phule and low Caste protest in nineteenth-century

western India. New York: Cambridge University Press, 1985.

- Oommen, T.K. Protest and Change: Studies in Social Movements. New Delhi: Sage Publications, 1990.
- Omvedt, Gail. Dalits and the Democratic Revolution. New Delhi: Sage Publications, 1994.
- ———— Dalit Visions: Tracts for the Times. New Delhi: Orient Longman, 1995.
- Pai, Sudha. State Politics: New Dimensions. Delhi: Shipra Publications, 2000.
- ———— Dalit Assertion and the Unfinished Democratic Revolution: The Bahujan Samaj Party in Uttar Pradesh. New Delhi: Sage Publications, 2002.
- Parish, Steven M. Hierarchy and its Discontents: Culture and the Politics of Consciousness in Caste Society. Philadelphia: University of Pennsylvania Press, 1996.
- Paswan, Sanjay and Jaideva, Pramanshi. Encyclopedia of Dalits in India: General Study. Vol.I- XI. Delhi: Kalpaz Publications, 2001.
- Patil, P.G. (Tr.). Collected Works of Mahatma Jotrao Phule Vol. II: Sections. II, First Bombay, Education Dept. Govt. of Maharashtra, 1991.
- Pende, Sandeep. At Cross-roads Dalit Movement today. Bombay: Vikas Adhyayan Kendra, 1994.
- Pieterse, Jan Nederveen. Emancipations, Modern and Post-Modern. London: Sage Publication, 1992.
- Poddar, Bhagirath. The Untouchables in Modern India., New Delhi: Sarup & Sons, 2001.
- Prakash, Gyan. Bonded Histories: Genealogies of Labour Servitude in Colonial India. Cambridge: Cambridge University Press, 1990.
- Prasad, Vijay. Untouchable Freedom: A Social History of

a Dalit Community. New Delhi: Oxford University Press, 2000.

- Prasad, Ravi D.M. Dalit Youth: A Sociological Study. New Delhi: A.P.H. Publishing Corporation, 1997.
- Ram, Nandu. Beyond Ambedkar: Essays on Dalits in India. New Delhi: Har-Anand Publications, 1995.
- Robb, Peter. Ed. Dalit Movements and the Meanings of Labour in India. New Delhi: Oxford University Press, 1993.
- Rodrigues, Valerian. The Essential Writings of B.R. Ambedkar. New Delhi: Oxford University Press, 2002.
- Sangwan, Om Prakash. Dalit Society and the Challenge of Development. New Delhi: Commonwealth Publishers, 1996.
- Sebastian, M. Liberating the Caged Dalit Panther. Madras: Emerald Publishers, 1994.
- Shah, Ghanshyam. Dalit Identity and Politics. New Delhi: Sage Publications, 2001.
- ——— Caste and Democratic Politics in India. Delhi: Permanent Black, 2002.
- Sharma, R.S. The State and Varna Formation in the mid-Ganga Plains: An Ethnographic View. Delhi: Manohar, 2001.
- Singh, Rajendra. Social Movements: Old and New – A Post- Modernist Critique. New Delhi: Sage Publications, 2001.
- Singh, S.K. Dalit Women: Socio Economic Status and Issues. Lucknow: New Royal Book Co., 2000.
- Sharma, G.S. Legislation and Cases on Untouchability and Scheduled Castes in India. New Delhi: Allied Publishers, 1975.
- Shyamlal. The Bhangi: A Sweeper Caste Its Socio-Economic Portraits: With Special Reference to Jodhpur City. Bombay: Popular Prakashan, 1992.
- ——— From Higher Caste to Lower Caste: The

Process of Asprashyeekaran & the Myth of Sanskritisation. Jaipur: Rawat Publications, 1997.

- Srinivas, M.N. (Ed). Caste: Its Twentieth Century Avatar. New Delhi: Viking, 1996.
- Srivastava, B.N. Manual Scavenging in India. New Delhi: Concept Publishing Company, 1997.
- Teltumbde, Anand. Ambedkar in And For The Post-Ambedkar Dalit Movement. Pune: Sugawa Prakashan, 1997.
- Vaidyanthan, A. and P.R.Gopinathan Nair (ed). Elementary Education in Rural India: A Grassroots View. New Delhi: Sage Publications, 2001.
- Zelliot, Eleanor. From Untouchable to Dalit: Essays on the Ambedkar Movement. Delhi: Manohar, 1996.

Articles:

- Agnivesh, Swami (et. al). Discrimination that must be cast away. New Delhi, 'The Hindu' June 6, 2001.
- Alex, Binu. Dalit Movement Comes of Age. 'Humanscape' 8 (8): September 2001, 6-8.
- Ali, Amir. Durban and After. 'Economic and Political Weekly' 36 (37): 15-21 September 2001: 3508-3509.
- Anaimuthu, V. Durban World Congress on Racism: Caste must be discussed. 'Periyar Era' 7 (10): July 2001: 1-5.
- Assian Human Rights Commission. Occupation and Descent-Based Discrimination Against Dalits. 'Human Rights Solidarity' 11 (4): April 2001: 3-10.
- APWLD. Double Discrimination for Marginalised Women in Asia. 'Human Rights Solidarity' 11 (9): September 2001: 8-9.
- Bal, Gian Singh. Caste Discrimination and Durban Conference. 'Mainstream' 39 (38): 8 September 2001: 18.
- Bhagwati, P.N. The Caste & Race Debate. 'PUCL' 21 (7): July 2001: 3-8.

- Bhanutej, N. Naked Assault: Dalit woman is stripped and paraded for two hours in Karnataka. 'The Week' 19 (39): 9 September 2001: 43.
- Barik, Satyasundar. Wash my feet, it's your dirt. 'Humanscape' 8 (8): 8 September 2001: 25-26.
- Biswas, A.K. Discrimination – Caste or Racial, How does it matter for the discriminated. 'Mainstream' 39 (30): 14 July 2001: 21-23.
- Bandyopadhay, Sarbani. Class conflict. 'The Statesmen' June 06, 2001.
- Beteille, Andre. Caste Consciousness. 'The Times of India' August 30, 2001.
- ———————— Race and Caste. 'The Hindu' March 10, 2001.
- ———————— Caste Consciousness: Initiate an Open Discussion in Durban. 'Times of India' August 30, 2001.
- Bhardwaj, Mukesh. Upper caste bias hits new law: Human waste. 'Indian Express' April 13, 2000.
- Chowdhary, Kameshwar. Violation of Human Rights: the Case of Dalits in Gujarat. 'Indian journal of Human Rights' 4 (1&2): January-December 2000: 158-172.
- Chopra, Perm. Let it Burn up Caste. 'The Hindu' March 16, 1999.
- Chandhoke, Neera. Backlash against affirmative action. 'The Hindu' June 2, 2001.
- Das, Soumitro. Caste and Race: Physiological Difference and alien Origin. 'The Statesmen' June 5, 2001.
- Dang Satyapal. Caste Discrimination and Communist Parties. 'Mainstream' 39 (35): 18 August 2001: 20
- Das Soumitro. Dalit Challenges: No change in pattern of oppression. 'The Statesmen' September 4, 2001.
- Desai, Radhika. India's ugliness in the Kutchi Mirror. 'The Hindu' May 4, 2001.

- Duffee, Richard, Z. Prejudicial Exploitation: The Issue of Caste and Race. 'Indian Journal of Human Rights' 4 (1&2): January-December, 2000: 25-64.
- Dhavan, Rajeev. India's apartheid. 'The Hindu' August 24, 2001.
- Dogra, Bharat. Battling caste and gender stigmas. 'The Statesmen' July 12, 2001.
- Dutt, Anuradha. The afternoon of the caste system. 'The Pioneer' July 10, 2001.
- Elliott, Michael. The Disgrace In Durban. 'Time' 158 (11): September 17, 2001: 33.
- Ganguly, Meenakshi, (et al). The Revolution Against Caste. 'Time' April 13, 1992: 10 – 17.
- Gundimeda, Sambaiah. Emergence of Caste Consciousness among the Madigas of Andhra Pradesh. USA, 'Dalit International Newsletter' 6 (1): February 2001: 5- 9.
- Gupta, Dipanker. Caste is not Race but, Let's go to the UN Forum Anyway. 'The Times of India' August 18, 2001.
- Guru, Gopal. The Left and the caste question. 'The Hindu' December 20, 2000.
- ———————— "Politics of Representation". Seminar 508 – December 2001: 29-33.
- Gatade, Subhash. Silence of the Lambs? Durban and the Indian elite. 'Mainstream' 39 (31): July 21, 2001: 23-26.
- Haragopal, G. Dalit Consciousness in Andhra: A Hypothesis. 'Indian Journal of Human Rights' 4 (1&2): January -December, 2000: 137-148.
- Haslam, David. Caste and the World Conference Against Racism. USA, 'Dalit International Newsletter' 6 (2): June 2001: 6 –7, 12.
- Ilaiah, Kancha. Durban, Caste and Indian democracy. 'The Hindu' June 11, 2001.

- ———— Caste and the U.N. Meet. 'The Hindu' August 21, 2001.
- Iyer, Lakshmi. Dalit women bear the burden of untouchability. 'The Pioneer' December 21, 1998, 5.
- Jain, Devaki. Slavery, then and now. 'Indian Express' September 10, 2001.
- Jhunjhunwala, Bharat. Discuss caste at Durban. 'The Pioneer' August 21, 2001.
- Jogdand, P.G. Human Rights Violation of the Dalits: An Inquiry into Indian Social Reality. 'Indian Journal of Human Rights' 4 (1&2): January-December, 2000: 121-134.
- Kannabiran, K. G. We, the other people. 'The Hindu' June 8, 2001.
- Kannabiran, Kalpana. Caste, the democracy and Dalit women. 'The Hindu' June 20, 2001.
- Kalidas, Rajendra. Prevention of Discrimination and Protection of Indigenous Peoples and Minorities. USA 'Human Rights Solidarity' 11 (9): September. 2001, 3-7.
- Kumar, Davinder. The Race To Be Heard. 'The Outlook'. 61 (35); September 10, 2001: 26.
- Kumar, Vivek. A blow from Dalit dignity and pride. 'The Pioneer' September 25, 2001.
- Louis, Prakash. Caste and Hatred: Violence on the Dalits. 'Social Action' 50 (3): July-September 2000: 287-302.
- ———— Doors of Durban Conference Closed for the Dalits. 'Mainstream' 39 (31): July 21, 2001: 27-29.
- ———— "Dalits" Even In Disaster: The Politics of Relief Operation in Gujarat. 'Indian Journal of Human Rights' 4 (1&2): January-December, 2000: 208-222.
- ———— "Dalit Human Rights: Problems and Opportunities". 'Humanscape' 8 (8): September 2001: 14-15.

- ———————— "Regaining our lost Faith". Seminar 508 – December 2001: 25-29.
- ———————— Scheduled Castes and Tribes: The Reservation Debate. Economic and Political Weekly. vol. XXXVIII. No. 25, June 21-27, 2003, p. 2475-2478.
- Malekar, Anosh. Noise from the Fringes. 'The Week' 19 (41) September 23, 2001, 10.
- ———————— Race Against Injustice. 'The Week' 19 (39) September 9, 2001, 40-41.
- Mungekar, B.L. Globalization and the Dalits. 'Radical Humanist' 65 (1): April, 2001: 9-10.
- Mehta, Pratap Bhanu. Dalits & economic Liberalization. 'The Hindu' September 5, 2000.
- Menon, N.R. Madhavan. Tackling discrimination. 'The Hindu' August 3, 2001.
- Menon, Sreelatha. SC – ST panel seeks quota in Judiciary. 'Indian Express' September 1, 2001.
- Mistry, Mihir. Dalits forced indoors as fear stalks Gujarat hamlet. 'The Times of India' November 20, 1998, 8.
- Mohan, Surendra. The Deeply embedded Caste system. 'The Hindu' November 27, 1998.
- Mukerjee, Hiren. Casteist Infamies: India must not Equivocate in Durban. 'The Statesmen' August 22, 2001.
- Nauttyal, Shefali. They hurt them without touching them. 'Indian Express' July 15, 2001.
- Nayar. Kuldip. Dalit, Durban and a lost chance. 'The Pioneer' September 11, 2001.
- Narnag, A.S. Caste at Durban: Why and How. 'Mainstream' 39 (31): July 21, 2001: 21-22.
- Oommen, T.K. Dalits & Production of Knowledge. 'The Hindu' September 13, 1999.
- Omvedt, Gail. The U.N., racism and caste. 'The Hindu' April 4, 2001.

- ——————— Caste, race and sociologist. 'The Hindu' October 18, 2001.
- Pai, Sudha. New Social and Political Movements of Dalits: A Study of Meerut District. 'Contributions to Indian Sociology', 34,2: 2000, 189-220.
- ——————— Social Capital, Panchayats and Grass Roots Democracy: Politics of Dalit Assertion in Uttar Pradesh. 'Economic and Political Weekly', February 24, 2001, 645-654.
- Pal R. M. Remembering M. N. Roy and his heresy. Human rights of Dalits On the Agenda of UN. 'Mainstream' 39 (14): March 24, 2001: 23-25.
- ——————— Durban: A Victims' Conference. 'Mainstream', 39 (40): September 22, 2001: 6-8.
- ——————— Caste Based Discrimination on UN Agenda. 'Radical Humanist' 65 (6): September, 2001:1-6.
- Pand, Rajaram. Phoolan's Killing fuels Polarisation of Caste Politics. 'Mainstream' 39 (34): August 11, 2001: 7-11.
- Panini, M. N. Caste, Race and Human Rights. 'Economic and Political Weekly' 36 (35): September 1-7, 2001: 3344-3346.
- Pathak, Bindeshwar. Untouchability Still stalks India. 'The Pioneer' October 01, 1998, 9.
- ——————— Sore on Indian's Social Structure. 'The Pioneer' March 3, 2000.
- Pinto, Ambrose. UN Conference Against Racism: Is Caste Race? 'Economic and Political Weekly' July 28, 2001: 2817 – 2820.
- Prabhudesai, Sandesh. Dalits still struggling. 'The Pioneer' September 25, 2001.
- Prasad, M. Madhava. Touching others: Perceptions of the Dalit struggle are shaped by upper caste fantasies. 'The Telegraph' May 25, 2000.

- Prasad, Chandrabhan. Blacks in US media and blackouts in India. 'The Pioneer' April 8, 2001.
- ———————————— The Durban dip can cleanse a billion sins. 'The Pioneer' August 12, 2001.
- Radhakrishnan P. Dalits and Durban New Delhi. 'The Hindu' August 27, 2001.
- Raina, Badri. Caste and Race: Discrimination by any Name. 'Economic and Political Weekly' 36 (32): August 11, 2001: 3025-3026.
- Reddy, S. Gopinath. Upper Caste obstinacy crushes fight for equality. 'Indian Express' May 4, 1999.
- Rajappa, Sam. Caste Cauldron Boils Over. 'The Statesmen' October 24, 1998.
- Raju, K. Where Dalits are forced to bathe with buffaloes. 'Indian Express' December 8, 1998.
- Raj, Felix. Dalit Identity: The Search for equality and Dignity. 'The Statesmen' May 2, 2001.
- Sankaran. S. R. Fifty Years of the Indian Constitution – Human Rights of Davits. 'Indian Journal of Human Rights' 4 (1&2): January- December 2000: 69-82.
- Setalvad, Teesta. A Date With Durban. 'Communalism Combat' 9 (71): September, 2001: 39-41.
- ———————— Demons in their mind. 'The Hindu' August 28, 2001.
- Shah, Ghanshyam. Dalit Movements and the Search for Identity. 'Social Action'. October 1990, p 317-335.
- Singh, Shubha. Caste – iron discrimination. 'The Pioneer' August 20, 2001.
- Singh, Vir. Is Durban the answer? 'The Hindu' September 2, 2001.
- Sabrang Team. Dalit Drishti. 'Communalism Combat' 8 (65): January, 2001: 31

- ———— Dalit Drishti. 'Communalism Combat' 8 (66): February, 2001: 30
- ———— Elected Reps, Officials fall foul of SC/ST Act. 'Communalism Combat' 8 (67): March 2001: 36-37.
- ———— A Question of Caste. 'Communalism Combat' 8 (68) April, 2001: 7-18.
- ———— Dalit and Muslim Women Grapple with the Triple Burden of Caste, Community, Class and Gender. 'Communalism Combat' 8 (69): May 2001: 8-11.
- Sob, Durga. The Triple Oppression of Dalit Women in Nepal. USA "Human Rights Solidarity' 11 (8) August, 2001: 8-10.
- Subramaniam, K. S. Violence Against Scheduled Caste in India Overview, Problems & Prospects. 'Man and Development' 9 (1): March 1987: 26 – 42.
- Thekkekara, Mari Marcel. What next for India's Dalit? 'The Hindu' September 13, 2001.
- The Editorial Team. No International Policing! Racial vs. Caste Discrimination. 'Manthan' 22 (3): July-September 2001: 7-45.
- ———— Scheduled Castes and Tribes: The Reservation Debate. Economic and Political Weekly. Vol. XXXVIII. No. 25, June 21-27, 2003, p. 2475-2478.
- Varma, N.M.P. Educational Deprivation of Women and Dalits in South Asia. 'Indian Journal of Human Rights' 4 (1&2): January -December, 2000: 181-192.
- Verma, Amita. Dalit songwriter paraded naked. 'The Asian Age' June 21, 2001.
- Verma, A.K. UP: BJP's Caste Card. 'Economic and political Weekly', December 1, 2001, 4452-4455.
- Vishwanathan, Shiv. The Race for Caste: Prolegomena to the Durban Conference. 'Economic and Political Weekly' July 7, 2001: 2512-2516.

————————— Durban and Dalit Discourse. 'Economic and political Weekly' 36 (33): August 18-24, 2001: 3123-3127.

Note: the following issues of Seminar was fully devoted to the issues relating to Dalits:
Voices, Visions and Political Assertions of the Dalits. Seminar 471, November 1998.
Exclusion. Seminar 508, December 2001.

Reports:

- Amnesty International - Using the International Human Rights system to combat racial discrimination, UK, Amnesty International Publication, 2001.
- Amnesty International - racism and the administration of Justice, UK, Amnesty International Publication, 2001.
- Chennaiah, P. Dalit Activists Protesting Panchayat Election Results Illegally Detained, Stripped, Tortured and Paraded naked in Chillamanur by Police of Venkatagiri Circle, Nellore District, Update Collective, (134): September 19, 2001: 1-4.
- Divakar, N. Paul, (et al). A Historical Overview of Achievements and Future Action Agenda. 'National Campaign for Dalit Human Rights' New Delhi, 2001.
- Human Rights Watch. Broken People: Caste violence against India's "Untouchables", USA, Human Rights Watch Publication, 1999.
- Indian Social Institute. Murder and Mayhem in Pankhan: Atrocities on the Dalits of Gujarat. A Report submitted to the National Human Rights Commission, New Delhi 2000.
- Louis, Prakash. Caste Discrimination is Draconian than Racial Discrimination: An Appeal to address in the World Conference against Racism. 'Update Collective' (133): June 2001: 1- 8.
- ————————— Durban and Post – Durban Dalit Discourse: Retrospect and Prospect, New Delhi, Indian Social Institute, 2001.

- Martin, Macwan. Caste May not be Race, New Delhi, National Campaign on Dalit Human Rights, 2001.
- Oommen, T. K., (et al). Caste is race and Plus, say Academic Jurists and Civil society groups at Delhi Conference, New Delhi, 2001.
- Reservation for Backward Classes: Mandal Commission Report of the Backward Classes Commission, 1980, Delhi: Alankar Publications.
- UN - United Nations Declaration and International Convention on the Elimination of All Forms of racial Discrimination, USA, United Nations Department of Public Information, 1997.
- UN - World Conference Against Racism, New Delhi, United Nations Information Centre Lodi Estate, 2001.
- UN – Declaration and Programme of Action. World Conference Against Racism, Racial Discrimination, Xenophobia and Related Forms of Intolerance. New York. March 2002.

Index